The Economics and Sociology of Management Consulting

Management consultancy is a key sector in the economic change toward a service and knowledge economy. This book explains the mechanisms of the management consulting market and the management of consulting firms from both economic and sociological perspectives. It also examines the strategies, marketing approaches, knowledge management, and human resource management techniques of consulting firms. After outlining the relationships between transaction cost economics, signaling theory, embeddedness theory, and sociological neoinstitutionalism, Thomas Armbrüster applies these theories to some central questions. Why does the consulting sector exist and grow? Which institutions connect supply and demand? And which factors influence the relationship between clients and consultants? By applying both economic and sociological approaches, the book explains the general economic changes of the past thirty years and sharpens the relationship between the academic disciplines.

Thomas Armbrüster is Professor of Business Administration in the Department of Management and Economics at Witten/Herdecke University, Germany.

The Economics and Sociology of Management Consulting

THOMAS ARMBRÜSTER

CAMBRIDGE
UNIVERSITY PRESS

CAMBRIDGE UNIVERSITY PRESS
Cambridge, New York, Melbourne, Madrid, Cape Town, Singapore, São Paulo

Cambridge University Press
The Edinburgh Building, Cambridge CB2 2RU, UK

Published in the United States of America by Cambridge University Press, New York

www.cambridge.org
Information on this title: www.cambridge.org/9780521857154

© Thomas Armbrüster 2006

First published 2006

Printed in the United Kingdom at the University Press, Cambridge

A catalog record for this publication is available from the British Library

ISBN-13 978-0-521-85715-4 hardback
ISBN-10 0-521-85715-5 hardback

Contents

List of figures   *page* vii

List of tables   viii

Preface and acknowledgments   ix

1 Management consultancy viewed from economic and
  sociological perspectives   1

Part I: The mechanisms of the consulting market   39

2 Why do consulting firms exist and grow? The economics
  and sociology of knowledge   41

3 How do supply and demand meet? Competition and the
  role of social institutions   68

4 Who is more powerful? Consulting influence and client
  authority   86

5 Substitutes or supplements? Internal versus external
  consulting   101

Part II: The drivers of managing a consulting firm   117

6 Diversified services or niche focus? Strategies of
  consulting firms   119

7 Fostering reputation and growth? Marketing consulting
  services   140

8 The economics and sociology of knowledge
  distribution: organizational structure and governance   152

9 Gaining talent and signaling quality: human resource
    management   178

Part III: Conclusions   203

10 The knowledge economy, management consultancy,
    and the multitheoretical approach   205

References   223
Index   247

Figures

1.1 Differences between the theoretical approaches 32
2.1 Global management consulting revenues, 1970–2001 42
2.2 Efficient versus inefficient use of consultants 48
2.3 Forecast demand intensity of tasks and
   make-or-buy solutions 51
2.4 Acquisition volume as a percentage of average
   total stock market capitalization, 1968–1999 59
2.5 Ruef's model of consulting growth 65
3.1 Market mechanisms in management consulting 79
4.1 The consulting business cycle: per annum growth rates,
   1970–2005 93
5.1 The cost-effectiveness of internal versus external
   consultancy 104
5.2 Task characteristics and make-or-(also)-buy
   solutions 106
6.1 Project structures of "procedural" versus "brains"
   consulting 127
7.1 Approaches to marketing in the consulting sector 144
7.2 Marketing types in the consulting market 146
8.1 Three basic elements in the consulting
   knowledge system and their interrelations 167

Tables

1.1 Four theories and their focus   18
2.1 Roles of consultants   43
2.2 Outbound FDI, developed economies, 1980–2000   56
2.3 Intra-industry trade indices for OECD countries, 1964–1990   57
2.4 Four theories and their explanations of consulting growth   66
7.1 Components and loading items of marketing measures   142
7.2 Loadings of marketing clusters on the individual components   144
7.3 Marketing cluster distribution per firm growth, 1997–2002   148
8.1 Two types of knowledge management   169
8.2 Consultants' firm-internal publishing strategies to gain attention   175

Preface and acknowledgments

THIS BOOK on management consulting is based on several sources of inspiration, and it is hard to say which the most important one has been. A first source was my own employment as a management consultant, first at a medium-sized information technology (IT) and organizational consultancy in Berlin, then at a small mergers and acquisitions (M&A) consulting firm in London, and eventually as a summer associate at a large strategy consultancy. The vicissitudes of these firms inspired my interest in management consulting as an academic topic, and after completing my PhD thesis on a different subject I started doing research on the advice sector. Without personal involvement in the consulting sphere and the insights gained there, I would have been unable to write the book.

A second source was my journey between academic disciplines and exposure to the ongoing discussion between economics and sociology. As an undergraduate and graduate student in management and industrial engineering, I attended lectures and tutorials in micro- and macroeconomics. I was disappointed by them and felt that daily newspapers and weekly magazines taught me more about the economy than the models I learned at university. I felt that these models, and thus economics as an academic discipline, were mere skeletons that contributed little to the explanation of ongoing events in the real world. Courses such as organizational behavior provided much more stimulation for me, and I finished my first degree by focusing on behavioral aspects without economic modeling.

In the course of my PhD thesis I came to be familiar with sociology in general, and with the British, critical tradition of economic sociology in particular. At the time, I perceived sociology as a relief. After all, academics were able to see the world as it is rather than as some models assumed it would be, and the application of sociology to management consultancy matched some of my experiences as a consultant. During and shortly after finishing my PhD thesis I was

interested in the critical tradition of sociology and applied these ways
of thinking to management consultancy.

At some point, however, I felt that many approaches to consultancy
in the critical tradition of sociology overdid it. The denial of prudent
and informed calculation on the clients' side, and the preoccupation
with what I came to consider oversocialized views, drove me back to
look at market mechanisms and cost considerations as outlined in
institutional economics and US-based economic sociology. Books such
as Swedberg's (1990) interviews with economists and sociologists, and
the tension between these two disciplines, became my fascination and
motivated me to look at consultancy along this line. I relearned
institutional economics autodidactically as far as possible and enjoyed
comparing it to economic sociology.

The list of sources of inspiration would be incomplete if I did not
mention the people with whom I had many discussions about
consultancy and who influenced my thinking. In the earliest stage of
my research I benefitted from many conversations and a first joint
conference paper with Raimund Schmolze, a friend for many years.
Later on, Johannes Glückler and Matthias Kipping became the most
important colleagues on the consultancy topic. Matthias was the
head of a research team with the EU-funded project 'The Creation of
European Management Practices' (CEMP). When I joined the team,
Matthias had already published widely on the history of management
consultancy. He introduced me to the literature and we started
publishing together. A revised version of a common article by us has
become chapter 6 of the present book.

Johannes drew my attention to embeddedness theory, and after this
discovery we dived into US-based economic sociology and published
a paper together, which I have shortened and revised to become
chapter 3 of this book. In the meantime, he has published subsequent
research on consultancy based on embeddedness theory (Glückler
2004, 2005, 2006), in which he has extended the notion of reputation
networks to a geography of reputation. I am grateful to both Johannes
and Matthias for our frequent discussions on consultancy, for the time
we spent together writing papers, and for their permission to use
revised versions of co-authored articles as chapters of this book.

In the organizational behavior section at the University of
Mannheim I could develop many ideas, and did most of the writing.
Its director, Alfred Kieser, gave me the freedom to co-assign topics

for diploma theses, and I had the pleasure of supervising highly talented graduate students, some of whose results have been integrated in this book. Christoph Barchewitz wrote an excellent piece on the marketing of consulting services, which we published as a German-language paperback and on which chapter 7 of this book draws. Judith Eichner wrote on careers and women in consultancy, and her interviews with female consultants nurtured a section of chapter 9. Sebastian Wind wrote a fine piece on internal versus external consultancy and his interviews informed chapter 5. I am thankful for and proud of having cooperated with them.

I also benefitted a great deal from visiting stays at the Scandinavian Consortium for Organization Research at Stanford University, and at the Department of Economics and Business of the University Pompeu Fabra, Barcelona. In these institutions I presented papers, discussed ideas, and learned a lot from colleagues and their comments. At Stanford I could also conduct interviews with clients and consultants in the Silicon Valley and San Francisco. A grant from the Stiegler Foundation in Mannheim enabled my visiting stay at Stanford; the MBA program at Pompeu Fabra hosted my stay in Barcelona. The support of these institutions is gratefully acknowledged.

A previous version of the manuscript was accepted at the Department of Economics and Management of the Technical University of Berlin as a formal qualification for full professorships at German-language universities (*habilitation*). I am grateful to the dean and faculty members for the uncomplicated procedure, especially to Diether Gebert and Hans Gemünden, who were important advisors. Diether Gebert was my most important mentor over many years; his support involved many more issues than just research.

As the final manuscript was taking shape, Henning Piezunka, Johannes Glückler, Achim Oberg, Christoph Barchewitz, and Sebastian Wind read it, or large parts of it. They provided additional ideas and literature sources, and they helped to clarify and sharpen my arguments. Katharina Mol edited the manuscript patiently and accurately. Chris Harrison, Katy Plowright, Lynn Dunlop and Paula Parish of Cambridge University Press steered the work through the review and production processes. I am grateful to all of them, as much as to the fifty consultants and clients in Germany and the United States who were interviewed in the context of this book.

Regarding the use of revised versions of articles as chapters in this book, my thanks go not only to the above-mentioned co-authors but also to the publishers for their permissions. Chapter 3 is a shortened and revised version of 'Bridging uncertainty in management consulting', by Johannes Glückler and Thomas Armbrüster, *Organization Studies*, 24/2, pp. 269–97, by permission of Sage Publications Ltd. Chapter 6 is a revised version of 'Strategy consulting at the crossroads', by Thomas Armbrüster and Matthias Kipping, *International Studies of Management and Organization*, 32/4, pp. 19–42, by permission of M. E. Sharpe, Inc. Chapter 7 draws on 'Marketing instruments of management-consulting firms: an empirical study', by Thomas Armbrüster and Christoph Barchewitz, *Academy of Management Best Paper Proceedings* 2004, Management Consulting Division, pp. E1–E6. Chapter 9 is a revised and expanded version of 'Rationality and its symbols: signaling effects and subjectification in management consulting', by Thomas Armbrüster, *Journal of Management Studies*, 41/8, pp. 1247–69, by permission of Blackwell Publishing Ltd. Figures 2.1 and 4.1 are reprinted with permission of Kennedy Information, Inc., Peterborough, NH 03458, United States.

A few more words on the relationship between economics and sociology in connection with this book are in order. To take up Akerlof's (interview with Akerlof in Swedberg 1990: 70) notion of the interplay between economics and sociology, A + B does not always equal C but often just remains A + B. That is, trying to use both economics and sociology on the same topic does not always lead to an integrated perspective, but often simply remains economics plus sociology or sociology plus economics. The perspectives may complement each other and add up to a more comprehensive view, but they do not always amalgamate. I think this is true, but it is not a tragedy. The results of using both economics and sociology come in different shades of integration, and can in any case be used to cross-check each other. For example, regarding the question of why the consulting sector has grown so rapidly over the past three decades, economic and sociological explanations complement each other but do not necessarily merge (see chapter 2). There are several reasons why the consulting market has grown, some of which can be best described in economic terms and others in sociological terms, and there is no need to marry them at gunpoint. Discussing both economic and sociological mechanisms leads to a more comprehensive view than just discussing one viewpoint. In other words, A + B is more than A or B alone, even if they do not merge to C.

As regards other topics of consultancy, such as the mechanisms that connect supply and demand, or human resource management (chapters 3 and 9), there is more room for interweaving the two disciplines. With regard to market mechanisms, chapter 3 discusses the role of trust between consultants and long-term clients, and it is a matter of terminology and empirical research, rather than academic discipline, how much calculativeness such a relationship entails and to what extent the term "trust" applies. Moreover, sociological insights often shed light on the limits of economic efficiency, and are thus indispensable for a full understanding of market mechanisms. With regard to human resource management, I aim to demonstrate that an interweaving of economic and sociological insights leads to a better account of personnel selection and career discrimination. My intention is to show that we can learn most about an industry or market if we do not tie ourselves to a single discipline but use insights from other disciplines to question, check, or test our assumptions, methods, and results. I consider this, rather than a merger of disciplines, as the essence of scientific progress, and outline this in chapters 1 and 10 from the viewpoint of critical rationalism.

I limit the scope to two theories of each discipline: transaction cost theory and signaling theory represent the economic approach, and sociological neoinstitutionalism and embeddedness theory the sociological one. These are four central theories to deal with the increased role of knowledge and uncertainty in the economy, of which management consultancy represents a central phenomenon. In comparison to other knowledge industries, such as biotechnology, management consultancy is less research-intensive and more customer-driven, and it brings about intangible results. Only the results of IT consulting are more tangible, and the results of financial consulting are often measurable. In general, however, consulting services represent intangible and hard to evaluate resources, and involve information asymmetries between economic actors as well as uncertainties about service quality, actor behavior, and business transactions. This highlights the questions of how clients gain quality certainty and how supply and demand meet, and transaction cost economics and embeddedness theory suggest themselves as representatives of economic and sociological perspectives. Moreover, consultancy represents a market of symbolic resources and has an institutionalized market stratification. Thus it is beset with phenomena external to the immediate exchange relationship between clients and consultants, and signaling theory and sociological neoinstitutionalism deal with these phenomena explicitly. While further theories could have been added, the selection of transaction cost economics, embeddedness theory, signaling theory, and sociological neoinstitutionalism was based on a tradeoff between redundancies and gains of omitting one theory or taking a fifth on board.

In the future, an application of game theory to management consultancy may sharpen the insights gained by the theories used here. This is not only due to game theory's modeling capacities but, first and foremost, due to its capability to take up arguments from different strands. In a few sections in the book I mention game theory in passing, but, at this point of the debate on consultancy, taking game theory fully on board would have overloaded the approach. Transaction cost economics, signaling theory, embeddedness theory and sociological neoinstitutionalism all make specific and irreplaceable contributions to the current state of scholarly writing on consultancy.

Chapter 1 outlines these four theories and their relationships to each other. After this, the book is divided into three parts. Part I looks at the mechanisms of the consulting market. By "mechanisms" I mean those institutions, such as trust, power, reputation, and price, that connect supply and demand and that determine the relationship between buyer and seller. These institutions are results of the features of consulting services, especially their intangible character and quality uncertainty. Hence Part I focuses on the questions of why consulting firms exist as independent firms and why the sector grows (chapter 2), which procedures connect supply and demand (chapter 3), which factors generate power between clients and consultants (chapter 4), and in which cases internal consultancies accompany or compete with external advice (chapter 5). Interviews with consultants and clients have been integrated as far as this seemed useful for illustrating or comparing the theories.

Part II seeks to explain the drivers of managing consulting firms. By "drivers" I mean the circumstances of strategy, marketing, organization, and human resource management which lead to decisions of senior consultants and which shape the fortunes of firms. Part II relies on Part I in that it refers to the market mechanisms outlined there and explains the management of consulting firms on their basis. The individual sections then look at the strategies of large providers (chapter 6), at the marketing of consulting services (chapter 7), at organizational governance and knowledge management (chapter 8), and at human resource management in the form of personnel selection and promotion mechanisms (chapter 9). Like Part I, it keeps the presentation of empirical material at a minimum and focuses on the comparison of theories. The concluding Part III summarizes the insights gained from the multidisciplinary perspective, puts them in the context of past and ongoing shifts to a knowledge economy, and discusses the relationship between economics and sociology on the basis of critical rationalism (chapter 10).

If the details of one theory or a particular aspect of the market or of managing a consulting firm had been in the foreground, then each topic – such as the consulting industry's growth, firm strategies, or personnel selection and promotion policies – would have been worth a full book. For example, an analysis of selection and promotion policies in management consultancy could usefully have been expanded to a monograph on personnel economics (see Pudack 2004 for a useful example, in German, based on signaling theory). However, the intention of this book is a different one. It seeks to provide a theory-guided overview of consulting market mechanisms and firm management. The book limits the degree of detail for each theory and gives center stage to a comparison of theories, seeking to enhance our knowledge on individual topics and phenomena.

For each subject I select an economic perspective as the point of departure, and complement, criticize or adjust it from the viewpoint of at least one sociological theory. I put a particular question in the foreground (e.g. why does consultancy grow? Why have strategy consulting firms moved less into IT consulting than accounting firms? Why do consulting firms select personnel by case studies rather than assessment centers?) and use the theories as different or complementary tools of explanation. This specialization on topics rather than theory or method represents a phenomenon-oriented rather than paradigm-driven work. Inevitably, this comes with the risk of being sketchy or eclectic. It is a hazard we must bear if we want to reap the benefits of a theory-comparative approach.

I hope that this book attracts not only scholars of management consulting, but also a broader audience of scholars interested in the economic shifts to a knowledge economy and in the relationship between economics and sociology. The literature on the knowledge economy often refers to knowledge workers as a general phenomenon, but tends to abstract from differences between them. Hence this book seeks to specify management consultancy as a part and a result of the considerable changes toward a knowledge and service economy. If we can sensibly explain why management consulting – as a pivotal sector of these changes – has grown, how supply and demand in such a market meet, why consulting firms are managed the way they are, and how careers in such firms develop, then we contribute to an encompassing understanding of economic and social developments that affect countless professional and private lives.

1 | Management consultancy viewed from economic and sociological perspectives

The literature on management consulting

Only since the 1990s has management consultancy prompted a great deal of attention in management research. Until then little had been written on this service sector, probably because it was not yet recognized as a mainstay in the economy. Management research, organization studies, and industrial sociology had primarily concerned themselves with larger industries and corporations, and the management consulting business was still too small to be recognized as an industry with considerable influence. Only a few authors, for example Hagedorn (1955), Higdon (1969), and Havelock and Guskin (1971), had begun to recognize the role of consultants in the transmission of business techniques. Other early publications on management consulting were concerned with organizational development, a consulting approach to help clients help themselves (Schein 1969; Argyris 1970).

Throughout the 1980s publications in the sociology of professions (Stanback 1979; Stanback *et al.* 1981; Noyelle and Dutka 1988; and later Tordoir 1995) referred to management consulting as one of the service sectors toward which industrialized economies shift. It became recognized as an emerging profession in which formal professional qualification has given way to professional work independent of a formal professional background (Abbott 1988; Brint 1994). At about the same time, Greiner and Metzger (1983) wrote a first advisory book for consultants, and the International Labour Organization (Kubr 1986) issued the second edition of a landmark book on best practices in management consulting, to which prominent management scholars and practitioners contributed and which aimed to cover a broad range of aspects from both consulting and client perspectives.

Despite these advances in the 1980s, the number of studies on management consulting remained low in comparison to the growth of the literature in the subsequent decade. Presumably it was assumed that not much could be added to the established view of consultants as transmitters of business techniques and carriers of organizational change methods. Not even the history of management consulting as a service sector and profession (McKenna 1995, 2001, 2006; Kipping 1996, 1997, 1999) was available to the scientific community before the 1990s. Only in the first half of the 1990s, following the rapid growth in the industry, did the significance and influence of management consulting become more recognized in the academic literature. Globally active consulting firms had achieved a high level of visibility, and management scholars could no longer ignore the influence of these firms on management knowledge, decisions, and practices. In the 1990s a large number of books appeared on the subject, oriented toward the markets for practitioners (e.g. Maister 1993; Kubr 1996), for MBA graduates applying to major consulting firms (e.g. Wet Feet Press 1996; Wickham 1999), or for those interested in starting their own consulting business (e.g. Kishel and Kishel 1996; Biech 1999).

At about the same time, a growing number of popular books on the potential dangers of hiring consultants appeared on the book market. These were mainly written by journalists or former consultants and had suggestive titles such as *The Inside Story* (Rassam and Oates 1992), *Dangerous Company* (O'Shea and Madigan 1997), or *Consulting Demons* (Pinault 2000). Even the Dilbert comics ridiculed consultants as shallow advisors. In this high tide of consulting bashing, well-known management scholars joined the ranks of those warning of *Flawed Advice* (Argyris 2000). Indeed, one of the salient characteristics of the consulting literature has been, and continues to be, that both journalists and academic commentators tend to have strong feelings about the business, considering consultants to be anywhere in a broad spectrum from shallow charlatans to modern carriers of economic growth.

Based on these images of the business, one can broadly distinguish between a functionalist and a critical view on consulting. The functionalist view sees consulting firms as carriers and transmitters of management knowledge. For example, Bessant and Rush (1995) distinguish between two knowledge-based roles for consultants: an intermediary one that supports clients' acquisition of knowledge and technological developments; and a capability-building one that supports clients' adoption and implementation of changes. Along this line, many authors have pointed out that consulting firms possess knowledge about analytical procedures which enables them to provide a variety of services and tasks that clients cannot perform on their own (Starbuck 1992; Moore and Birkinshaw 1998; Morris and Empson 1998; Sarvary 1999; Werr et al. 1997; Werr 1999, 2002; Armbrüster and Kipping 2002). Traditional organizations are assumed not to have the human resources, analytical skills, and procedural potential, with the result that taking management consultants into service has become a matter of course rather than an exceptional case, as it was some decades ago (Alvesson 1995; Faust 2002; Suddaby and Greenwood 2001). This perspective will be taken up in chapter 2 and integrated into a transaction cost perspective.

The functionalist view also points out other features of large consulting firms: the worldwide representation, the familiarity with a wide variety of industrial sectors, and the "one-firm" governance concept (for details, see chapter 8). These features ensure that consulting firms can obtain knowledge from a large variety of sources and, potentially, apply experiences gained in other industrial sectors or parts of the world. From this perspective, the methods to generate data and information outside and within the client organization constitute the primary driver of the consulting business and its growth. The recruitment of talented personnel, an extraordinary work ethic, and the strong commitment to an achievement culture represent a fundamental aspect of their performance and of the demand for their services. From the functionalist perspective, systematic knowledge management allows consulting firms to stay up to date with industry practices and market information, and it also enables them to distribute knowledge resources in a manner unequaled by conventional organizations (Larsen 2001; Hansen 1999, 2002; Hansen et al. 1999; Hansen and Haas 2001). I shall come back to these arguments in the transaction cost approach to consulting in chapters 2 and 8.

The critical literature on consulting does not necessarily doubt the usefulness of consulting for clients, but argues that the view that "consultants are experts and provide knowledge and analyses to clients for a fee" is too narrow to grasp what is going on in consulting projects (Clark and Fincham 2002). For example, Abrahamson (1996), Kieser (2002) and Ernst and Kieser (2002) refer to the faddish character of many management activities and argue that, among others, consulting firms have an economic interest in the up- and downswings of management concepts and substantially contribute to fashion setting. Berglund and Werr (2000) point to consultants' communicative flexibility, for example in their use of rationality and pragmatism myths to legitimate their approaches. Benders *et al.* (1998) have done empirical work in this context, finding that consultants use the term "business process reengineering" for a large variety of services that have often little to do with Hammer and Champy's (1993) original call for radical changes. Benders *et al.* (1998) argue that consultants separate the label from the contents of this management concept and create a sense of urgency by using a particular term without relating project contents to it. Similarly, Fincham (1995) argues that, in particular, business reengineering is constructed and marketed as a saleable commodity in order to meet the needs of the "managerial consumer." Ernst and Kieser (2002) and Kieser (2002) draw on these ideas to suggest that the circulation of management concepts and fashions contributes to managerial insecurity and fuels the demand for consulting services.

In a micropolitical view of consulting, Jackall (1988: 140–4) argues that consultants often trade in the troubles between the internal factions of a client organization, and that consultants often have to work on the problem as defined rather than develop a solution autonomously. As in an earlier approach by Moore (1984), client firms are not conceptualized as organizations as a whole, but as consisting of competing actors and groups. Using IT consulting as an example, Bloomfield and Danieli (1995) argue that the socio-political skills of consultants are indissoluble from their technical expertise, because technology cannot be separated from its communicative representation and thus from vested interests within a client firm. During the elaboration and implementation of advice, consultants and clients mobilize discursive and symbolic resources, which render it impossible to conduct consulting without any micropolitical involvement (see also Bloomfield and Best 1992). As with the other approaches, the micropolitical view draws on the insight that consultancy services are intangible and that their commercial impact is difficult to evaluate. But, rather than focusing on the consequential market mechanisms, the critical perspective on consultancy looks at the ways in which consulting assignments and client–consultant interactions are open to distortion.

In this context, Czarniawska-Joerges (1990) holds that the use of metaphors and labels that are new to the client organization can give meaning to situations and engender action through sense making. Seen from this perspective, the communicative resources of consultants provide some potential to obfuscate issues, to interpret situations for vested interests, or to manipulate definitions of success and failure. For Alvesson (1993), the point of departure is the uncertain character of all types of knowledge, even scientific knowledge. He argues that knowledge work needs to be viewed in the context of institutionalized myths of rationality, since there is no objectively determinable knowledge. Claims of knowledge, and therefore of communicative performance, may move into the foreground of this business, as credible stories about the world need to be delivered. The work of Clark (1995) has been influential in this respect. Given the lack of objective criteria for quality assessment, he argues, convincing clients of consulting quality requires considerable communicative skills and thus promotes consultants' impression management and rhetorical abilities. Along these lines, Clark and Salaman suggest viewing management consultants as "systems of persuasion creating compelling images which persuade clients of their quality and work" (Clark and Salaman 1998: 18).

In summary, the critical view argues that consulting results and project achievements are too problematic to be sufficiently theorized in terms of knowledge transfer. Authors in this paradigm point to the contestable nature of consulting knowledge, to the involvement of consultants in vested interests in client organizations, and to the potentially flexible mode of "consultancy speak." In so doing, they are expressing much of the concern, or even distaste, of an academic research community regarding consultants (March 1991), contributing to a more emancipated comprehension of the business. This critical take on consultancy will be taken up in chapter 4.

Theories used in this book

Publications of the above two types, the functionalist and the critical views, today characterize the literature on consultancy and have considerably advanced our knowledge of the industry and its mechanisms. Nevertheless, to date both are beset with limitations. The functionalist view lacks a systematic outline of why clients have increasingly externalized management services and continue to do so, and the critical view lacks an acknowledgment of economic processes and clients' rational deliberations. More precisely, the functionalist view presents useful lists or outlines of the economic role of consulting firms, but it lacks an analytical grounding. Neither theoretically nor empirically does it engage with the question of why client firms do not perform the services themselves or hire experts as employees rather than making use of external consultancies. It has not delved into the question of how clients gain quality certainty or why they hire a particular consultancy in preference to another, and a more theoretical analysis and elaboration suggests itself.

For its part, the critical view exhibits a limitation that is at least equally serious. As Salaman (2002) points out, it is preoccupied with consultants' truth claims, with consultants' supposedly unscientific approaches, and with an ostensibly dark side to consultancy. It either focuses on management fashions that clients supposedly fall for – which represents an oversocialized conception of the consulting market, to use Granovetter's (1985) term – or it portrays consultants as opportunistic agents who exploit clients' lack of quality certainty – which represents an undersocialized conception of management consulting. In some cases, the critical approach mixes over- and undersocialized views by portraying clients as somewhat retarded victims of both opportunistic consultants and mesmerizing management fads. This way, it has no concept of situations in which clients know exactly what they are doing when they hire consultants, and of conditions in which social ties and reputation effects preclude opportunistic action by consultants. Much of the literature from the critical camp seems based on an anti-consulting attitude, and scholars reproduce and reinforce their attitude in their research. The neglect, or even denial, of client prudence and economic deliberations is reminiscent of what W. O. Coleman (2002) has recently pointed out as anti-economics. I shall take up this discussion in chapter 4 and in the conclusion.

Sociological neoinstitutionalism

The only theory that the previous literature on consultancy has systematically drawn on is sociological neoinstitutionalism. For example, many articles in the volumes edited by Sahlin-Andersson and

Engwall (2002) and Kipping and Engwall (2002) draw on Meyer and Rowan (1977), DiMaggio and Powell (1983), Powell and DiMaggio (1991), or Tolbert and Zucker (1996). Sociological neoinstitutionalism is based on the argument that it is belief in the efficiency of particular practices or solutions, rather than any proven efficiency, that determines or influences economic action. According to this view, legitimacy toward the organizational environment rather than technical efficiency represents the core of organizing. If the efficiency or efficacy of organizational innovations or management ideas cannot be objectively evaluated, then they are oriented toward what the environment or decision-makers themselves believe to be efficient or effective. This leads to a number of effects — such as the institutionalization of management ideas — that are deemed efficient but are not necessarily so, or to pressure on organizations to adopt the same practices or structures as other firms (isomorphism) in order to gain legitimacy. Issues such as the legitimacy of organizational structures, the enforceability of change processes, and the validation of management decisions have taken center stage in the literature on consultancy (Sahlin-Andersson and Engwall 2002; Kipping and Engwall 2002; Alvesson 1993, 2004). The large and renowned consultancies in particular have duly been described as carriers not only of knowledge but also of legitimacy, as their analyses and reputation validate management decisions.

The diffusion of management concepts and innovations also touches upon elements of isomorphism in the neoinstitutional sense. If the efficiency and effectiveness of change initiatives or innovations often remain uncertain, then organizational decisions are frequently — on a normative or mimetic basis — oriented toward the behavior of other organizations. If a number of firms adopt a particular practice or innovation, then this is taken as signifying that these practices or innovations generate improvements. Even if it remains impossible to determine with certainty whether an innovation triggers progress or more efficient operations, a firm at least puts itself on equal footing with other firms if it adopts the same practices, and for this it often needs agents of change (such as consultants) as transmitters. Observations of McKinsey interventions, for example, have given rise to one of the founding publications of neoinstitutional theory, the article by DiMaggio and Powell (1983), which was based on the two authors' observation that McKinsey advice led to a number of isomorphic changes in public- and private-sector organizations.

Sociological neoinstitutionalism has been somewhat appropriated by the critical view on consultancy, as the theory seems to fit nicely into the critical camp's doubts about efficient outcomes from consulting assignments. However, the theory does not lend itself fully to the critical view. In fact, it has some elements of functionalism. For example, consultants as traders of legitimacy provide a service to a client *even if* their solution is similar to others, because it puts the consulted firm on a par with the others. Moreover, the sheer otherness of consultants in relation to client firms plays a central role in their ability to provide advice and gain legitimacy for it (Meyer 1996). And, as a central point, in their article on the institutional conditions for diffusion (of innovations, management practices, etc.), Strang and Meyer (1993) argue that any process of diffusion is accompanied or even preceded by a process of institutionalization. That is, before anything can disseminate as an idea or practice, it must be conceptualized and commodified as a term and concept, for only a communicatively transferable concept or explicit theory stands a chance of diffusing within or between professional groups. Consultants represent interpreters and theorists of individual cases and events. They often frame ambiguous information in new terms and theories, and thus develop and sharpen an interpretive consciousness within the client firm. Only this preceding theorization and term-building process enables an idea to diffuse. And, again, it is especially those consulting firms with a high public reputation that play a part in this process.

Signaling theory

The application of sociological neoinstitutionalism to management consultancy has been a useful and important advance, as it has highlighted the role of consultants in legitimation processes and in the communicative framing that precedes the diffusion of management concepts. Nevertheless, relying solely on sociological neoinstitutionalism may narrow the focus on societal norms and divert researchers from looking at the deliberative processes of individuals. Although sociological neoinstitutionalism acknowledges the possibility of different degrees of deliberation in economic action (Meyer and Rowan 1977; DiMaggio and Powell 1983), the question of the conscious behavior of economic actors represents the Achilles heel of this theory. As DiMaggio (1988: 9) observes, "[s]elf interested behavior tend[s] to be smuggled into institutional arguments rather than theorized explicitly." Sociological neoinstitutionalism has been developed to model the influence of norms on economic action, but it has difficulties with modeling autonomous action in the context of norms that economic actors are aware of. DiMaggio's (1988) distinction between institutionalization as a process and as an actual state then allows us to conceive of individual action at least in processes of institutionalization (see, in this context, Tolbert and Zucker 1996 and Barley and Tolbert 1997). If we take into account the possibility that clients are experienced and knowledgeable executives who can reflect on norms and act deliberately, then sociological neoinstitutionalism meets its limits and other theories suggest themselves.

In particular, economic signaling theory (Spence 1973, 1974, 1976) models deliberate signaling processes in the context of known norms. Signaling theory argues that, in markets of credence goods and quality uncertainty, providers invest in product or service features that signal status, quality, and reliability. Spence models graduate education (essentially, the reputation that different kinds of education involve) as a signal for graduates' future productivities. At the center of attention are the costs of signaling (e.g. for graduates on the job market the costs of education such as loans and household credit, and the effort put into attaining the degree), the effects of signaling (type of job, salary, promotions of the hired employee), and the incentive structures to invest in signals. If a provider cannot prove the quality of the outcome prior to purchase, and not even for some period after purchase, then he resorts to proving input factors as an indicator for the quality of the outcome. Signals such as certificates concerning educational background reduce the information asymmetry between supply (graduate) and demand (employers) of labor. Spence's central point is that a good education works as an efficient mechanism to signal a graduate's future productivity because, for someone with lower future productivity, it would be much more costly (investments, efforts) to attain a renowned degree. A conceptually simple but methodologically unfeasible test of signaling theory would be, for example, to gather people of identical ability and randomly assign some of them a degree certificate. If those with the certificate later earn more, then signaling theory would be supported.

There is one fundamental difference between economic signaling theory and sociological neoinstitutionalism. The former assumes that the signaling mechanism works as an efficient device to connect supply and demand, the latter looks at deviations from economic efficiency that legitimacy-seeking behavior brings about. In other words, signaling theory assumes that the market clears efficiently and conceptualizes how this comes about by signaling mechanisms. This assumption of efficiency may appear absurd to sociological neoinstitutionalists, because they observe economic action oriented toward norms and anticipated expectations independent of or detrimental to economic efficiency. Indeed, the explanation of economic actions in cases where efficiency remains unclear is the main purpose of the theory.

Nevertheless, the two theories have two important aspects in common. First, both view the essence of economic behavior in aspects external to the immediate exchange relationship, such as the status of education at prestigious colleges/universities or the status of particular concepts of organizational structure. In other words, both focus on the orientation of economic behavior toward the norms within which exchange partners act, rather than toward the immediate features of the exchange partners. The second commonality is that both theories imply a decoupling of reputation from the actual quality of a service. For sociological neoinstitutionalists, the legitimacy effect is decoupled from the economic quality of a decision (e.g. regarding organizational structure). Alternatively, an economically positive effect arises as a result of the gained legitimacy rather than from any intrinsic economic quality of the decision. Firms make particular decisions not because they have proven economic effects but because the environment considers them useful. Signaling theory, too, relies on the assumed rather than the actual quality of education. That is, a graduate from a college of high reputation may have undergone a worse preparation for a job than someone from an unknown college. Nevertheless, the graduate from the high-reputation college is rightly assumed to have a higher future productivity. This is because those individuals with a high future productivity independent of the education have less costly access to colleges of high reputation. Thus the signaling mechanism works irrespective of the actual quality of the education.

Important for our purposes is the notion that whether the behavior of market participants leads to efficient or inefficient outcomes cannot be assumed a priori, hence there can be no prior nonnormative preference for either of the two theories. Rather, the essence is to compare the theories with regard to individual phenomena.

Management consultancy can be perfectly modeled in terms of signaling theory. It represents a market of experience if not credence goods, and the quality of a consulting service is very difficult or impossible to prove in advance. As a result, management consulting firms signal output quality by input quality – i.e. by the quality of their human resources (see chapter 9 for details, and Pudack 2004). Although they accept applications from all universities, they hire actively only from the top business schools and universities. Independent of whether these institutions really deliver higher educational quality, these are the places that highly talented people covet and have less costly access to than less talented people, and therefore these are the places where the best graduates can be hired.

In fact, the large and renowned management consulting firms play a crucial role in what could be theorized as a signaling economy. The most talented students are drawn to the most renowned universities, irrespective of whether the educational quality is proven to be better there. Renowned management consulting firms hire from the most renowned universities and actually obtain better graduates than from other universities, again irrespective of proven educational quality. By hiring from these universities, the renowned consulting firms signal high output quality, can charge higher fees to their clients, and thus can offer higher salaries to their graduates. For consulting firms of lower reputation which cannot charge such high fees, it would be more costly to hire the same graduates, as they cannot carry over the higher personnel costs to clients in the same way. The renowned business schools, in turn, can signal quality by referring to the coveted jobs their graduates obtain, which, again, renders it more costly for less talented people to secure placement there.

This signaling circle can be extended to consulting clients. Large corporations hire the most renowned consultancies because the latter signal better consulting quality through their top business school graduates. Signaling high-quality advice means gaining legitimacy for management decisions and thus signaling management quality, which leads to advantages in the capital market. If the capital market rewards better talented students with less expensive loans and thus lower costs of obtaining access to coveted universities, then the signaling circle would be closed. But this might drive the signaling argument to the extreme and be too far-fetched to apply to future consultants. This point is taken up in the conclusion (chapter 10).

Transaction cost economics

The orientation toward norms external to the immediate business relationship is an important factor influencing the consulting market, but only one factor. If we take into account the possibility that clients can make rational decisions about whether to hire consultants or not, then we need to look more closely at the deliberations that characterize the immediate exchange relationship. Transaction cost economics (Coase 1937; Williamson 1975, 1985, 1986, 1988) helps theorizing when or for which business problems internal solutions or market provisions are beneficial. From this viewpoint, cost considerations are the crux of economic action, but more closely related to the immediate features of the transaction than signaling theory suggests. To transaction cost theorists, rationality (bounded by the available information and processing capabilities), calculativeness, and opportunistic behavior in business relationships represent an imperfect yet still the best possible set of assumptions for modeling economic behavior. The point of departure is the assumption that a company's costs can be classified in two categories: production costs and transaction costs. Production costs are those directly attributable to the productive capacities, such as manufacturing or logistics. Transaction costs, by contrast, are those associated with organizing economic activity. The latter comprise costs that occur prior to or that lead to a transaction, such as costs for gathering information, for negotiation, and for finalizing a contract, and costs that emerge after a transaction has been agreed upon, such as costs for interpreting contract clauses, enforcing contractual conditions, monitoring, conflict solving, or adjusting the contract. The decision of whether a task or service is to be conducted in-house ("hierarchy solution") or purchased in the market ("market solution") is based on a comparison of the sum of production and transaction costs.

Due to the detailed consideration of make-or-buy decisions, transaction cost economics is useful to outline clients' decision if and when to hire external consultants. Williamson conceptualizes make-or-buy decisions on the basis of three factors: the uncertainty, frequency, and asset specificity of a transaction. The argument is that, the higher the uncertainty, frequency, and asset specificity of a transaction, the more efficient an in-house solution is, because the transaction costs of elaborating and enforcing a reliable contract with an external provider would be higher than monitoring internal personnel. Vice versa, transactions with a low degree of uncertainty, frequency, and asset specificity can more sensibly be outsourced.

The question of which management functions are better conducted in-house and which should be outsourced to a consulting firm can be approached with the transaction cost tool by a trivial example. Suppose a chemical engineering company faces continuous engineering challenges in order to maintain and improve its products and production processes. These core engineering activities demand a highly specialized workforce and engineering equipment (high asset specificity), the challenges occur on a regular basis in the context of process maintenance (high frequency), and uncertainty is relatively high because the challenges are often accompanied by research and development (R&D) issues. As a result, outsourcing those activities would be inefficient, and the company will retain an internal workforce of chemical engineers to take care of them.

The same chemical engineering firm may face a new challenge, for example an opportunity to acquire or set up a plant in a new region with a much lower cost structure. Such a situation requires an analysis that represents a one-off activity (low frequency), it does not involve specialized machinery (low asset specificity), and the process of *analyzing* the situation is less burdened by long-term uncertainty than research and development processes. As a result, the chemical engineering firm may reasonably outsource this analytical service to an external provider, for example a consulting firm. This may be a trivial example of applying transaction cost economics to the consulting business, but it conveys the consideration that explicitly or implicitly underlies a decision to hire consultants.

Information economics (Stigler 1961; Alchian and Demsetz 1972) belongs to the same family of theories as transaction cost economics. It compares the usefulness of information with the costs of obtaining it. With regard to a comparison between an internal and an external solution to gaining the necessary information, its existence is attributable to the advantages of monitoring joint inputs. That is, in comparison to a market solution, it is easier for a firm to monitor internally those inputs that are not attributable to individual providers, such as employees. Put differently, "The ability to detect shirking among owners of jointly used inputs in team production is enhanced (detection costs are reduced) by this arrangement and the discipline (by revision of contracts) of input owners is made more economic" (Alchian and Demsetz 1972: 794). The limit to a firm's size is reached when the "specialized knowledge about inputs becomes as expensive to transmit across divisions of the firms as it does across markets to other firms" (794). To translate the argument to the consulting market, in simplified terms the limit to a client firm size is reached when the costs of transferring information within the firm, for example from the bottom of the hierarchy to the chief executive officer (CEO) or between divisions, are higher than transferring this information through an external provider. In a similar vein, the limits to a firm's size are reached when labor law renders it difficult to dismiss employees. Hiring consultants may often mean purchasing short-term enhancement of analytical capacities that are in principle available for in-house employment but that would constitute over-capacity after the task has been finished.

With regard to management consulting, one of the points is that clients economize on the acquisition of knowledge and information when hiring an external consultant. They do not necessarily buy the direct supply of information but, rather, information-gathering or knowledge acquisition skills. If internal employees had (inexpensive) methodological means to collect and distribute them internally, or if collecting this information represented an interplay of joint inputs rather than a service attributable to a particular party, then the use of external consultants would be less economical. In short, methodological skills for tasks which occur rarely or aperiodically in any one firm, which involve high costs of internal coordination and distribution, which can be attributed to a particular provider, and which can be more economically acquired and applied across firms are the crux of the consulting business. It is indeed surprising that few scholars of management consultancy have drawn on transaction or information cost economics (Canbäck 1998a, 1998b, 1999 and Kehrer and Schade 1995 represent notable exceptions), although these arguments explicitly address the alternatives from the client perspective. Chapter 2 will provide more detailed analyses and examples.

Embeddedness theory

In conceptualizing mechanisms internal to the immediate exchange relationship, transaction cost economics has been challenged over the past twenty years by embeddedness theorists (Granovetter 1985; Powell 1990; Granovetter and Swedberg 1992; Uzzi 1996, 1997; Dacin *et al.* 1999). To them, transaction cost considerations represent an "undersocialized" (Granovetter 1985) conception of economic action. Embeddedness theory argues that organizational economists are not necessarily wrong in their cost comparisons and assumption of calculativeness, but that they ignore or underestimate the point that most economic action takes place in established lanes of social ties and networks. Calculativeness is not absent, but it is often bounded by social ties, and the efficiency of a transaction is only one consideration or possibility.

Embeddedness theorists distance themselves from transaction cost economics by arguing that management decisions, for example between subcontractors or make-or-buy alternatives, are primarily based on the structure and quality of the relations between decision-making executives of different companies, which can only imperfectly be captured in terms of transaction costs. At the heart of the embeddedness paradigm is the structural aspect of social relations, especially the significance of personal and business networks for economic transactions. Business relationships, for example between consultants and their clients, are rarely characterized by arm's-length relations and opportunistic behavior by the two parties, but typically by long-term relationships of trust and/or a social embeddedness in networks of business partners. As a result, transactions may be inefficient without the participants either noticing or calculating it as such. A transaction cost analysis of such processes may then represent an *ex post* rationalization of an otherwise inefficient solution.

From this perspective, the question emerges as to how consulting assignments come about and under which circumstances consulting firms compete with each other. For example, from the embeddedness perspective the make-or-buy decision is not based primarily on a calculative comparison of costs between hierarchy and market solutions, but the very question of whether to outsource or not emerges only from social ties. For example, a client may learn about a particular kind of consulting service only through business contacts and social ties to clients, suppliers, or competitors. Calculative cost considerations may then be a complementary feature of the make-or-buy decision, but the primary mechanism is a social relation one.

More often than not, the decision-making process does not follow the sequence of, first, deciding about making or buying, and, second (in the case of buying), checking who would be a good provider. Rather, the social interaction with business partners is often the trigger for a buy decision, and possibilities of in-house solutions or other external providers are not considered.

Indeed, empirical findings suggest that competition between providers in the consulting sector is not based on price or costs (Dawes *et al.* 1992; File *et al.* 1994; Clark 1995; Page 1998). The degree and significance of the uncertainty that clients face when choosing and interacting with a consulting firm is high. Objective quality measurement of the mostly immaterial consulting services is difficult to achieve, and management consulting (as well as most other knowledge-intensive business services) is performed subsequent to the contract, which shifts the risk as to quality or partner adequacy toward the client. In such situations, informal social institutions such as trust, reputation, and word-of-mouth effects take center stage. These may also save costs, such as for gaining information or screening quality, but they may also prevent price or cost considerations on the buyer's side. As a result, the quality of a network tie to a client decision-maker is the main competitive advantage of a consulting firm. Chapter 3 outlines these circumstances in greater detail.

Embeddedness theory offers an additional perspective: applying the focus on social ties and networks to firm-internal matters. In the literature on knowledge management, the "communities of practice" approach (Brown and Duguid 1996, 1998) has obtained broad attention. While this approach tries to develop its own theory from the knowledge-based theory of the firm (Spender 1996; Grant 1996a, 1996b), it places the effects of strong and weak ties on knowledge creation within the firm at the center of attention. For example, Brown and Duguid (1998: 97) write,

[M]ost formal organizations are not single communities of practice, but, rather, hybrid groups of overlapping and interdependent communities. Such hybrid collectives represent another level in the complex process of knowledge creation. Intercommunal relationships allow the organization to develop collective, coherent, synergistic organizational knowledge out of the potentially separate, independent contributions of the individual communities.

While Brown and Duguid, and others who pursue the communities of practice approach, rarely refer to embeddedness theory as a point of orientation and source of information, the above quote shows that their arguments are practically the same. Not only strong ties (within a community of practice) but also weak ties (between communities of practice) lie at the center of their attention. Hence, their approach can duly be seen as an application of embeddedness notions to firm-internal matters − with one difference: authors such as Brown and Duguid praise communities of practice as being functional for firms but do not look at the inefficiencies that embeddedness effects may involve. In fact, one of the key insights that embeddedness research has brought about is that economic exchange does not always follow the lines of efficiency, precisely because it is bound by social ties. In a similar vein to the communities of practice approach, Högl and Gemünden (2001) and Högl *et al.* (2004) show that not just teamwork quality but inter-team coordination as well are crucial factors for the success of innovative projects. Thus, it is not only the quality of strong ties but also the management of weak ties within a firm that matter for innovativeness and corporate performance. But, unlike embeddedness research, Högl and Gemünden (2001) and Högl *et al.* (2004) do not look at the limits to efficiency that network ties often involve. This discussion will be taken up in chapter 8 on organizational design, governance, and knowledge management in consulting firms.

In summary, all four theories have important things to say about management consulting, although they are based on different assumptions and look at different issues. Signaling theory and transaction cost economics are both driven by the assumption that observations of calculativeness and cost considerations teach us most about economic behavior, while sociological neoinstitutionalism and embeddedness theory argue that observations of social mechanisms and the limits to calculativeness are more informative. Signaling theory and sociological neoinstitutionalism, by contrast, have in common their orientation toward norms and thus on mechanisms external to the immediate transaction partners, while transaction cost theory and embeddedness theory focus on the immediate features of the transaction and its participants. Table 1.1 summarizes these juxtapositions.

Table 1.1. Four theories and their focus

	Focus on cost considerations ("economics")	Focus on social mechanisms ("sociology")
Mechanisms external to the immediate exchange relationship	Signaling theory	Sociological neoinstitutionalism
Mechanisms internal to the immediate exchange relationship	Transaction cost economics	Embeddedness theory

Distinguishing and debating the four theories

At this point, the differences and applications of the three theories need to be outlined more thoroughly. The scientific community is often split in its assumptions concerning the nature of business relations and human behavior, and this split is reflected in the use of theories. Typically, the divide lies between the disciplines of economics and sociology (Swedberg 1990; Zukin and DiMaggio 1990; Friedland and Robertson 1990; Lie 1997). The debate between transaction cost economics and embeddedness theory represents this divide and, accordingly, is outlined first. The difference between transaction cost economics and sociological neoinstitutionalism follows different lines but is equally representative of the two disciplines. However, there are differences even between theories of the same academic discipline. As mentioned above, neither embeddedness theory and sociological neoinstitutionalism nor transaction cost economics and signaling theory form coherent approaches, as they differ in their assumption as to whether mechanisms outside or inside the immediate transaction relationship are more important. These theories cannot be applied to management consulting without discussing their differences or without discussing the debate on paradigm incommensurability, which will be carried out on the basis of critical rationalism.

Transaction cost economics versus embeddedness theory

Transaction cost economists tend to conceive of economic action in terms of the calculativeness (bounded rationality) and opportunism of market participants. This does not mean that market participants have to have egoistic motives; *Homo economicus* may have egoistic or perfectly altruistic motives. What is important for the economic paradigm is only that he pursues these (possibly altruistic) motives in a calculative and opportunistic manner. Through this lens, modeling business decisions in terms of cost considerations is a logical consequence, for costs represent a useful unit for invested effort.

Embeddedness theorists, by contrast, do not consider this approach particularly useful. As outlined above, they hold that the degree of calculativeness in economic transactions is often limited, because actors are embedded in social relations. These may be direct trust relations between suppliers and clients, or webs of social relations in which weak ties enable transactions between participants who are not connected through direct ties. From the embeddedness perspective, calculativeness and opportunism, in the sense of cheating when the cost of reputation damage is lower than the gains of cheating, be it modeled by transaction cost or game theorists (von Neumann and Morgenstern 1944; Axelrod 1984; Fudenberg and Tirole 1991; Kreps 1991), represent an "undersocialized" (Granovetter 1985) image of economic behavior. Bound by social ties, economic transactions may be inefficient, and transaction cost economics may at best be able to rationalize individual behavior *ex post* rather than sketch the reality of economic transactions at the time of decision-making. The arm's-length relationships between economic actors that economists often assume by default might be an accurate assumption for a consumer transaction such as buying a shirt or a pair of shoes, but not for purchasing business services in markets of credence goods and quality uncertainty (DiMaggio and Louch 1998).

Such theories are often considered either or paradigms for scholars. Either one models business relations as arm's-length ones with opportunistic behavior (essentially, as relationships in which cooperation is based on calculation, as game theory does), or as embedded relations with limited calculativeness. However, this either or relationship must be put in perspective. Embeddedness theorists emphasize that buyers often choose transaction partners within preexisting noncommercial ties. If these ties do not entail an appropriate provider, they seek recommendations from noncommercial and trust-based commercial ties to identify and assess transaction partners with whom they did not previously have relations. This is a process of actively pursuing word-of-mouth effects, which DiMaggio and Louch (1998) call "search embeddedness." It does not preclude economizing behavior but emphasizes its limits. As Powell (1990: 323) argues in his article on network forms of organization,

Economizing is obviously a relevant concern in many instances, especially in infant industries where competitive preserves are strong. But it alone is not a particularly robust story, it is but one among a number of theoretically possible motives for action – all of which are consonant with a broad view of self-interest. Clearly many of the arrangements discussed above [network forms of organization] actually increase transaction costs, but in return they provide concrete benefits or intangible assets that are far more valuable.

This argument is supported by the analyses of Burt (1992, 2004), who finds that good ideas are connected with brokerage positions between network holes, which feed back on individuals in terms of performance evaluation, compensation, and promotions.

Since the embeddedness approach has become prominent, econo-mists have come to be aware that networks play a critical role in economic transactions. Williamson (1991: 291), for example, outlines a network as "a nonhierarchical contracting relation in which reputation effects are quickly and accurately communicated." He has become aware of the role of social ties in economic transactions, but insists that acting within strong and weak social ties still entails a lot of economizing:

It's my feeling that a rather huge fraction of what is going on in these network enterprises can be interpreted usefully in transaction cost terms. Actually, one of the things that is probably frustrating to noneconomists is that economics is so incredibly elastic. Once the economic content of a concept is understood, economics finds a way to embrace it. So I anticipate that networks can probably be incorporated – at least to some degree – into an extended version of transaction cost economic. (interview with Williamson in Swedberg 1990: 122)

And, indeed, game theory (von Neumann and Morgenstern 1944; Fudenberg and Tirole 1991) is based on exactly this notion: that an offeror gives trust as a specific investment if he reckons with rents, if reciprocated, or with comparatively lower costs, if not. The other part, the decision-maker, reciprocates trust if it involves advantages (Axelrod 1984; Raub and Weesie 1990; Kreps 1991).

From this perspective, nothing stands in the way of modeling trust in cost terms. Network ties simply enable actors to save the costs of searching and assessing product or service quality, and pursuing transactions in webs of strong or weak ties saves the monitoring and contract enforcement costs. Even reputation then emerges as a result of iterated games of calculative refraining from monitoring (Raub and Weesie 1990). Hence, economists are perfectly able to model co-operating and gaining a reputation as a fair player, which could then be called "trust," as a result of calculative behavior (Ripperger 1998; Axelrod 1984). Williamson (1993) reserves the term "trust" for purely noncalculative relationships and argues that calculative trust is a contradiction in terms. On this basis, he argues that economic relationships simply do not entail trust, but only calculative coopera-tion. By contrast, Ripperger (1998) argues, in line with game theory, that trust and calculativeness cannot sensibly be divided. Reserving trust for purely noneconomic relationships assumes a schizophrenic concept of human beings, whose deliberations and behavior precisely distinguish between different spheres of life. Ripperger (1998: 247−8) further argues that calculativeness forms a basis for trust rather than a contradiction of it, because moral behavior such as trustfulness cannot be learned without reason, deliberations, and thus calculation.

As a result, trust in economic relationships can be conceptualized as the degree to which an actor refrains from screening, monitoring, or demanding explicit contractual security or incentives. In games of iterated prisoners' dilemmas, cooperating, in terms of refraining from short-term opportunism, may pay off in the long run, and an eco-nomics of trust emerges as the calculation of when this makes sense (Fudenberg and Tirole 1991; Kreps 1991; Ripperger 1998). Such deliberations can be perfectly virtuous if the ends and motives are altruistic. Vice versa, monitoring may lead to a spiral of distrust and thus to an inefficient economic transaction (Ripperger 1998: 70). The assumption of opportunistic behavior is no contradiction of this notion: only the possibility and danger of opportunistic behavior establishes those risks without which trust would not exist as a social institution (Ripperger 1998: 60). Tacit collusion, defined as two organizations using cues but without direct communication in order to achieve mutual gain, may then result in the formation of implicit cartels (for an overview, see Ivaldi *et al.* 2003).

To embeddedness theorists, however, such models encapsulate precisely the undersocialized conception of economic action. As Granovetter (1985: 490) puts it, "Economists have pointed out that one incentive not to cheat is the cost of damage to one's reputation, but this is an undersocialized conception of reputation as a generalized commodity, a ratio of cheating to opportunities to cheat." Embeddedness theorists, therefore, are aware that network effects can be modeled in terms of search, information, and assessment costs, but they doubt that such models correspond to the real world of economic actors. The transfer of information from previous transactions, the refraining from market screening or from monitoring transaction partners, are not necessarily calculative processes but often the result of the social ties within which the actors move. Even in endgames, when actors are about to withdraw from a market or social environment, do they not necessarily abuse trust but may act on a broad continuum between trust-fulfilling and -abusing behavior. Transaction cost economics and game theory model only one end of this spectrum, namely the calculative one. Calculus-based models of transactions may underestimate or even ignore the web of reciprocal obligations in which bilateral relationships are embedded. Economic transactions can often not be isolated from the social environment in which particular outcomes or ways of behaving have an impact. Transaction cost and game theorists, by contrast, reply that such a web of multiple rather than bilateral obligations can in principle be addressed in cost terms, but concede that integrating them would render a model very complex (Raub and Weesie 1990; Williamson 1991).

A client–consultant relationship can be taken as an example. Transaction cost economists can model clients' cost-based decisions between alternative providers. The relevance of trust relations between consultants and clients can, in principle, be acknowledged and integrated in terms of search, information, and anticipated monitoring costs. From the embeddedness viewpoint, by contrast, such cost considerations either fail to be precise enough to guide a client's decision, or they do not even emerge between trusted business partners. According to this view, it is not that transaction cost considerations are absent but that they are often overruled by qualitative decisions based on social tie quality.

The point that cost considerations cannot be precise enough to guide a purchasing decision is an important one. The exact comparison of search, information, monitoring, and enforcement costs between different purchasing options – or the estimation of the costs of a damaged reputation when discontinuing the cooperation – might be a fascinating task for academics, but it is rarely a matter that executives can spend their time on. In the consulting market, such cost estimation between different service providers would be so complex that it would require a consulting project of its own – before the actual project can be started with the selected provider. In addition, many of the costs would have to be forecast based on previous experiences without precise information about the incurred *ex post* costs of the transaction (i.e. the costs of monitoring, contract enforcement, contract adjustment, etc.). Transaction cost economics may be able to model decisions after the event, but, in the actual decision-making process, transaction costs and costs for damaged reputation can only roughly be estimated – and the quality of the social relation strongly influences or determines this estimation. As far as credence goods are concerned, it may be impossible to say whether or not a solution was optimal. Hence, it is not surprising if executives make such decisions largely on the basis of social tie quality. This, however, may in turn be calculative even if the result is immeasurable. The very decision to rely on social ties may implicitly be a cost-based one, since any search or information gathering beyond the social ties may be more costly. Moreover, as soon as some dissatisfaction emerges, client executives may automatically engage in considerations of alternatives, and, even if the final decision is not based on precise estimates of future costs, cost issues are indissolubly interwoven with social tie considerations.

What emerges here is a central problem of monotheoretical perspectives. Adopting only one perspective may result in losing sight of phenomena that the other perspective would discover. For example, for the duration of one or two projects, a client may be perfectly satisfied with a provider's services, and a trust relation emerges between the executive and the senior consultant. This trust may go so far as to prevent the manager from seriously considering alternative providers (so-called "overembeddedness"; Uzzi 1997: 59). Even if a competing consultant enters the scene and offers a potentially better or more economical service, the manager cannot or does not want to examine the new provider's quality and thus may not seriously consider him. In particular in such a market for credence goods, a client may not engage in serious cost-benefit analyses, and he may not even think of disappointing his present partner. Thus, cost considerations interwoven with social tie considerations cannot be expressed purely in cost terms; real events rarely follow the clear lines of a single theory. This discussion will be taken up in chapter 10.

Transaction cost economics versus sociological neoinstitutionalism

The distinction between transaction cost economics and sociological neoinstitutionalism follows a different line: the emergence and nature of social institutions. For a transaction cost economist, social institutions such as contracts and laws, and even trust and reputation, are arrangements that emerge in the context of economizing on negotiations, monitoring, and enforcement. As DiMaggio and Powell (1991: 3–4) put it in their demarcation of sociological neoinstitutionalism from other approaches, to economists "[i]nstitutions arise and persist when they confer benefits greater than the transaction costs...incurred in creating and sustaining them." Information is costly, people behave opportunistically, and rationality is bounded; thus the features of transactions such as asset specificity, uncertainty, and frequency give rise to economic institutions. DiMaggio and Powell (8–11) usefully outline the difference between new institutionalism in economics and new institutionalism in organizational sociology along three lines: (a) the degree of consciousness and deliberation in creating institutions; (b) whether institutions are considered results of individual actors' preferences and interests, or outcomes of collective social constructs; and (c) the degree to which institutions are malleable according to the imperatives of efficiency.

Transaction cost economics conceives of institutions as results of calculative action in order to save search, information, monitoring, and enforcement costs in economic transactions. They may be collective in the sense that groups of individuals have collectively designed them, but economists do not conceive of them as outcomes of collective social constructions that cannot be reduced to individual or groups' deliberations (DiMaggio and Powell 1991: 9–10). Moreover, economists assume that institutions are also subject to change according to the deliberations of individuals or groups. Sociological neoinstitutionalists, in contrast, take the opposite stance on these matters. They conceive of institutions as social constructs without preceding processes of calculativeness; they argue that institutions cannot be reduced to the interests or preferences of individuals or groups; and they hold that changing or adapting them is highly complex, if not impossible.

Again, these differences can be applied to the consulting business, for example to the choice of organizational structures or outsourcing decisions that consultants may recommend. To an organizational economist, institutionalizations such as the multidivisional organizational structure (M-form) in the decades after the Second World War (in North America it began before the war) or the establishment of in-house consultancies in the 1980s and 1990s (see chapter 5) represent deliberate solutions in order to save transaction costs. In the case of the M-form, the divisionalization of the organizational structure was considered the best means of coordinating multinational corporations to respond to the increasing internationalization. It was assumed to reduce the information overload on top management and to reduce communication problems via standardization. Moreover, the divisions of an M-form have no excuse for poor performance and thus use resources more efficiently, which accounts for the cost advantages triggered by motivation (Chandler 1962; Williamson 1975).

To a sociological neoinstitutionalist, this may be true, but the amazing dissemination of the M-form cannot be fully explained by proven efficiency. The M-form may or may not represent an efficient solution for some corporations; much more important has been the collective belief in its efficiency, which has accounted for its widespread, international adoption. To an individual firm or a decision-making executive, it was probably impossible to ascertain the economic benefits or drawbacks of adopting the M-form. Nevertheless, the institutionalization of this solution as a good organizational structure constituted a strong normative pressure to adopt it. Whether an executive actually believed in the efficiency of a solution, whether he was forced by legal standards, or whether he just reproduced it because comparable firms did the same, the crucial criterion of implementation was the firm's increasing legitimacy in the environment if it adopted the M-form. Moreover, as Bartlett and Ghoshal (1993) and Hoskisson *et al.* (1993) have pointed out, the term "M-form" covers a large variety of solutions. It is very questionable whether these different forms subsumed under the term represent more efficient responses to corporate internationalization than others. From a sociological neoinstitutional perspective, the diffusion of the M-form may have been a classical case of an institutionalized rationality myth.

A similar argument applies to the growth of internal management consulting in the 1980s (North America) and 1990s (Europe). A transaction cost consideration suggests that, if certain features apply to an analytical task, then in-house consulting may be a more economical solution than external consultancy (see chapters 2 and 5 for details). Again, from a neoinstitutional perspective this may be the case, but a transaction cost view does not suffice to explain the sudden wave of internal consultancies being founded in the 1980s. From a sociological neoinstitutional perspective, these processes of organizational isomorphism were a matter of normative or mimetic adaptation to perceived expectations − that is, to institutionalizations of what was considered efficient rather than as economic responses to what actually was efficient. Nevertheless, to economist and historian North (1990), for example, even broadly shared ideologies represent means to curb opportunistic behavior and to substitute formal rules. As an empirical proof for either theory cannot finally be achieved, it is again the case that more than one theory may inform the explanation of the phenomenon.

Signaling theory versus transaction cost economics

Signaling theory and transaction cost economics have several commonalities. Not only do they both take root in the economic paradigm and view cost considerations as the crux of economic action, but they also consider institutions such as contracts or trust as efficient outcomes of deliberate and calculative behavior. Moreover, both are concerned with mechanisms to reduce adverse-selection problems and information asymmetry between transaction partners. Nevertheless, the two theories have dividing lines. First, signaling theory looks at cost alternatives (different kinds of education) that emerge in anticipation of future productivity ascribed by a third party, such as an employer for graduates in the labor market. In transaction cost economics, at least in the basic model there is no such third party, and the alternatives are oneself (make) and a second party (buy). Thus, signaling theory is oriented toward mechanisms external to the immediate alternatives, while transaction cost economics is oriented toward the attributes of the immediate transaction alternatives. Like sociological neoinstitutionalism, therefore, signaling theory involves a macro component of societal expectations or norms, while transaction cost economics operates at the meso level of immediate transaction alternatives.

The second difference is that signaling theory models the behavior of the better-informed party to reduce information asymmetry, while transaction cost economics models the behavior of the worse-informed party. Signaling costs emerge for those who know about their future productivity and have to convey it to the other. Transaction costs of screening, selecting, monitoring, and enforcing emerge for those who have to learn about their transaction partner rather than convey information about themselves. The question of which party takes the initiative to reduce information asymmetry gives rise to the question of market power, which will be addressed in chapter 4.

Sociological neoinstitutionalism versus signaling theory

Sociological neoinstitutionalism conceives of institutions as social and cultural constructs in the sense of unreflective routine behavior and taken-for-granted norms and views. From this perspective, signaling theory seems just the opposite – intentional participation in signaling games based on a full awareness of norms such as good education. Yet sociological neoinstitutionalism and economic signaling theory address two sides of the same coin. The former tries to explain the emergence and effects of norms and institutions, the latter models the way how individuals act in the context of these taken-for-granted norms. Sociological neoinstitutionalists, for example, observe the decoupling of an official organizational structure from the actual functioning of an organization (Meyer and Rowan 1977). Signaling theory, by contrast, observes how individuals such as job-seeking graduates behave in a market that is characterized by taken-for-granted institutions and thus provides a cost consideration of decoupling effects.

Nevertheless, important differences remain. The most important one has been mentioned above: sociological neoinstitutionalism does not suppose that economic decisions, for example selection principles in job markets, are particularly rational or efficient (as signaling theory holds). Rather, sociological neoinstitutionalism is interested in systematic distortions from economic efficiency, for example in hiring graduates from renowned universities *although* they may be less productive. These doubts about economic efficiency are particularly relevant in markets of credence goods. Consulting services comprise a variety of procedures on a continuum between experience and credence goods. To sociological neoinstitutionalists, it is unclear how approaches such as signaling theory can sensibly model such markets on efficiency assumptions. Hence, sociological neoinstitutionalism looks at symbolical and cultural processes within which institutions emerge and inefficiencies persist, while signaling theory is concerned with deliberate investments in sending imperfect signals, which result in efficient matching processes between supply and demand.

Because of its focus on the influence of institutions, sociological neoinstitutionalism may lead researchers to underestimate the intentionality with which market participants act. Calculative behavior by individuals who are aware of social institutions is a possibility, but the thrust of sociological neoinstitutionalism is the unconscious effect of institutions on individual behavior. Self-interested behavior tends to be "smuggled into institutional theory" (DiMaggio 1988: 9) after the original setting has abstained from it. Indeed, if empirical research increasingly identifies actors' behavior as calculative and aware of institutions, sociological neoinstitutionalism gradually loses its explanatory power. By contrast, signaling theory may lead researchers to erroneously assume efficient outcomes of economic action. Job market signaling, for example, is considered an effective way that leads the market to clear (Spence 1973, 1974). The theory is interested in explanations of how and why a market clears, rather than in market failure. For credence goods, such assumptions are shaky. If empirical research finds that a job market does not clear, or that individuals with lower productivity do not have higher signaling costs than high potentials, then signaling theory meets its limits. If the degree of intentionality of market participants varies, or if market clearance is but one out of several observed results, then the juxtaposition of signaling theory and sociological neoinstitutionalism may lead to learning effects.

Signaling theory versus embeddedness theory

Signaling theory and embeddedness theory may appear intellectually too far away from each other to be sensibly compared. Interestingly, however, both are rooted in observations of the same topic: job markets. Granovetter's (1974) study of job market participants introduces the now common distinction between strong ties as direct trust relations and weak ties as rooted in rare encounters, mutual acquaintances, or mechanisms of recommendation. It gives center stage to the notion that weak ties can make the difference in accomplishing a transaction such as getting a desired job. From the embeddedness perspective, the essence of successful job market behavior is the mobilization of weak ties, rather than applications without previous contacts or reliance on strong ties. This represents a big difference from Spence's (1974) study of job market signaling, where both strong and weak ties are largely left out of the picture. Job market signaling is based on the assumption of arm's-length relationships, or even complete anonymity, between seekers and providers of jobs. A commonality is that both theories portray the job seeker as the one who takes the initiative in reducing the other party's informational disadvantage. In real life, the two ways of reducing information asymmetry may complement each other. For example, the mobilization of weak ties may be strongly facilitated when diplomas from renowned educational institutes can be presented. And women or ethnic minorities may not succeed in the job market as much as white males do, even though they have the same contacts, because their signaling costs are higher, which may render it more difficult for them to build on their contacts. Alternatively, they may not even obtain these contacts because of their higher costs of signaling future productivity. In fact, if job market participants obtain contacts by way of attending a renowned educational institute, then the two effects reinforce each other and are only analytically distinct.

Nevertheless, these analytical differences are important. First, embeddedness-based analyses of job markets tend to play down the cost aspect of contacts. Obtaining or maintaining strong and weak ties does not come for free but requires investments. And signaling theory, rather than embeddedness theory, looks at these investments in reducing information asymmetry. Second, embeddedness theory looks at the immediate features of the relationship through which a transaction comes about. In the case of job markets, this is the quality of the relationship to a potential employer. Signaling theory, by contrast, neglects these immediate features and focuses on mechanisms external to the immediate exchange relationship; in the case of job markets, on the reputation and therefore the value of education and on the investments in obtaining it. Like the difference between transaction cost economics and signaling theory, the levels of observation are meso versus macro. I will return to this discussion in the conclusion in Part III.

Embeddedness theory versus sociological neoinstitutionalism

Both embeddedness theory and sociological neoinstitutionalism represent critiques of transaction cost economics, but important differences between them remain. Embeddedness theorists see the essence of economic transactions in the social relations between individual actors and in webs of mutual obligations. They focus on the quality of social relations in terms of strong or weak ties. Sociological neoinstitutionalists, in contrast, consider economic action to be driven by systems of rules or assumptions about efficiency that are shared not only by members of a business network but by larger entities, such as entire business sectors, organizational fields, nation states and their cultures, or even "world society."

In the field of management consulting, the diffusion of innovations and the role of consultants in this process constitute good cases for outlining the difference between the two theories. As mentioned above, embeddedness theorists try to reconstruct or explain the diffusion of innovations by looking at the social ties within which innovative products are brought about or disseminated. Extensive studies of social networks account for detailed analyses of the relationship between network position and innovation success (Burt 1992, 2004; Powell 1996, 1998; Powell *et al.* 1996; Tsai 2001; Beckman and Haunschild 2002; Reagans and McEvily 2003; Ritter and Gemünden 2003). Management consultants are considered in the context of technology transfer and bridges of innovation between formerly unconnected actors or firms. The analysis of innovations and their diffusion is thus located at a meso level of social relations and their effects.

From a neoinstitutional perspective, such analyses are useful, but they may not represent the first stage or essence of the innovation process. Through this lens, innovations are accompanied or even preceded by a process of institutionalization. That is, before anything can disseminate as an idea or practice it must be conceptualized and commodified as a term and concept, for only communicatively transferable concepts or explicit theories have a chance to diffuse within or between professional groups (Strang and Meyer 1997). An analysis of economic action along these lines would ascertain how some ideas institutionalize in such a way that they become a transferable commodity while others remain uninstitutionalized and are not transferred, even though the conditions of social relations are the same. The diffusion of ideas or practices, therefore, is based not only on interaction and exchange but also on a theorization of and abstraction from individual cases. The role of consultants may then be reinterpreted in that they operate not just as network-related bridges to sources of innovation or as advisors and facilitators in change processes, but as interpreters and theorists of individual cases and events. They often frame ambiguous information in new terms and theories and thus develop and sharpen an interpretive consciousness within the client firm. Only this theorization and term-building process allows for the possibility of diffusion within social structures.

Apart from this reinterpretation of consultants as carriers of economic functions, neoinstitutionalism views them in yet another role. Those consulting firms with a high public reputation may bestow legitimacy upon an innovation or business idea and thus validate a management concept. Consultants contribute to the institutionalization of an innovation not only through interpretation and term-building processes but also by being an icon of management knowledge. The top consulting firms in particular represent rationality and quantitative-analytical competence. Embeddedness theorists may reply that being an icon of management knowledge at a macro level of institutionalized myths may be useful but barely suffices to get a consulting contract. Only social tie quality at a meso level enables this, and this is true for large as much as for small providers. Thus, embeddedness operates at a meso level while sociological neoinstitutionalism represents a macro level of sociological inquiry.

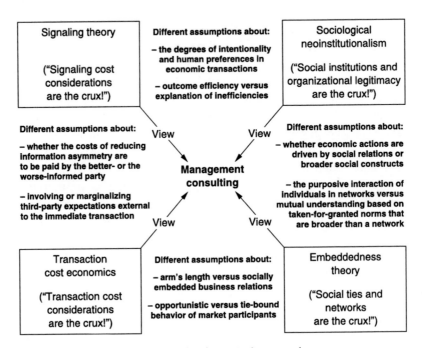

Figure 1.1. Differences between the theoretical approaches

In summary, the differences between the four theories can be sketched in figure 1.1.

The case against incommensurability

Looking at these differences between theories, the immediate concern of incommensurability may emerge. In organization theory, the assumption that different paradigms are incommensurable was first proposed by Burrell and Morgan (1979). They argue that the four paradigms of organizational analysis that they identify (radical humanist; radical structuralist; interpretive; functionalist) are based on entirely different assumptions about human nature and about the nature of social science (ontology, epistemology, methodology). Hence they say that researchers should adopt one perspective and contribute to research and knowledge production within it. Since all four theories outlined above represent different approaches to economic phenomena and are based on different assumptions about the nature of business relations and human behavior, how can they all be applied to management consulting in one book? Signaling theory and transaction cost economics assume calculative behavior and model it in cost terms. Sociological neoinstitutionalism and embeddedness theory look at the limits of calculative behavior and point to social phenomena that guide or at least influence the behavior of market participants. The gulf between, for example, embeddedness theory and transaction cost economics appears to many scholars to be too large to be bridged. The argument is that one can only either assume that human behavior is fully calculative or that it is bound by social ties, or one can only either assume that individuals act opportunistically or that they do not. The potential for integration seems low.

However, the above debate between embeddedness theory and transaction cost economics has indicated that actual business relations — for example between clients and consultants — are characterized by a mixture of personal trust, calculative cost considerations, reliance on weak ties, and arm's-length search behavior. These elements of the business relationship and their individual weight vary from case to case, or even overlap within a single decision-making process. Ignoring either embeddedness theory or organizational economics may be appropriate in one situation but misleading in another. Screening out one category by defining strict assumptions of human behavior may lead to a clean model but distract from a comprehensive image of what is really going on.

Likewise, transaction cost economics and sociological neoinstitutionalism are analytically different too. Social institutions emerge through calculative behavior (economics) or through norm-based conduct (sociological neoinstitutionalism). Nonetheless, scholars such as Ruef (2002) point out that some elements are compatible. The process of interpreting and framing ambiguous information in new terms — which, for example, consultants perform — is a central element of social institutionalization processes. At the same time, it represents a service to clients who would incur higher transaction costs if it was carried out internally. As mentioned above, before anything can disseminate as an idea or practice, it must be conceptualized and commodified as a communicatively transferable concept. As interpreters and theorists of individual cases and events, consultants form a part of institutionalization processes, and at the same time save clients transaction costs by sharpening an interpretive consciousness at lower costs than in-house personnel could.

Acknowledging that human behavior does not cleanly follow the assumptions of any particular theory, and that observable phenomena refer to elements of originally different theories, the argument of paradigm incommensurability[1] emerges as increasingly problematic. Burrell and Morgan's (1979) suggestion of paradigm incommensurability has always been contested. Willmott (1990, 1993) and Deetz (1996) have suggested considering Burrell and Morgan's conceptualization as heuristic rather than instrumental. The point is not only that observable phenomena − such as consultants' framing of information and solutions − refer to elements of theories with different assumptions, but also that analyses and results obtained from one perspective open people's eyes to the shortcomings and limits of other perspectives. Scientific progress *may* be achieved by using only one theory and testing ideas on that basis. However, it also grows on the comparison and mutual critique of different views − even, and in particular, if this critique concerns the very assumptions.

The person who rejected the thesis of paradigm incommensurability early and most forcefully was Karl Popper. In his book *The Myth of the Framework* (1994; based on articles he wrote in the 1960s and 1970s) he explicitly deals with the argument that paradigm incommensurability − in his words "the doctrine that truth is relative to our intellectual background and changes from one framework to another" − builds an appropriate basis for scientific progress. In fact, he considers this doctrine an intellectual fashion, and points out that its supporters are either ideologists who seek to render their theory immune to critique, or relativists who assume that truth is relative to the applied framework.

This doctrine [paradigm incommensurability] is, logically, an outcome of the mistaken view that all rational discussion must start from some *principle* or, as they are often called, *axioms*, which in their turn must be accepted dogmatically if we wish to avoid infinite regress. [...] Usually those who have seen this situation either insist dogmatically upon the truth of a

---

[1] For a summary of this debate, see Scherer (1998). For significant contributions, see Gioia and Pitre (1990), the edited volume by Hassard and Pym (1990), Jackson and Carter (1991), the debate in *Organization Studies*, 1993, volume 14, no. 5, and the "Comments" in the special issue of *Organization*, 1998, volume 5, no. 2.

framework of principles or axioms, or they become relativists: they say that there are different frameworks and that there is no rational discussion between them, and thus no rational choice.

But all this is mistaken. For behind it is the tacit assumption that a rational discussion must have the character of a justification, or of a proof, or of a demonstration, or of a logical derivation from admitted premises. But the kind of discussion which is going on in the natural sciences might have taught our philosophers that there is also another kind of rational discussion: a critical discussion, which does not seek to prove or to justify or to establish a theory, least of all by deriving it from some higher premises, but which tries to test the theory under discussion... (Popper 1994: 60; emphasis in original)

Popper elaborates on the point that proponents of paradigm incommensurability are either ideologists or relativists, or both, by outlining the consequences of this attitude:

One of the components of modern irrationalism is relativism (the doctrine that truth is relative to our intellectual background, which is supposed to determine somehow the framework within which we are able to think: that truth may change from one framework to another), and, in particular, the doctrine of the impossibility of mutual understanding between different cultures, generations, or historical periods – even within science, even within physics. [...]

The proponents of relativism put before us standards of mutual understanding which are unrealistically high. And when we fail to meet those standards, they claim that understanding is impossible. Against this, I argue that if common goodwill and a lot of effort are put into it, then very far-reaching understanding is possible. Furthermore, the effort is amply rewarded by what we learn in the process about our own views, as well as about those we are setting out to understand. (33–4)

Popper thus makes two points. First, the doctrine of paradigm incommensurability errs in its assumption that mutual understanding or communication between paradigms is impossible. Rather, as he points out later in the book (48–53), communicating between paradigms is like learning a different language: it is difficult but not impossible. The proponents of paradigm incommensurability confuse difficulty and impossibility. In other words, they do not make an appropriate effort and are content simply with working within one paradigm, and they justify their lack of effort by saying that another paradigm is incommensurable with their own. The doctrine thus represents a comfortable excuse for not making oneself familiar with a different theory or method.

Second, and more importantly, Popper argues that the doctrine of paradigm incommensurability errs with regard to scientific progress. Certainly, scientific progress can take place within the framework of a single theory. However, this is only one possibility, and probably not the best one. Rather, a mutual critique represents the central basis for scientific progress, and in particular a mutual critique between different theories and their assumptions. Rather than a declaration of intellectual independence, the comparison and mutual critique of different theories is the hallmark of scientific progress, in both the natural and the social sciences.

There is a third shortcoming of paradigm incommensurability, and Popper considers this one not only futile but even dangerous: the encouragement and justification of intolerance between theories.

The myth of the framework can be stated in one sentence, as follows. A rational and fruitful discussion is impossible unless the participants share a common framework of basic assumptions or, at least, unless they have agreed on such a framework for the purpose of the discussion. [...] As I have formulated it here, the myth sounds like a sober statement, or like a sensible warning to which we ought to pay attention in order to further rational discussion. Some people even think that what I describe as a myth is a logical principle, or based on a logical principle. I think, on the contrary, that it is not only a false statement, but also a vicious statement which, if widely believed, must undermine the unity of mankind, and so must greatly increase the likelihood of violence and of war. (34–5)

Thus, in addition to the concern that the assumption of paradigm incommensurability limits scientific progress, we have an even more forceful statement here. Thinking in terms of incommensurability immunizes one's viewpoint against critique, because one can always say: "Your critique of my viewpoint is not valid because your paradigm is a different one," or "... because your ontological assumptions are different from mine." This self-immunization against critique fosters a belief in the infallibility of one's standpoint and nurtures intolerance of others – other theories, other ways of thinking, and, ultimately, other ways of life. As a result, thinking in terms of paradigm incommensurability increases the likelihood of using force, communicatively and – ultimately – physically, against people who think differently.

It is important to note that rejecting the doctrine of paradigm incommensurability does not mean that an agreement between different theories should or can be achieved. This is not the point, and Popper makes this very clear when he argues that expecting agreement between different theories is utopian (37). There is no need to amalgamate different theories in such a way that they are made to agree. Rather, the point is to allow for comparing different assumptions, enabling the mutual critique and reciprocal testing of assumptions. This offers a more differentiated and thus a more precise view of empirical phenomena, and nurtures both tolerance and scientific progress. The point is to exchange views, to be open to critique from other viewpoints, and to learn from this, rather than close one's theory off against outside critique.

The remainder of this book is based on these principles and draws on the four theories outlined above. These theories do not need to agree and the degree to which they complement or contradict each other will vary. But in their complementarities or mutual critique they will illuminate the aspects of management consultancy in a way that individual theories could not achieve. From now on, the phenomena of management consultancy shall take center stage, and the theories will be taken as searchlights to shed light on them.

PART I

The mechanisms of the consulting market

2 | Why do consulting firms exist and grow? The economics and sociology of knowledge

The era of strategy and organization consultancies commenced in the 1960s, when the demand for engineering-based advice on the shop floor diminished and the upturn in international trade and corporate expansion began to shift the demand for consulting services to the boardroom level (Kipping 1996, 1997, 2002). McKenna (1995, 2006) points out that the first wave of advice on finance, strategy, and organization was triggered by the Glass-Steagall Banking Act in the 1930s. From the 1950s onwards the strategy and organization consultancies not only expanded their activities considerably in the United States but also opened offices in Europe and, later, in Asia and Latin America. With the growth of these firms in the 1980s and 1990s the consulting market took off, gaining considerable importance in relation to national gross domestic product (GDP). Figure 2.1 represents the global management consulting revenues between 1970 and 2001.

The data indicate an impressive growth of the market in the 1980s and 1990s in terms of annual revenue and proportion of the gross world product (Kennedy Information 2002: 58). When they prepared their 2002–2005 projections Kennedy Information were forecasting a general economic upswing in 2002, and did not predict the stagnation of the consulting industry between 2001 and 2003, and as a result the figures were (over-)estimated. Since 2003 the consulting market has been recovering, in Europe with growth rates of 3.5 percent (2003), 3.7 percent (2004), and between 8 and 14 percent (2005) (FEACO 2006: 2–6). For the purposes of this chapter, the historical development represented in figure 2.1 takes center stage.

A look at figure 2.1 shows that there are two "elbows" in the curve, one in the early 1980s and another one in the mid-1990s. The growth figures of the individual market segments in the 1980s and 1990s (strategy, organization, IT, human resources) suggest that the first elbow can be attributed to the increasing

41

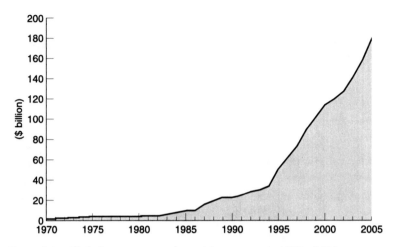

Figure 2.1. Global management consulting revenues, 1970–2001
Source: Kennedy Information (2002: 56). Reprinted with permission.

demand for strategy and organization consultancies. The second one, from 1994 onwards, was driven by both strategy and information technology advice. This corresponds broadly to Kipping's (2002) hypothesis of different consulting waves, but, in contrast to his prediction, strategy and organization consultancy is not in decline.

In the second half of the 1980s the big accounting firms entered the IT consulting segment. The then Big Eight, now Big Four, accounting firms (PricewaterhouseCoopers; KPMG; Ernst and Young; Deloitte Touche Tohmatsu) had always offered advice in addition to their traditional services, but from the late 1980s onwards these activities became increasingly important in relation to the maturing market of accounting and auditing (Allen and McDermott 1993; Ghoshal 1993; Jones 1995). By the mid-1990s these firms had outgrown those service providers focusing on corporate strategy and organization (see chapter 6 for details). While three of the Big Four legally divided the different service lines after the Enron scandals and the ensuing breakdown of Arthur Andersen, they are now back in the consulting business (on the consequences of the Enron collapse for management consultancy, see McKenna 2006: 216–44).

We start by highlighting the consulting market from the viewpoint of transaction cost economics. To do so, we can begin with a typical outline of consulting functions, as often found in the literature.

Turner (1982) was probably the first to list the various functions of consulting services using the following eight task categories.

1. Providing information to a client.
2. Solving a client's problem.
3. Making a diagnosis, which may necessitate redefinition of the problem.
4. Making recommendations based on the diagnosis.
5. Assisting with the implementation of the recommended actions.
6. Building a consensus and commitment around the corrective actions.
7. Facilitating client learning.
8. Permanently improving organizational effectiveness.

Bessant and Rush (1995) provide another systematization of ways in which consultants benefit client businesses (see table 2.1). They distinguish between six different user needs and list the activities of consultants as bridges for information and knowledge, especially in the context of technology transfer. Bessant and Rush suggest that externals can provide these bridging services more economically than

Table 2.1. Roles of consultants

User needs	Bridging activity of consultants
Technology	Articulation of specific needs
	Selection of appropriate options
Skills and human resources	Identification of needs
	Selection, training, and development
Financial support	Investment appraisal
	Making a business case
Business and innovation strategy	Identification and development
	Communication and development
Knowledge about new technology	Education, information, and communication
	Locating key sources of new knowledge
	Building linkages with the external knowledge system
Implementation	Project management
	Managing external resources
	Training and skill development

Source: Bessant and Rush 1995: 101.

client firms themselves, hence their arguments imply transaction cost considerations, although they do not mention them explicitly.

Such lists are useful, but they leave open the question as to why clients hire consultants for these kinds of activities rather than perform them by themselves or hire additional staff. Without a further comparison of costs and benefits between in-house and external solutions, all the activities listed above could, in principle, be performed by an internal function established for this purpose. Turner's (1982) and Bessant and Rush's (1995) lists, therefore, may represent useful systematizations of consulting functions, but they do not answer the question as to why consulting firms exist as independent firms. Rather, the fact that in 1980 there were only five consulting firms with more than 1,000 consultants worldwide, whereas now there are more than thirty firms of this size (Canbäck 1998a: 7), requires a theoretically informed answer. In particular, Turner's point 8, "permanently improving organizational effectiveness," is an example. Improving organizational effectiveness is the very task of a client manager.

Marvin Bower (1982), McKinsey's long-term director, has mentioned the benefits of externality. He argues that the main benefits of consultants are: (1) they provide competence not available internally; (2) they have varied experience outside the client company; (3) they have time to study the problems; (4) they are professionals; (5) they are independent; and (6) they have the ability to bring about action based on their recommendations. Bower's list certainly implies considerable advertisement for consultancy, but he was the first to mention that externality is an important point. Yet even Bower's list does not deal with the crucial question: if consultants provide competence not available internally, if they have time to study the problems, and if they have made varied experiences outside, why does the client not hire personnel with these competencies as employees? If competencies that are not available internally are the critical issue, then a client can in principle hire a former external person who possesses these competencies. As Canbäck (1998a: 16) points out, the degree of a consultant's professionalism is not automatically higher than that at the client firm, and the ability to bring about action is a matter of training and methods rather than being intrinsic to the consulting business.

Transaction cost analysis of consultancy

Transaction cost theory provides the central framework for solving this puzzle. The question is: in which cases and for which tasks is the externalization of analytical or management functions more efficient than an in-house solution? In the case of outsourcing a task to a consulting firm (the market solution), *ex ante* transaction costs occur as a result of searching for consulting firms, assessing their competencies, selecting between several firms, negotiating, and finalizing the contract. *Ex post* transaction costs occur for monitoring consultants' work, for reinforcing contract clauses, or for resolving conflicts in the case of project difficulties. In an in-house solution, *ex ante* transaction costs occur in the context of internal changes, such as changing administrative fiat, reallocating tasks within the firm, training staff, adjusting an incentive system for motivational purposes, or hiring new personnel; *ex post* transaction costs occur for monitoring and maintaining employee effort, performance, and motivation. When considering whether a hierarchy or a market solution is more efficient, consultants openly present their production costs (consulting fees) to clients and only the transaction costs need to be estimated. Regarding the in-house solution, clients need to estimate both the production and transaction costs. The latter may involve costs for researching information, setting up an internal function, selecting and hiring personnel, monitoring employees, and coordinating functions within the firm.

The decision between a market solution and a hierarchy solution depends mainly on three factors. First, the frequency with which a particular task occurs — i.e. the frequency with which a particular service is required. The more often a task occurs the more efficient a hierarchy solution will be, because the costs for repetitive contracts will at some point be higher than the costs for the in-house administration. The second factor is the specificity of the assets (technical equipment, human resources) that are necessary to conduct the task. This represents the extent to which the assets for a particular task cannot be transferred to other uses. The more specific the necessary assets are the more efficient an in-house solution will be, because, if the supplier rather than the client is supposed to invest in the specific assets, then this involves high contract costs for safeguarding against hold-up risks. Moreover, as Canbäck (1998a: 39) argues,

[c]onsultants know that it will take time for the client to find, evaluate, and build the knowledge of a new consultant. In the end, it may be easier for the client to avoid the hold-up situation by using internal resources rather than go through a painful negotiation with outsiders. Thus, all other things being equal, external consultants can be expected to work on issues that have low human asset specificity, while internal experts deal with issues close to the heart of the organization.

The third point, the uncertainty of the task, is the extent to which the task can be defined and framed, and the extent to which the quality can be measured. It also involves the extent to which the outcome is volatile and dependent on factors that cannot be fully controlled. Most important – and possibly crucial for the decision – is the uncertainty about the adequacy of human resources and technical equipment. The higher the uncertainty of a task the more likely that an in-house solution will be more efficient. This is because it is difficult (and thus expensive in terms of transaction costs) to formulate and enforce a contract with an external provider in which all aspects and uncertainties are covered. As far as make-or-buy questions concerning analytical operations are concerned, it is unlikely that all the above factors will point in one direction (either hiring an external consultancy or establishing an in-house function). Rather, they are likely to represent tradeoff decisions, requiring weights to the above decision-making criteria.

Canbäck (1998a) makes an important point related to the rise of the knowledge economy: the more complex organizations have become the more the internal coordination costs have risen. While, fifty years ago, executive meetings were concerned with issues closely related to the production process, today's organizations face more abstract and complex issues of strategic, financial and organizational importance. "[S]enior executives today deal primarily with abstract issues relating to transaction costs, while fifty or a hundred years ago they concentrated on more concrete tasks aimed at reducing production costs. Therefore, the role of top management in a large company has changed beyond recognition" (Canbäck 1998a: 32). Canbäck uses Sloan's (1964) description of General Motors under his stewardship as an illustration. The book is almost exclusively concerned with production cost issues in sales, marketing, and production itself. Even the finance issues concerned production costs rather than transaction costs, and there was an insignificant amount of abstraction regarding strategic and organizational issues. (This broadly corresponds to Fligstein's research, which shows that during the twentieth century there was a shift of power from production executives to marketing and ultimately to finance executives – a shift that represents the increasing degree of necessary abstraction; see Fligstein 1983, 1990.)

Canbäck (1998a, 1998b, 1999) argues that this rise of transaction costs in comparison to production costs gives rise to an increased relevance of two factors: clients' internal (bureaucratic) coordination costs, and the human asset specificity of tasks. As far as clients' internal coordination costs are concerned, he argues that the higher these are the more efficient it is to use external consultants. As far as human asset specificity is concerned, the opposite is the case because of the hold-up risk (see above).

Consultants have specialized on tasks that would involve high internal coordination costs for clients, such as organization-wide changes or the implementation of information technology. In addition, because of economies of scale, their focus and experience in gathering information worldwide and across industries renders their information search less costly than for clients. Services exhibit economies of scale when the costs per unit decline over a range of output, for example by way of learning effects, by spreading fixed costs over increasing output, or by better technology that pays off its up-front investment after a certain production level. Economies of scope emerge when the costs of producing a variety of services in one firm are lower than producing them in two or more firms. This can be due to transferring learning effects between different services or sharing fixed costs (Besanko *et al.* 2000: 72–4). If a particular task emerges for a firm and it considers whether or not to do it in-house, then it looks at scale and scope economies. Does the task emerge often enough for it to economize on scale at some point, or is it related to an existing task of the firm so as to economize on scope? Canbäck also offers a graphical illustration of his arguments, presented in figure 2.2.

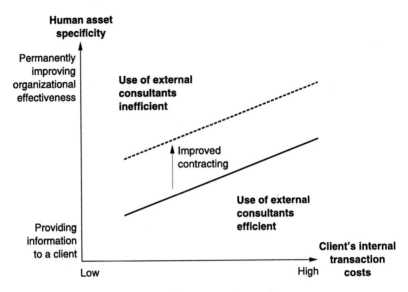

Figure 2.2. Efficient versus inefficient use of consultants
Source: Canbäck (1998a: 43).

To illustrate Canbäck's figure, we can take up the example mentioned in chapter 1, the chemical engineering firm. Before a chemical
engineer is able to improve the effectiveness of chemical procedures
permanently, a firm needs to invest heavily in his on-the-job training
and familiarity with the specific processes (i.e. there is high human asset
specificity). At the same time, permanently improving the effectiveness
of chemical processes does not require a lot of coordination between
departments, hence the client's internal coordination costs are low. As a
result, it would be inefficient to use external consultants for such tasks.
By contrast, if the same chemical engineering firm faces IT-related
changes in the market, for example the connection of corporate
functions by enterprise resource planning (ERP) systems, in such cases
the internal coordination costs of the chemical engineering firm would
be very high, since such changes involve enormous coordination
between departments. At the same time, the knowledge required is not
specific to the chemical engineering firm, but requires knowledge that is
applicable to a large variety of corporations. This means that the
human asset specificity is low and it would be efficient to outsource
such an IT-related task to external providers.

The same applies if the firm faces a challenge related to its strategy, such as a sudden change of market conditions or legal requirements. Such issues, too, require services of low human asset specificity but high internal coordination costs, and outsourcing to a consulting firm makes sense. Consider the following example.

Marcia Blenko, for example, a partner in Bain's London office, had to consider a difficult strategy problem for a large British financial institution. The client wanted Bain to help it expand by offering new products and services. The assignment required geographic and product-line expertise, a broad understanding of the industry, and a large dose of creative thinking. Blenko, who had been with Bain for 12 years, knew several partners with expertise relevant to this particular problem. She left voice mail messages with them and checked Bain's "people finder" database for more contacts. Eventually she connected with the nine partners and several managers who had developed growth strategies for financial service institutions. She met with a group of them in Europe, had videoconferences with others from Singapore and Sydney, and made a quick trip to Boston to attend a meeting of the financial services practice. A few of these colleagues became ongoing advisors to the project, and one of the Asian managers was assigned full time to the case team. During the next four months, Blenko and her team consulted with expert partners regularly in meetings and through phone calls and email. In the process of developing a unique growth strategy, the team tapped into a worldwide network of colleagues' experience. (Hansen *et al.* 1999: 108)

This example illustrates how consulting firms economize on problems that are of a one-off kind for clients but recurrent for the firm. In this case a client has outsourced a creative procedure that has occurred infrequently, involves little asset specificity, is highly complex, and involves considerable coordination costs. Economies of scale and scope emerge in consulting firms, as they have learning effects across firms, industries, and regions. At the same time, the internal network of the consulting firm makes the knowledge available to the particular consultant or partner and allows for the cross-national and cross-functional transfer of information.

Canbäck (1998a) then adds one more component. The more experience a client gains in contracting consultants − i.e. the smaller the transaction costs a contract with consultants involves − the more a client can trade off the costs of human asset specificity against the costs of contracting consultants. In other words, the lower the transaction costs a consulting contract involves the more a client can replace internal personnel with consultants. Canbäck (1998a) marks this by varying the line between efficient and inefficient use of consultants along the human asset specificity axis (see figure 2.2).

In a German-language publication, Kehrer and Schade (1995) arrive at a very similar outline from a transaction cost perspective. They first point out that an internal solution comprises three possibilities rather than just one: the internal solution of the functional department, the delegation to an overhead function such as a staff department, and the delegation to an in-house consultancy (if there is one, which typically happens only in very large client corporations; see chapter 5). The question of internal versus external solution, therefore, depends on the question of what one considers internal, namely whether one defines the client as the particular micro system of the department in which a task occurs, or as a macro system of the whole company. In the former case, the delegation to a different department or an internal consultancy already represent an external solution. As a consequence, Kehrer and Schade consider internal consultants to constitute a hybrid solution between market and hierarchy, and include it in their models.

Kehrer and Schade then consider two aspects of the make-or-buy question: the specificity of the task for client operations, and the complexity of the task. As far as the former is concerned, Kehrer and Schade's argument parallels Canbäck's (1998a, 1998b, 1999) point that the higher the specificity of the task the more efficient an in-house solution becomes. As far as task complexity is concerned, Kehrer and Schade argue that consultants are specialized on methods and instruments to structure complex problems. External consultants have access to similar cases in other industrial or service sectors, and, in large consulting firms, project teams can approach a large variety of company-internal but worldwide resources and contact colleagues who may have dealt with similar issues. Kehrer and Schade's (1995) first model is similar to Canbäck's, only with exchanged axes and with internal consultancies positioned between department-internal solutions and external consultancy. (Canbäck was apparently not aware of Kehrer and Schade's model, probably because it was published in a German-language journal.)

In their second model, Kehrer and Schade go beyond Canbäck's conceptualization and add two components: the demand intensity for a task, and the similarity of the expected tasks to each other.

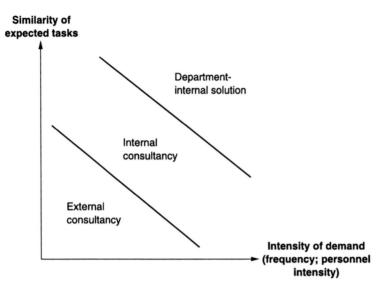

Figure 2.3. Forecast demand intensity of tasks and make-or-buy solutions
Source: Kehrer and Schade (1995: 472: author's translation).

Demand intensity is defined as the forecast frequency with which a task occurs and the number of required personnel. The greater the personnel requirement for a task, and the more often it occurs, the more efficient an in-house solution will be. As Kehrer and Schade further point out, however, demand intensity in itself is still meaningless if the similarity of the expected tasks to each other is not taken into account. That is, only those demand-intensive tasks that are dissimilar to each other justify outsourcing, whereas the more similar the expected tasks are the more efficient a department-internal solution will be. Again, internal consultancy represents a hybrid solution, as sketched in figure 2.3.

The issue of consulting knowledge, or the mastering of instruments and methods to structure complex problems, requires closer attention in the context of a transaction cost approach to the consulting business. As Kehrer and Schade (1995: 471) argue, the more complex a task or problem is the more an external consulting solution suggests itself, since consultants have specialized precisely on problems such as these, as opposed to clients, who are somewhat more concerned with routine business. The transaction cost argument for external solutions is ultimately based on the argument that consultants are specialized on problems other than clients' routine issues, because otherwise there could be no cost advantage to external solutions.

Methods as a special type of knowledge

Regarding consultants' specialization on particular methods and procedures to collect information and solve problems, the work of Werr (1999, 2002) and Werr *et al.* (1997) is central. Similar to any nonconsulting company, the work of consultants is based on experience and accumulated expertise, albeit in other types of expertise than clients'. Werr points out that consulting work (here: strategy and organization consultancies) is driven largely by particular methods, in the sense of particular ways to analyze and structure problems, and to trigger and manage change. The specialization in such methods renders consulting expertise dissimilar to client operations, and thus more efficient than an in-house solution if demand occurs sufficiently infrequently to build up in-house skills of this sort.

Werr *et al.* focus on methods of organizational change and define the terms "approach," "method," and "tool" in order to lay a terminological groundwork for their subsequent analyses. An "approach" describes "an overall perspective on the phenomenon of change and how to bring it about" (Werr *et al.* 1997: 288). An example would be the broad distinction between radical versus incremental change. "Methods" of change are subordinate to approaches; they describe the way of managing the change process, such as stepwise project models, "defining what should be done when, how, why and by whom" (289). "Tools" are, in turn, subordinate to methods. They support the process of specific problem solving and can take the form of checklists, software tools for analyzing processes, questionnaires to gather data, estimates or opinions, or statistical procedures to analyze client data.

Werr *et al.* (1997) and Werr (1999) undertook empirical investigations in five consulting firms (four large ones and a small one). They observed that the methods of the different consulting firms showed marked similarities in the area of process improvement, "regarding both content and structure, and regardless of the different traditional approaches of each [consulting] company" (Werr *et al.* 1997: 296). More precisely, apart from an emphasis on competency transfer, cooperation, and learning, Werr *et al.* (1997) and Werr (1999) emphasize that the change processes triggered by consultants cut across the functions of the client organization and involve most, if not all, organizational levels. Moreover, they use highly structured methods, with templates for analyses and checklists to support the individual steps. Thus, what Werr *et al.* have found is that consulting firms focus on methods that are linked to a low intensity of demand for individual clients but recurrent across firms (one-off issues for the client organization, involving few personnel in the project structure); their methods are characterized by high complexity, for the subject of analysis is cross-functional and involves a high degree of company-internal coordination costs; and the methods have a low degree of specificity in terms of the expected tasks – that is, the client does not expect the same project to occur again.

As Werr *et al.* (1997) and Werr (1999) further outline, the structured and detailed methods employed by consultants build the foundations for two-way learning between consultants and clients. Within the client organization, the methods and structures that consultants apply facilitate communication and competency transfer. They represent road maps for change, allow for coordinated action, and facilitate client employees' active participation through a common project language and structure. This does not mean that consultants make themselves obsolete, because bridging different functional and professional subcultures remains a perpetually new challenge, and the demand for the accumulated experience of a consulting firm resurfaces at the next dissimilar challenge. In a situation in which neither the solution nor the problem is apparent, clients' increasing familiarity with consultants' methods through knowledge transfer does not necessarily suffice to render consultants superfluous, because for the individual firm the newly emerging issues are, for the most part, dissimilar to the previous ones. The consultants' greater institutional exposure to different sectors, countries, and technologies renders them more prone to provide methods and solutions for the next, dissimilar task.

A point that Werr *et al.* (1997) do not further elaborate is the role of what they call "tools" – that is, checklists to map procedures, software tools for making processes transparent, questionnaires to collect and quantify opinions and estimations, workshop procedures, metrics to quantify process features, mathematical and statistical procedures to analyze data, etc. These tools are much more proprietary than the less concrete "methods," and here lies another key to client demand. While methods provide the means to structure and communicate projects, tools provide the more concrete means to analyze business processes. Pivotal to the transaction and information cost consideration is the argument that consultants can use these tools and the analytical experience that emerges from them with more than one client.

The use of tools leads back to the critical literature on management consulting. A recurring criticism leveled at consultants is that they provide "standardized" rather than customized solutions, or simply "copy" practices from one sector to another without further considering the idiosyncrasies of the organizations they advise. However, from a transaction cost perspective, this reproach is to a large extent misguided. The development and application of methods and tools that can be used in more than one case is exactly that kind of expertise that clients purchase in order to save costs. If business problems required completely idiosyncratic solutions then consultants would not exist, because, as the above transaction cost considerations have shown, in such cases in-house solutions would be more economical. The very reason why clients hire consulting firms is the fact that consultants have the ability to gain experience, expertise, methods, and tools in one industry or organization and then apply them in another, thereby saving the client the costs of developing them in-house.

Another recurring criticism leveled against consultants is that the only solutions they recommend are ones that the client or some client employees have already developed themselves. Indeed, in some cases an insincere consultant may claim knowledge or results as his own even though they have already been elaborated by client employees. But, in many cases in which this reproach may seem to apply, consultants may have provided a type of service that is fully compatible with transaction cost and information economics and that is economical for the client. They may have triggered the expression and extraction of knowledge that tacitly existed in the client organization, framed it into a coherent case, and transported it to decision-making bodies. This is no "stealing" of a solution from the client, but helping existing ideas become part of a solution. In situations in which information does not properly flow upward in client organizations, a consultant performs the legitimate role of a transmitter. Again, methods and tools rather than organization-specific knowledge are the economic reason for hiring consultants, and if these methods and tools help to express, extract, distill, or frame the knowledge of client employees then a consultant has achieved one of the objectives he is paid for rather than acted in an insincere way (see the above discussion of sociological neoinstitutionalism in this context).

The growth of consulting from a transaction cost perspective

A consideration of consultancy from a transaction cost perspective would be incomplete if we did not also look at the question of why the business has grown so considerably over the past twenty-five years (see figure 2.1). The theoretical basis for the answer has been laid out above. Clients use consultants efficiently for one-off tasks that are dissimilar to each other and dissimilar to client operations, and that would create high internal coordination costs. The reasons why such tasks have occurred increasingly since the 1980s would also explain why the consulting sector has grown. Hence, we need to look at the economic changes in this period, especially the intensification of international economic exchange (globalization), the increasing speed of information-technological change, the accelerating pace of product variation and innovation cycles, the increase in international capital variation and finance opportunities, and the politics of market liberalization and privatization. Empirical books on globalization (Held *et al.* 1999; Dicken 2003) and the data on trade and foreign direct investment available on the home page of the United Nations Conference on Trade and Development (www.unctad.org) provide ample evidence for these developments. They suggest that these changes are no longer rising in a linear fashion but at an ever more rapid rate in comparison to earlier periods.

I shall focus on two aspects: (a) the faster rate of change, as documented in the key indicators of international trade and foreign direct investment (FDI); and (b) the changing structure of economic transactions which these circumstances have triggered and continue to drive, especially the advancing international division of labor and progressively greater global competition.

As far as (a) is concerned, a useful indicator is the ratio between outbound FDI and GDP, which shows the proportion of international

Table 2.2. Outbound FDI, developed economies, 1980–2000
($ million)

	1980	1990	2000
FDI outflows	50,407	225,965	1,092,747
FDI outward stock	496,197	1,637,760	5,257,261

Source: UNCTAD (http://stats.unctad.org/fdi/).

economic activity in total output. Successive issues of the World
Investment Report, published by the United Nations Conference on
Trade and Development (UNCTAD) (downloadable from the
UNCTAD homepage), leave little doubt that outbound FDI has con-
sistently grown more rapidly than overall GDP. Table 2.2 presents
the aggregated figures of the developed economies (which are the
countries in which consultancy has grown most) in 1980, 1990,
and 2000.

The table shows that the compound annual growth rate of
FDI outflows was 16.2 percent per year between 1980 and 1990,
and 17.1 percent from 1990 to 2000. (The comparable figures for FDI
outward stock were 12.7 percent from 1980 to 1990, and 12.4 percent
between 1990 and 2000). During both these periods developed
economies' compound annual GDP growth rate was only about
3 percent per year. Hence the proportion of overseas economic
activity in developed countries' total GDP was growing during this
twenty-year period at a substantially faster rate than the growth of
their overall economic activity.[1]

From the perspective of the individual firm, this rise in the ratio
between outbound FDI and GDP means that output has expanded
relatively modestly, while the involvement of foreign markets and
investors in production, finance, and distribution has grown much
more steeply. This has had the effect of exposing the individual firm to
more complex decision frameworks with respect to procurement,
marketing, logistics, organizational structure, and strategy.

---

[1] After 2000 FDI outflows from developed economies dropped, beginning to rise
again only in 2004 (http://stats.unctad.org/fdi/). This corresponds to the
consulting market cycle.

Table 2.3. Intra-industry trade indices for selected OECD countries, 1964–1990

	1964	1970	1980	1990
United States	48.0	44.4	46.5	71.8
Germany	44.0	55.8	56.6	72.2
France	64.0	67.3	70.1	77.2
United Kingdom	46.0	53.2	74.4	84.6

Source: Held *et al.* (1999: 174).

As far as (b) is concerned, the structure of cross-border activities and relationships, trade has shifted and is continuing to shift from inter-industry to intra-industry exchange. Inter-industry (or intersectoral) trade represents the traditional form of trade, based on comparative cost advantage. However, since the 1980s intra-industry trade, which reflects the international division of labor, has risen with respect to previous decades. Table 2.3 looks at those Organisation for Economic Co-operation and Development (OECD) countries in which consultancy has grown most; it documents the rise of intra-industry trade, especially in the 1980s (in the United Kingdom it was already growing rapidly in the 1970s).

For the individual firm, this meant that, in order to manufacture a product in the 1980s, much more intra-industry trade in parts and half-finished products was necessary than previously. Trade requires more information about suppliers and markets, and each new step in the expansion of trade represents a one-off task that is different from clients' standard operations.

There is yet another shift in the international division of labor, which has emerged since the 1990s: the offshoring of production processes, IT services and business processes. While, traditionally, trade was about imports of raw materials and exports of finished products, the intensification of international economic exchange has offered new opportunities for firms to source semifinished products on a worldwide basis. Unfinished goods enter the production process for further processing or assembly in other parts of global commodity chains. The increasing social division of labor in emerging global value chains is reflected in the increase of intermediate goods trade and intra-firm trade. Today, intermediate goods represent about a half of the total trade between the European Union and other OECD countries. Moreover, this does not yet include the goods exchanged between different units of the same multinational enterprise. Although data based on a coherent method are difficult to obtain, eleven years ago the United Nations estimated that the volume of intra-firm trade had already risen to about one-third of all world trade (UNCTAD 1995).

Firms must react to these increasing rates of change. Since innovation is the most important way of obtaining monopoly rents, an acceleration of innovation cycles and a growth of knowledge intensity in production have emerged. Since imitation and innovation activities raise the level of competition, firms can no longer exploit technological advantage over long periods, and innovation cycles become shorter. Multinational corporations earn most of their annual revenues from products that are younger than five years. The intensification of international economic exchange and the diffusion of modern information and communication technologies create precisely those tasks that trigger the demand for externalized management: dissimilar and singular for client firms, but recurrent across firms, industries, and regions.

The management consulting boom has paralleled the increase in global FDI and world trade volume. The more the international division of labor unravels the larger the number of new management tasks that are dissimilar to previous tasks (i.e. involve low human asset specificity). Many tasks and services occur too rarely for it to be efficient for an individual firm to render establishing an in-house function, but they occur recurrently across firms, industries, and regions. Certainly, client–consultant relations are typically long-term and based on repeated contracts. This is because each project represents a new task in the context of changing information technology, procurement, logistics, organizational structure, or strategy. Typically, each project is a subject on its own and represents a specific task for the client firm. The shifting patterns of global finance and the politics of market liberalization and privatization have reinforced this trend toward newly occurring one-off tasks, and thus toward the efficiency of externalized management. The boom in management consulting is a manifestation of this new social division of management labor (Wood 2002) as much as it is a manifestation of the economic changes requiring organizational responsiveness.

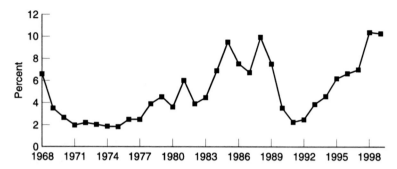

Figure 2.4. Acquisition volume as a percentage of average total stock market capitalization, 1968–1999
Source: Holmstrom and Kaplan (2001: 124), based on Mergerstat data and Holmstrom and Kaplan's calculations.

In addition to this argument, we can look at wider developments that characterized the twentieth century. Fligstein (1983, 1990) identifies a shift to investor capitalism in the second half of the century. That is, he notes a shift of power from engineering functions to marketing and sales positions, and ultimately to finance personnel. He supports this empirically by looking at the educational backgrounds of CEOs, with the turning point from engineering to marketing/sales taking place after the Second World War, and the shift to finance personnel in the 1970s and 1980s. It represents the evolution from an industrial to a service economy that Stanback (1979), Stanback et al. (1981), Noyelle and Dutka (1988) and Tordoir (1995) have pointed out. This shift in the second half of the twentieth century corresponds to Canbäck's (1998a, 1998b, 1999) argument that, fifty years ago, executive meetings were concerned with issues closely related to production costs, while today's executive meetings face more abstract and complex issues of transaction costs, for example regarding strategy and finance. It represents two issues: a move from the concrete (production) to the abstract (finance), and a move from internal issues (production) to external issues (markets for products and services), and on to even more volatile external issues (capital markets).

At this point, another two trends of the 1980s can be outlined: the wave of mergers and acquisitions, and the deregulation of industries and privatization of firms in a range of sectors, including aviation, telecommunication, energy and utilities, rail, mail services, health care, and hospitals. Figure 2.4 presents the wave of mergers in the United States, which took off in 1984 having already been growing since the late 1970s.

The 1990s saw a resurgence of mergers and acquisitions, which exceeded the wave of the 1980s. Interestingly, the two phases of particular growth, one from 1982 and the other from 1993, correspond exactly to the "elbows" in the consulting growth curve (see figure 2.1). Again, viewed from a transaction cost perspective, mergers and acquisitions represent aperiodical or one-off activities for individual clients, while consulting firms serve several customers and can economize on acquisition strategies or post-merger integration. In the aftermath of mergers and acquisitions in particular, the number of tasks that are dissimilar to client routines rises: post-merger integration involves a homogenization of the value chain of the merged firms, merging functions and departments, examining and transforming previously different corporate cultures, and homogenizing IT. The parallel development of consulting growth and M&A activities is another indicator of how consultants economize on aperiodical services.

In the context of the deregulation of industries that began in the 1980s, another set of tasks emerged for external management. One example is the deregulation of the energy and utility sector. New governance mechanisms for utility firms trigger challenges for strategy and organizational design. Utility firms have to be prepared for competition, which entails developing strategies for trading energy rights or for regional coverage, creating new functions such as marketing, bearing down more strongly on overhead costs, and fostering a client-oriented organizational culture. For energy and utility firms, the change was fairly abrupt: the nature of the challenges was uncertain, as market developments could not be foreseen; the demand for organizational innovations was high; and the character of coordination was integrated, since all organizational functions were involved. In short, the deregulation of markets that began in the 1980s and, in Europe, unfolded in the 1990s prompted tasks which were disparate and had a unique character for client firms, which involved high coordination costs within the firm, and which required a different type of knowledge with low human asset specificity.

The growth of consulting from other theoretical perspectives

A counterargument to the transaction cost explanation of consulting growth could be twofold. First, client firms become increasingly accustomed to the new ways of production and services, and thus the frequency of tasks of dissimilar kinds decreases. This would render in-house solutions increasingly efficient over time. Second, if the transaction cost argument is so compelling, why are relationships between clients and consultants often characterized by strong rather than arm's-length ties?

The first point may underestimate the disparate and often unrelated nature of the changes that clients face. Every step into a new market or toward a more dispersed value chain of manufacturing or service represents a new type of task: countries are different from each other, information-technological and logistical possibilities change, and regulatory or deregulatory conditions vary. Clients certainly learn from consulting projects, but not at the same pace at which the conditions of production change.

The second point is harder to answer, and from this perspective it is indeed surprising that strong ties have long remained the dominant form of organizing client–consultant relationships (see chapter 3). Only in the past five years has there been a trend toward selecting consultants in systematic procedures and toward involving cost-calculating purchasing or procurement departments in the decision-making process. However, with the rise of the knowledge economy in the 1980s and 1990s there has been another development that has nurtured, and continues to nurture, the reliance on network forms of organization. Powell (1990) suggests that this rests on three factors:

- the increasing role of know-how;
- the demand for speed; and
- the increasing reliance on trust in the knowledge economy.

The increase of knowledge-intensive activities gives rise to network forms of organizing because know-how is intangible and mobile. Tacit knowledge assets

exist in the minds of talented people whose expertise cannot be easily purchased or appropriated and who commonly prefer to ply their trade in a work setting that is not imposed on them "from above" or dictated to them by an outside authority. Indeed, markets or hierarchical governance structures may hinder the development of these capabilities because the most critical assets – the individuals themselves – may choose to walk away. (Powell 1990: 324)

In addition, the rise of costly products that have short life spans

now rewards many of the key strengths of network forms of organization: fast access to information, flexibility, and responsiveness to changing tastes... This advantage [of networks in terms of disseminating and interpreting information] is seen most clearly when networks are contrasted with markets and hierarchies. Passing information up or down a corporate hierarchy or purchasing information in the market place is merely a way of processing information or acquiring a commodity. In either case the flow of information is controlled. No new meanings or interpretations are generated. (Powell 1990: 325)

Finally, exchange relations have become long-term and continuous because they are well suited to watching intangible and mobile assets such as knowledge. "Monitoring is generally easier and more effective when done by peers than when done by superiors. Consensual ideologies substitute for formal rules and compliance procedures" (326).

These three points – the increased role of intangible and mobile assets, the demand for speed, and the increased reliance on trust – thus operationalize the emergence of the knowledge economy and account for the rise of network forms of organization. Further analyses, for example those by Powell (1996, 1998), Powell *et al.* (1996), Tsai (2001), Beckman and Haunschild (2002), Reagans and McEvily (2003), and Ritter and Gemünden (2003), show that the innovative success of a firm is strongly related to its position and its ability to act in networks of business and research relations. In fact, much of the traditional research on the diffusion of innovations (Katz *et al.* 1963; Rogers 1995; Robertson *et al.* 1996) is implicitly based on embeddedness notions.

From an embeddedness viewpoint, the rise of consulting rests not only on an increasing rate of innovation that renders the use of trusted agents of change and external providers of informational cues increasingly useful, but also on the network-based ways of generating innovations. Frequently, it is the embeddedness in a network of different institutions such as universities, research firms, and professional service firms that makes the difference for innovations, in addition to company-internal specialization. The lower the extent to which innovations are created through human asset specificity, and the more innovation success is related to a position in a network of business and research relations, the more the transfer function of consultants is in demand. Silicon Valley, or particular regions in Italy, are often taken as references for networks of innovation. There is a whole culture of engaging in webs of strong and weak ties. In this respect, the embeddedness-based account of consulting growth complements rather than contradicts the transaction cost account.

The same applies to a sociological neoinstitutional account of consulting growth. From this perspective, the development from ownership-based to managerial capitalism in the twentieth century, and thus the increasing separation between owners and managers, have triggered an escalating need to legitimate the decisions of managers toward principals and the public. Due to changes in financial markets, a stronger orientation toward shareholder value, the growth of institutional investors such as mutual funds, and the privatization of formerly public services, the need to legitimate decisions to the outside grew particularly in the 1980s and 1990s. As a result, the analytical preparation and implicit accreditation of managerial decisions by large consulting firms became increasingly important to executives, and contributed to the growth of consulting in these two decades.

This development was reinforced by another phenomenon: the increase of lawsuits against board members. McKenna (2006: 228) writes that – due to changed adjudication in corporate liability law – between 1985 and 1988 the number of lawsuits against directors grew by a factor of five, and the associated monetary judgments by 750 percent. This fostered the demand for certifications of good management. In addition, the increase of legal-institutional complexity in the 1980s and of technological complexity in the 1990s required (and continue to require) cognitive abstractions with respect to administrative and strategic rules. In this process of increasing detachment from company- and industry-specific rules, consultants have adopted a high degree of both analytical and symbolical capital (Reich 1992; Ruef 2002) and thus operate as symbolical guarantors of management quality.

McKenna (1995, 2006) points to one more issue going further back in history. The original emergence and growth of consulting firms in the United States was triggered by a legal and institutional shift in the 1930s: the Glass—Steagall Banking Act passed by Congress in 1933 in the aftermath of the 1929 crash. Apart from introducing Federal Deposit Insurance Corporation (FDIC) insurance to guarantee banks and placing a cap on the interest paid on savings accounts, the Act prohibited commercial banks from owning brokerages, thus separating commercial and investment banking.[2] This separation provided those firms able to conduct performance analyses of entire firms with an opportunity to offer advice independently of banks or commissioned by banks. Moreover, Congress established the Securities and Exchange Commission (SEC) in 1934 to enforce the newly passed securities laws and to protect investors. The SEC increased the public surveillance of corporations in order to prevent breakdowns of financial corporations as in the Great Depression, leading investment bankers to hire management consultants for analyzing their situation and shielding themselves against potential corporate lawsuits (McKenna 2006: 16—20). McKenna (1995) shows how the number of consulting firms in the United States rose between 1930 and 1940 from around 100 to an estimated 400. The legitimation or certification function of management consulting, therefore, was not new in the 1980s but had historical precedent.

Based on the increasing level of abstraction and detachment from internal issues, Ruef (2002) suggests another model of consulting growth (see figure 2.5). Although framed in neoinstitutional terms, his model is consistent with transaction cost economics, which he acknowledges himself (81). The increasing detachment from the specific administrative procedures of production and the increasing need for cognitive abstraction account for a decline of human asset specificity and for corporate governance structures that increasingly favor outside contracting. The growth of standardized rules and increased rates of corporate restructuring add to this picture. In combination with the increasing internationalization of markets and trade, they account for a growth of aperiodical issues that are dissimilar from each other and from standard corporate functions.

---

[2] On 12 November 1999 President Clinton signed into law the Gramm—Leach—Bliley Act, which replaced the Glass—Steagall Act. As a consequence, certain advisory activities of banks are now regulated by the Investment Advisor Act of 1940 (see http://www.wordiq.com/definition/Glass-Steagall_Act).

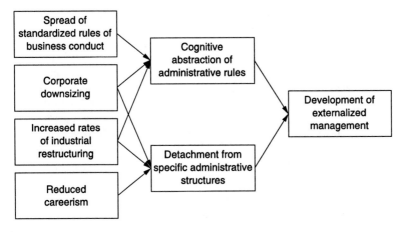

Figure 2.5. Ruef's model of consulting growth
Source: Ruef (2002: 82).

As discussed in chapter 1, the process of interpreting and framing ambiguous information in new terms, which consultants perform, is a central element of social institutionalization processes. At the same time, it represents a service to client firms, which would incur higher transaction costs if the process was carried out internally. Consultants act as interpreters and theorists of individual cases and events, and thus they form a part of institutionalization processes and at the same time save clients transaction costs by sharpening an interpretive consciousness at lower costs than in-house personnel could. Even signaling theory forms a complement to this approach. If we accept the argument that there has been an increasing need to signal management quality to stakeholders and shareholders, then hiring external consultants represents such a signal for a firm as much as education represents a device to signal the future productivity of an employee. Hiring expensive consultancies, i.e. the large strategy and organization firms, represents a signal as stakeholders and shareholders of the client firm ascribe consulting quality to these firms. And, indeed, large providers have grown more rapidly than small and medium-sized consulting firms (FEACO 2002: 5, 8).[3]

---

[3] This development ended only with the 2001–2003 crisis, which hit large consulting firms more than others. However, this can be attributed to the decline in demand for IT services, which are mostly provided by large service firms.

Table 2.4. Four theories and their explanations of consulting growth

Theory	Basic explanation for consulting growth
Transaction cost economics	Due to globalization, technological, and legal-institutional changes, there has been and continues to be a rise of those tasks for which external solutions are more efficient.
Embeddedness theory	There has been and continues to be a rise in the number of challenges for which network forms of operation, cooperation, and connectedness are essential.
Sociological neoinstitutionalism	There has been and continues to be an increasing need to legitimate management decisions toward shareholders and stakeholders, and to frame decision in ways that the institutional environment associates with high-quality management.
Signaling theory	With involving abstractions, management decisions increasingly there has been and continues to be an increasing need to signal management quality to stakeholders and shareholders.

Neoinstitutional and signaling theory help to explain the growth of both IT consulting and strategy and organization consultancy. Changes to the IT infrastructure are not only based on technical matters but come with particular images of how to organize a firm. In particular, the establishment of enterprise resource planning systems, which were a major driver of consulting growth in the 1990s, is based on the idea of planning and rationalizing the firm as a whole. Consultants are not just factual but symbolic experts of such rationalization processes (Alvesson 1993; Meyer 1996; Berglund and Werr 2000; see also chapter 9). The expansion of externalized management is accounted for not only by the actual but also by the symbolic emergence of market forces, the symbolic strength of institutional investors, and the symbolic decline in state authority and national corporate communities (Meyer 2002). The four theories, which in this case complement rather than contradict each other, can be summarized in table 2.4.

Keeping the complementary character of the four theories with respect to the growth of consulting in mind, the following chapters now outline topics in which the relationship between the theories is more complicated.

3 | How do supply and demand meet? Competition and the role of social institutions

There are two weak areas in transaction cost economics: the personal compatibility between clients and consultants, and the abstractness of transaction cost analysis and its lack of applicability to real-life problems for clients. In their transaction-cost-based article on consulting, Kehrer and Schade (1995: 468; author's translation) admit to these vulnerable points as follows: "This form of compatibility [in terms of personal and organizational features] can only be sensibly investigated between concrete consultants and clients, that is, on a case-by-case basis. In this article, in which a general comparison of the benefits of internal versus external solutions is in the foreground, we exclude these compatibility issues from the analysis." Kehrer and Schade (1995: 476) further admit that their analysis cannot be applied immediately to a concrete decision-making problem, for their economic comparison between making and buying consulting services is too abstract.

Admitting the existence of these weak aspects is music to the ears of some sociologists, such is their distaste for the other discipline. What economists may consider a minor blind spot of the theory is, according to some sociologists, a weakness that renders many economic analyses void. The argument is that, because of these weaknesses, cost considerations are overruled by tie quality. Granovetter (1985) was not the first to recognize these problems of economic analyses, but he was the first to realize that an entire theory emerges through these blind spots.

The debate on management consulting has paid only scant attention to the competitive mechanisms of the consulting market and the specific constraints and characteristics of consulting transactions. Although empirical findings suggest that competition in this service sector is not primarily based on price or cost (Dawes *et al.* 1992; Clark 1993, 1995; Page 1998; Lindahl and Beyers 1999), contributions to a theoretical account of the market mechanisms and the competitive logic in management consulting have remained rare. Nayyar (1990), Clark (1993), and Schade (1997) have suggested important accounts from the perspective of information economics. They have analyzed the information asymmetries in the consultant–client interaction, and their findings indicate that, under conditions of uncertainty, neither price nor institutional regulation can reduce information asymmetries. Instead, personal experience that evolves from interaction between clients and consultants becomes most important in reducing the uncertainty and controlling for opportunistic behavior. This chapter explores the impact of informal social institutions on competition in the consulting sector and analyzes their implications for firm growth. The point of departure is the different sources of quality uncertainty, which give rise to the social institutions that determine the market mechanisms.

The sources of quality uncertainty

Formal institutional uncertainty

Ideally, business activity is segmented into sectors with clearly defined markets, legally and culturally agreed professional standards, and discrete products. However, these features do not really apply to the consulting market. Their absence reduces the degree of system trust (Giddens 1990) or institutional trust (Zucker 1986), which can be conceived of as a general institutional framework that coordinates actors' expectations, and thus reduces uncertainty in interactions independent of individual sympathy or specific personal experience (Bachmann 2001: 348).

Unbounded profession

Ever since the origin of management consulting, the spectrum of firms has been characterized by a variety of backgrounds, such as engineering, accounting, law, or banking. National associations from various countries have made several efforts to obtain protective designation of the term "management consultant," similar to that enjoyed by lawyers, medical doctors, engineers, accountants, and auditors. While the CMC (Certified Management Consultant) certification of the International Council of Management Consulting

Institutes (ICMCI) possesses some visibility in the United States and internationally, it does not yet represent an equivalent to the status of the institutionalized professions. This implies very low market entry barriers at the lower end of the market, and permits any individual or firm to label their services as "consulting." As a consequence, client firms face a remarkable degree of uncertainty, because there are no institutional clues to distinguish qualified from nonqualified consulting providers (Nayyar 1990; Alvesson 1993; Clark 1995; Schade 1997). In addition, there are no measures for client firms to respond to inadequate consulting work. The absence of licensing standards, qualification requirements, or codes of conduct means that malpractice cannot be defined against a set of determined norms. In the United States, most courts hearing negligence cases against business consultants are unable to rule on malpractice, because there are no standards to judge them against (UNCTAD 1993: 20; Brockhaus 1977).

Unbounded industry

The fact that management consulting is not a legally or institutionally protected profession has consequences in the consulting market. The combination of growth potential and low institutional market entry barriers has led to extraordinarily high entry rates. An exemplary survey from the Cambridge Centre for Business Research (Keeble and Schwalbach 1995) demonstrates that, in Britain between 1985 and 1992, management consulting had the highest rate of new firm creation (117.8 percent) compared with all other services (13.8 percent on average). Nearly 98 percent of this growth in the number of establishments is accounted for by small and medium-sized firms. The dynamics of startups are further confirmed by the fact that 57 percent of the firms surveyed were established after 1980 and 37 percent after 1985. However, the high rate of growth of startups is compensated for by a comparably high mortality rate. One-third of the firms operating in 1985 had withdrawn from the market by 1990 (Keeble and Schwalbach 1995). Uncertainty about the sustainability of the consulting firms, their professional background and status, and the qualifications of their staff leads to a low degree of market transparency.

Unbounded service lines and product standards

The term "blurred boundaries" applies not only to the consulting sector as a whole, and to the background of its service providers, but also to the differentiation of service types. Although public reputation differentiates distinct core competencies, such as strategy or information technology, among the top consulting firms, different kinds of services often overlap within a single consulting project, and the separation and distinction of these services is often artificial. For example, the boundary between strategy consulting and IT advice has been blurred ever since the consulting arms of the big accounting firms entered the IT consulting market and conducted mixtures of IT and strategy projects on a large scale (see chapter 6 for more details). Another example is that the term "business process reengineering" encompasses a large variety of different services, and often it is not clear which type of service is actually planned and provided (Benders *et al.* 1998; see also chapter 1).

Consequently, the grouping of consulting services into the categories of strategy, information technology, operations, human resources, and marketing is based on the public reputation of consulting firms rather than on clear-cut differences in services. This can also be seen in the fact that agencies or institutions that survey the demand for consulting services use different classifications of service lines and publish different and inconsistent data. For example, the private market research agency Alpha Publications (1996) ascertained the market shares of IT services in Europe to be 44 percent and of strategy services to be 14 percent in the mid-1990s. For about the same period, the European Federation of Management Consulting Associations (FEACO 1998) calculated figures less than half these for the former category and double for the latter. For clients in the management consulting market, then, it is difficult to obtain unequivocal information about clearly defined market segments. Such ambiguities of service line classification render the market nontransparent for clients and the choice of adequate consultants additionally uncertain. The only information available to clients is the public reputation of firms for a particular area of expertise, but, as will be discussed later, this alone is not a reliable source (cf. Clark 1993).

In sum, the regulation of the consulting business in terms of legal or organizational norms and standards is minimal, which opens the market potentially to any individual or firm, increases quality risk, and renders the choice uncertain. There are no formal requirements for the products and no institutional means to respond to malpractice, which makes it difficult for clients to choose a consulting firm for an assignment. The absence of general regulation engenders a lack of institutional or system trust (Zucker 1986; Giddens 1990; Bachmann 2001).

Transactional uncertainty

Formal institutions of legal, professional, market, and product standards are fundamental to informed action, since they absorb some of the information asymmetry between service providers and potential clients. Conversely, the more that formal institutions are missing the more the uncertainty of economic action increases (Beckert 1999). Institutions evolve in a historically contingent process, easing transactions and creating institutional trust between transaction partners. From this angle, one would expect uncertainty to be only a temporary problem in the management consulting sector. Yet the consulting business is riddled with another source of uncertainty, associated with most knowledge-intensive services, namely its confidentiality, intangibility, and interdependency. These aspects can be referred to as transactional uncertainty.

Confidentiality and relational risk

The nature of consulting projects often allows consultants to access confidential information within client organizations. They enquire about, sketch out, and assess client members' activities, obtain access to and analyze data that the client's competitors must not get hold of, and gain insights into internal operations, specific knowledge, and sociopolitical constellations within client firms. This knowledge renders the client potentially vulnerable to opportunistic behavior by the consultant (Nayyar 1990; Clark 1993; Schade 1997). The opportunity for misuse does not necessarily refer to a straightforward transfer of information to competitors. This would either be subject to law or be regulated by nondisclosure agreements. Nevertheless, the consulting firm may handle confidential information in a wide range of ways, which could become detrimental to the client in an imperceptible fashion, rendering it immune to statutory protection. As part of a consultancy's knowledge management, for example, client information may be benchmarked with data from other firms without the client's knowing; project reports, presentations, and analyses are saved in internal knowledge databases and downloaded when similar projects come up (see chapter 8). Moreover, approaches and methods of handling problems that the client firm has developed itself may tacitly be appropriated for another client of the consultancy. These aspects together make for what Das and Teng (2001) call relational risk – i.e. the uncertainty associated with a consultant's tendency to act opportunistically in the course of a project. In addition, the job mobility of consultants implies risk for the client firm because an individual consultant may work for a competitor in the near future.

Except for criminal law, which is hard to enforce in such cases, there are hardly any institutional means of reducing these risks. In order to create institutional trust with member firms, consulting associations "urge" their members to practice according to ethical guidelines and codes of conduct. However, guidelines lack a legal framework and cannot be enforced by sanctions. Consequently, client firms have no guarantee that members of the association adhere to them. Monitoring a consulting firm's compliance with these guidelines would be extremely costly. Codes of conduct at best encourage appropriate behavior, but there is no institutional guarantee against the possibility of abuse. Uncertainty and risk shift to the client, who is forced to be vigilant.

Product intangibility

In markets of commodified goods, price and quality information suffice to make decisions and carry out transactions. However, these strategies are inadequate in the management consulting market, since service quality is difficult to measure. In spot exchange commodities it is the producer who takes the risk of production measures, because customers can see, compare, and often test the product prior to purchase (Levitt 1981). Knowledge-intensive services, by contrast, represent a case of deferred compliance, since consulting clients do not purchase ready-made products but contract a consulting firm to perform a service in subsequent cooperation.

The point is that the quality of consulting services cannot be assessed prior to the assignment, a circumstance that again raises the issue of performance risk (Das and Teng 2001). Moreover, because corporate success is contingent on a wide variety of decisions and conditions, the influence of a specific consulting project is hard to assess even long after the project has been finished. Performance evaluation is a subjective procedure, with few objective criteria to refer to (Ernst and Kieser 2002). If the quality of a consulting firm or a contracted performance is not objectively assessable, price is not a reliable indicator of quality (Akerlof 1970). Project results are unique and hard to compare with other projects, hence the intangibility of consulting services inhibits objective price building. Consequently, prices do not resolve the uncertainty that clients face when screening the consulting market for the best providers. Accordingly, as Lindahl and Beyers (1999) have found, service firms hardly ever pursue cost-leadership strategies.

Interdependent cooperation

Management consulting is a two-way interaction and often represents a process of mutual learning and cooperation. Wood (1996: 656) observes that the more competent a firm the more likely it is to hire a consultant: "Generally, consultancies tend to reinforce the strategic strengths of experienced companies rather than compensate for the weaknesses of the inexperienced." Client firms certainly contract a consultant in order to improve on certain operations, but these firms tend to be on the competitive edge (see chapter 4), which implies that consultants profit and learn from their assignments as well. Reciprocal interaction and co-production between consultant and client render consulting services nontransparent. The co-production of consultants and client members during the actual delivery of the service also means that clients considerably influence the outcome of the interaction and the project. The course of an assignment is contingent, because it depends on the goals, strategies, and skills of both parties on the one hand, and on their ability to cooperate on the other. In this respect, uncertainty is mutual (Sturdy 1997).

As the critical perspective on consultancy has pointed out, consultants make a considerable effort to control the relationship (Clark 1995; Ernst and Kieser 2002). In contrast to professions such as medicine and accounting, consultants may actually benefit from the absence of a clearly defined and codified body of knowledge and from the resulting inability of clients to assess service quality objectively. The paradox resides in the fact that consultants are originally hired to reduce uncertainty (Ernst and Kieser 2002).

The absence of standards opens the door to performance surrogates, as demonstrated by the debate about the communicative performance of consultants, the aspect of consultants' impression management, or their involvement in sociopolitical struggles within client firms (see the critical perspective on consultancy, chapter 1). Consulting firms are required to mediate progress and detect the dominant party in order to ascertain the politically most acceptable solution. The degree of consent within a client firm, and between the client and consultant, is substantial in order for a consultant to stimulate a sell-on success − i.e. follow-up assignments with an existing client (Sturdy 1997).

In summary, there is a fundamental paradox in the consulting market. On the one hand, low system trust and high relational risk render the choice of a consultant extremely uncertain; on the other hand, industries are increasingly making use of management consultants, as documented by the worldwide market growth. Hence, there must be mechanisms that bridge uncertainty and enable companies to make the assignment decision.

Uncertainty reduction through trust and "networked reputation"

When uncertainty constrains economic exchange and institutional trust is missing, informal social institutions (Akerlof 1970; North 1990) are required in order to gain certainty for transactions. Economic sociology and institutional economics both emphasize the importance for economic relations of informal social institutions, such as culture and shared cognitive schemes (DiMaggio 1997), trust (Lane and Bachmann 1996; Nooteboom 1996; Lorenz 1999), and reputation (Kollock 1994; Kreps and Wilson 1982; Uzzi 1997).

In particular, three mechanisms can be identified which reduce institutional and transactional uncertainty: public reputation, experience-based trust, and "networked reputation." Networked reputation emerges from word-of-mouth recommendations and represents a central factor of growth under conditions of institutional and transactional uncertainty. In drawing on these three mechanisms, a client needs to trade off between choosing from a wide variety of consultants and gaining a maximum of certainty about them.

Public reputation
If markets are conceived of as institutions in which business partners are anonymous to one another, then their functioning is dependent on a substantial degree of system trust for the actors involved. However, as shown above, management consulting is not a delimited industry or subject to professional standards and clearly denoted products. Nevertheless, the market does provide an additional kind of information to clients: public reputation. Reputation is defined here as the perception of a consulting firm's past performance (see Clark 1995: 74). It is public when this perception has a general, anonymous source and circulates freely in the management arena. While there are few to no entry barriers at the lower end of the market, the public reputation and visibility of large firms represents a massive entry barrier to the upper end of the consulting market.

The public reputation of style, approach, and capability that the large consulting firms carry is transported in the media but cannot be attributed to individual experience. Consequently, the problem for the client is that such information remains at arm's length and is similar to a public good (Nayyar 1990). Public reputation discloses overt information that is known to everyone, so that no client has any particular information advantage over anyone else. Under conditions of high institutional and transactional uncertainty, public reputation alone is an unsatisfactory mechanism of partner choice. Although it may signify general areas of competency and help stratify the market into layers of large, international firms on the one hand and small to medium-sized domestic or regional consultancies on the other, it does not provide reliable information on concrete performance quality or relational certainty for the client.

Experience-based trust
In contrast to market interaction, personal experience is a very reliable basis on which to choose a transaction partner. When relations have been positive in the past, positive expectations guide future action (see the term "process-based trust" in Zucker 1986; Lane and Bachmann 1996). Experience is an authentic way of assessing another person's actions and it helps to establish trust in the sense of the expectation "that damage will not be caused even though there is both

an opportunity and an incentive for the partner to cause damage" (Nooteboom 2000: 921). The fact that personal trust in economic exchange is derived from mutual social commitment also provides control for the interacting partners. Malfeasance against a trusted partner may trigger sanctions by the betrayed. Trust stabilizes interaction over time and embeds meaning, control, and solidarity into a structure of economic exchange. Under conditions of uncertainty, therefore, partner choices are driven by personal trust based on previous transactions. Once established, experience-based trust enables reciprocal and enduring relations, and individuals or organizations tend to transact with trusted partners whenever they can.

However, experience-based trust has its limits, too. It evolves only slowly and its maintenance demands commitment and energy. Therefore, trust relations are limited to a small number of friends or business partners and do not encompass many partners in a market. Moreover, owing to the limited number of contacts, clients are biased to hire previous consultants even if their expertise does not cover the new problem area. Uzzi (1997: 59) has coined the term "over-embeddedness" for this phenomenon (see chapter 1). Hence, experience-based trust may imply two shortcomings. First, since uncertainty is high, client firms may cling to their accustomed consulting firms despite a lack of competency. Second, experience-based trust limits the scope of potential partners. Consulting firms that would perform better in certain problem areas will not be chosen, because there is no history of mutual experience.

Networked reputation

Each of the two mechanisms above is limited in its utility for a client regarding the process of choosing a consultant. Although public reputation provides clients with a wide range of consultants, the quality of the consultants' performance cannot be reliably assessed. Trust relations based on experience create certainty for transactions, but they do not allow access to those consulting firms that best meet the requirements for tackling a specific problem. However, there is a third mechanism, which reconciles the deficits of public reputation and experience-based trust: the reputation of a consulting firm within a network of client firms, which could be called "networked reputation" (Glückler 2004, 2005, 2006).

If a trusted party cannot provide the resources needed, its relations can be used in order to obtain trustworthy information about parties to which an actor is not connected. A friend's judgment about another party serves as an essential criterion for someone's evaluation of the unknown third party. This mechanism communicates certainty through an established network of trusted relations and thus helps to access additional resources. Networked reputation, therefore, is a result of referrals or repeated word-of-mouth information about a firm.

This kind of reputation is one of the very basic ways that social networks operate. In contrast to public reputation, where an assessment of a person or firm is known to everybody, networked reputation conveys a far more personal and reliable credibility, because it provides "thick information" about potential transaction partners (Clark 1993; File *et al.* 1994). As Granovetter puts it, "Better than the statement that someone is known to be reliable is information from a trusted informant that he has dealt with that individual and found him so" (1985: 490). The thickness and trustworthiness of information channeled through socially embedded networks inform the concept of networked reputation as opposed to public reputation.

Networked reputation, competition, and firm growth

The mechanisms of public reputation, trust, and networked reputation can be arranged along two dimensions: the degree of certainty on one axis, and the number of potential transaction partners (i.e. the "market scope") on the other (see figure 3.1a). For the client firm, public reputation conveys a high number of possible consulting partners independently of direct trust relations (see figure 3.1b, left-hand part). However, it is accompanied by a considerable degree of uncertainty. This is because choice based on overt market information cannot be validated by the client's own experience. If formal institutional certainty is missing, then system trust is too low and uncertainty too high. An assignment implies high expenses, high opportunity costs due to the involvement of client staff, the relational risk of sharing sensitive corporate information, and a loss of valuable time.

Experience from previous interaction, in contrast, provides the basis for establishing personal trust. It preserves existing relationships by

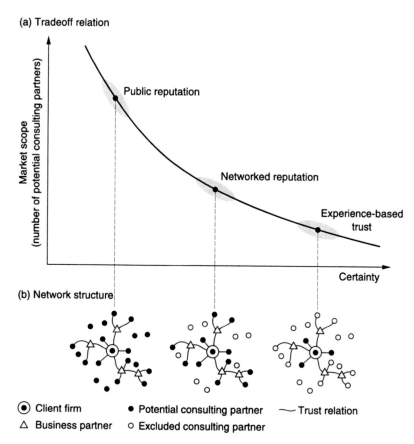

Figure 3.1. Market mechanisms in management consulting

reinforcing and stabilizing mutual commitment, rendering transactions very certain. However, based on experience-based trust, the number of potential consulting partners is limited to the client firm's set of direct trust relations (see figure 3.1b, right-hand part). Personal trust per se does not widen the realm of partners, and the size of one's network largely depends on the amount of effort one invests in making new acquaintances and in developing trust on a step-by-step basis (Kollock 1994; Lane and Bachmann 1996; Lorenz 1999). Typically, the number of partners with whom one shares positive experiences and has established a trust relationship is very limited. A partner network can grow only slowly, because any new trust relation is historically contingent and reduces the resources available to establish additional trust relations.

Networked reputation is a way of trading off both advantages: it offers considerable market scope and still communicates trustworthy information about transaction partners. Networked reputation as a result of word-of-mouth referrals thus emerges as a vital factor of firm growth, for several reasons.

- From the client's perspective, a trusted partner's recommendation endows a consulting firm with credibility and reduces transactional uncertainty between the consultant and the potential client.
- Networked reputation operates as a social substitute for service quality. If the future performance of a consultant cannot be evaluated, confidential reputation is used to draw conclusions from the evaluation of previous performance. The act of assessing the quality of a service is transferred to trusted partners. Networked reputation absorbs consulting quality and becomes a key factor of competition.
- The fact that networked reputation indicates quality and secures client networks implies higher entry barriers for competitors and newcomers. Keeble and Schwalbach (1995) find that a significant proportion of new consulting firms and startups already have contracts at the start of their business. This is remarkable, because entrants in other industries and markets often begin without a defined set of clients. It supports the importance of enduring client relations and networked reputation.
- The use of networked reputation widens the market scope − i.e. the range of potential consulting partners for a client. In addition to personal trust relations with a consultant, indirect contacts via a client's business partners are also taken into consideration (see figure 3.1b, central part). The number of potential partners increases exponentially with the number of network contacts.

From the consulting firm's perspective, the operation of networked reputation not only preserves its existing clients but also exponentially broadens the range of potential clients, since every satisfied customer might recommend a consultant to trusted third parties. Hence, networked reputation provides opportunities for both consulting and client firms. Clients benefit from networked reputation, in that the business partners' recommendations widen the market scope for alternative service providers. Consulting firms benefit, in that the number of potential clients increases as clients open their business networks to the services of a consulting firm.

Typical steps of assignment decisions

Public reputation, experience-based trust, and networked reputation appear to be the most critical criteria in the client's choice of a consultant. These mechanisms provide grounds for deriving a general pattern of assignment decisions. The social mechanisms for reducing uncertainty do not always have the same importance in comparison to each other. Rather, they are drawn on at different times and to different extents. Clients' decision-making processes may follow the sequence (1) public reputation, (2) experience-based trust, (3) networked reputation, and (4) competitive price. Although the steps in this sequence may overlap, their analytical distinction facilitates a heuristic analysis of a sequential decision-making process in terms of social relations.

(1) *Public reputation.* Public reputation stratifies the consulting market into at least two levels of firms: a stratum of highly prestigious consulting firms on the one hand, and a stratum of less prestigious ones on the other. The brand name of top consulting firms accounts for their distinction from the market segment of medium and small firms, as the research on status similarity in other industries suggests (Podolny 1994; Chung *et al.* 2000). In addition, within the layer of top-tier firms, public reputation accounts for a rough distinction between, for example, strategy and IT consulting firms. Large firms are associated with certain types of expert knowledge or approaches, despite the fact that service lines are often difficult to distinguish. In particular, long-established large firms benefit from their brand. Nevertheless, public reputation serves to attract only attention, not explicitly deals. Although it may account for the perception of a firm in the arena of management, the information is not thick or trustworthy enough to be the only basis for an assignment decision.

(2) *Experience-based trust.* Within a stratum of firms and field of specialty, defined by public reputation, the choice is driven by experience-based trust. Clients look for previous partners to carry on their relationship. If past interaction has been positive and

commitments have been reciprocated, then client–consultant relations tend to become embedded into a social mutuality of shared information, values, and problem comprehension. However, as soon as client firms face distinct challenges that cannot be met by those consulting firms with which they share a history of positive experience, then experience-based trust relations do not suffice to find an adequate partner. The number of relationships based on experience-based trust is often not large enough to find an adequate partner for a new task.

(3) *Networked reputation.* If the web of experience-based trust relations does not encompass the desired consultant, then clients ask trusted partners for their experiences with other providers. Clients approach business partners to share experiences with consultants in order to obtain thick, trustworthy judgments on consulting firms. This intermediate form of credibility is lower than in experience-based trust, but far higher than in public information. The process of intermediate referrals has been addressed in many other contexts, such as Granovetter's (1974) study on how to get a suitable job, research on consumer transactions (DiMaggio and Louch 1998), or in game theory (Raub and Weesie 1990; Kreps 1991). In contrast to DiMaggio and Louch's "search embeddedness," networked reputation is not limited to the active request for information, because a consulting assignment is not necessarily preceded by a search procedure (see the section on embeddedness in chapter 1). In many cases, a client recognizes a need for a project only after learning about a certain consulting firm and its services through business partners. Here, social networks and intermediary processes of networked reputation lead to contracts that may otherwise not come up as projects at all. Recommendations are a part of day-to-day communication and are exchanged independently of concrete demand and decision contexts. Firms gather this information on consulting firms and may draw on this pool of suppliers legitimized through networked reputation for future projects.

(4) *Price.* As suggested above, fees reflect public reputation but are not the primary driving force within a stratum of firms. Often, medium-sized client firms do not opt for a first-tier consulting firm simply because they are constrained by their budget. However, within a given budget range, price is not a very relevant decision

criterion. The significance of price is contingent on social institutions. There are two cases where the price mechanism may particularly matter. First, firms with a high degree of public reputation enjoy the opportunity to charge higher fees, because they benefit from a brand that signals a high degree of legitimacy. A top-tier firm enjoys a brand name because of, rather than in spite of, its high fees. Thus, the price mechanism follows a social rather than a purely economic logic, and the meaning of price remains contingent on the existence of social institutions, especially public reputation. Second, price becomes increasingly important (a) for consulting firms without public reputation, and (b) as uncertainty in the consultant–client interaction decreases. Regarding (a), for small and medium-sized consulting firms price matters much more than for large providers. This is because their services do not convey the same symbolic capital and do not automatically deliver legitimacy to management decisions. Regarding (b), bargaining over the terms of a project often begins only at the point where both consultant and client have made their commitment and developed a context of mutual expectations.

Several streams of thought about intermediary social processes have informed the concept of networked reputation proposed here. In his concept of third-party trust, Coleman (1990: 180–2) elaborates on the idea of intermediate actors who establish contacts and enable interaction between actors who otherwise would not have any confidence in each other. He distinguishes advisors from guarantors and entrepreneurial types of intermediary in trust, and argues that an advisor communicates trust between mutually unconnected parties and thus facilitates interaction between new partners. The mechanism of networked reputation corresponds to this, because an actor mediates trust at the risk of his own reputation if something goes wrong in the relation he or she has facilitated.

The importance of these issues has also been addressed in the concept of social capital. This notion draws on the benefits or returns that can be gained from the nonmonetary resources of the structure of social relations (Coleman 1988; Burt 1997; Portes 1998). Similar to Coleman's account, structural hole theory (Burt 1992, 2004) emphasizes the bridging of structural holes as a fundamental realization of social capital. When actors maintain exclusive relations with otherwise disconnected others – i.e. bridge structural holes – they maximize their chances of obtaining information advantages (Burt 1997) and improve their performance (Burt 2004). Strategically, consulting firms should of course increase the growth effect by engaging in several business networks rather than focusing on a single one.

Although the mechanisms of public and networked reputation are analytically distinct, in that they trade the advantage of market scope against that of transactional certainty, these advantages may in practice reinforce each other and jointly reduce uncertainty. Consultants typically try to achieve a combination of effects. As a matter of marketing (chapter 7), they expect public reputation to provide visibility, client awareness, and first contacts. Moreover, they try to establish a climate in which personal contacts become possible and personal trust builds up. In some cases, public reputation may also be the outcome of the long-term formation of reputation within networks of business relations. Thus, consulting firms, especially the established providers, benefit from combining the analytically distinct mechanisms of public and networked reputation.

Empirical support and extensions

Although the consulting market is ridden with uncertainties for clients, the demand for consulting services has been high over the past twenty-five years (apart from the phases of general economic slowdown). This is because public reputation, experience-based trust, and networked reputation bridge these uncertainties. Based on the finding that consulting relations are largely repetitive and long-lasting, networked reputation emerges as the driver of firm growth and as the key factor of competition.

The original article underlying this chapter (see preface and acknowledgments) presented data from the German consulting market, which illustrate the mechanisms elaborated above. Moreover, in his historical analysis of the postwar expansion of US-based consultancies into Europe, Kipping (1999) reconstructs instances of new assignments being acquired through local elite networks. He finds that the large US-based consulting firms systematically "relied on a small number of individuals from the host countries to play the role of 'connectors' and introduce them to potential clients" (Kipping 1999: 220). Moreover, Dawes *et al.* (1992) and Page (1998) asked senior managers of client companies in Australia and New Zealand to rate the most important criteria in the selection of a consultant. Their results are consistent with the market mechanism and hierarchy of partner choices suggested here. Furthermore, Clark (1995: 70–1) compares a number of empirical studies from the Anglo-American context to show that personal experience and recommendations within client networks play dominant roles in the choice of consultants. These studies suggest that the perspective presented is valid in a cross-cultural context.

Glückler (2004, 2005, 2006) has conducted further research on this basis. Focusing on the internationalization of consulting firms, he studied the market entry of consulting firms in Frankfurt, London, and Madrid. Glückler finds that most consulting firms enter a market via existing client firms that operate abroad, or via other business relations that did not yet belong to the client base but have international operations that potentially require consulting services. For most consulting firms, the decision to internationalize is a reaction to opportunities emerging from existing client relations. Only very few consulting firms tap into a foreign market without any previous experience, clients, or contacts there. Glückler (2004, 2005, 2006) hence argues that, for consulting firms, going abroad takes place in a relational context, which lends further support to the above outline of the market mechanisms. In his interviews in Madrid, consultants argued that gaining new clients without recommendations is practically impossible.

Overall, there can be little doubt that management consulting is a socially and culturally contextualized business. The growth, competitiveness, and market success of a consulting firm all depend on its ability to create long-lasting and trustworthy networks of client relations. In contrast to the lack of formal institutional or cost-based barriers to entry, business environments based on trust and networked reputation have distinct barriers of entry for competitors and newcomers. Market entry often seems to be subject to a paradox, which in an Australian study is encapsulated: "[w]inning contracts in Australia and New Zealand is possible when there is a prior relationship to draw on" (Page 1998: 56). A satisfied customer is a gateway to new clients, and the barriers that a positive reputation network creates against other providers are enormous.

Who is more powerful? Consulting influence and client authority

Strong feelings of the academic community

The subject of power between consultants and clients is a delicate one. As mentioned in chapter 1, many business journalists and academics have strong feelings about the consulting sector. Business journalists have published books entitled *The Inside Story* (Rassam and Oates 1992), *Dangerous Company* (O'Shea and Madigan 1997), and *Consulting Demons* (Pinault 2000). And some academics seem to agree with titles such as *Consultancy as the Management of Impressions* (Clark 1995) or *Flawed Advice* (Argyris 2000). In academic journals, the recent debate between Sturdy *et al.* (2004) and Clegg *et al.* (2004), and the article by Sorge and van Witteloostuijn (2004), indicate that there are strong reservations among academics regarding consultancy. O'Shea and Madigan's (1997) journalistic but well-investigated book is, of the critical kind, the most popular one worldwide. It has been reviewed in a number of US business journals and represents a well-known critique of management consultancy. The recent essay by Sorge and van Witteloostuijn (2004) refers to it several times as ostensible evidence for consultants' unsophisticated advice.

However, a detailed reading of the book shows that O'Shea and Madigan do not keep up the critical tone adopted in the book title and introduction. While the authors describe the failure of consulting projects at one particular corporation in detail and add a number of other consulting cases in which clients were not satisfied, the book then – somewhat surprisingly – describes a number of successful consulting cases in which the clients were very satisfied. Moreover, what the authors announce as a series of failed consulting projects turn out to be cases in which the shortcomings of client management were so great that consultants could not remedy them. The authors build up an image of powerful consultants and relatively powerless clients, but fail to prove that consultants deliver faulty performance. Rather, in spite of its anti-consulting title, the book shows that many consulting projects succeed (Armbrüster and Kieser 2001).

Nevertheless, a extent share the critical image of consultancy. In Europe in particular, academics have tended to portray consultants as persuasive opinion formers who impose solutions and methods on client companies that do not really need them, or as people who actively foster management fashions and create a sense of urgency against which clients are nearly powerless (see the review of the critical approach in chapter 1). Their arguments are based on an assumption: that consultants are in a position of power vis-à-vis their clients. Expressed in economic terms, the critical literature assumes that consultants have ample opportunity for opportunistic behavior, and exert it. However, this view ignores the market mechanisms outlined in chapter 3, and it confuses the power relations in the consultancy market.

A long-standing criticism leveled against economics is that it does not have a notion of power, or that economists are not interested in power and thus overlook a central feature of economic relationships. In order to remedy this picture, we start with a transaction cost perspective on consultants' power, before outlining embeddedness, signaling, and neoinstitutional notions. After that, the chapter charts the sources of client authority. It will conclude that characterizing management consultancy as a seller's market of consulting power is an error. The chapter suggests that management consultancy is a buyer's market and that, with few exceptions, client authority is overarching for client—consultant relationships.

Concepts of power and the sources of consultants' influence

Transaction cost economics is not oblivious to power but can integrate it as information asymmetry and asset specificity. The very reason that transaction costs emerge is information asymmetry to the detriment of one party (i.e. less power), resulting in information, screening and monitoring costs, etc. Moreover, specific investments involve high costs of switching to another provider or client, and thus involve hold-up risks. Specific investment implies transferring power to the other party, which must be mitigated by contractual measures that involve transaction costs. Thus, transaction cost economics is perfectly able to model power, once it has been operationalized in these terms. Williamson argues:

It is certainly true that power is a consideration and that [it] is out there. The thing I would urge is that just as transaction cost analysis needs to be operationalized, so does power. Now the definition of power, which in my opinion comes the closest to be operationalized, is what is called "resource dependency" (Pfeffer and Salancik 1978). Resource dependency is fairly close to what I would call "asset specificity"... But to get back to the power advocates: I think there is a great obligation on their part to say exactly what "power" is and how their power analysis works (interview with Williamson in Swedberg 1990: 123).

From this perspective, we can look at the power of consultants with regard to information asymmetry and asset specificity, manifested in hold-ups. Regarding information asymmetry (typically specified as hidden characteristics, hidden intentions, hidden information, and hidden action), consultants are certainly better informed about their capabilities and the extent to which they benefit clients. Chapter 2 has drawn attention to the tools and methods that characterize consulting firms vis-à-vis their clients. These tools are mostly proprietary, and consultants' familiarity with them, as well as their knowledge regarding their usefulness to the client's business, constitute the central information advantage of consultants. Moreover, throughout a consulting project, consultants apply these tools and collect data. Before a presentation reveals the data and results to the client, consultants hold information that client individuals are often keen to obtain. Thus, especially after data have been collected and analyzed and before the results have been presented, consultants possess considerable power to influence micropolitical action within the client firm.

Asset specificity, as the degree to which clients make transaction-specific investments that cannot be regained if a transaction is terminated, depends on the degree to which consultants have gained client-internal knowledge that it is difficult for the client to transfer to other consultants. The better a consultant knows the client business the more costly a potential transfer of this knowledge to a new provider becomes. Switching provider incurs costs for searching, selecting, new contract negotiations – and for transferring all necessary information to the new consultant. Due to an initial lack of quality certainty, it may also involve costs of monitoring and possibly contract enforcement if there is no embedded relationship to another provider. This is the central reason that clients typically engage consultants with a slowly increasing degree of project importance, as Glückler (2004, 2005) has found. It is a way of not falling into the hold-up trap. A trusted advisor is costly to exchange, whereas a relationship with a new advisor can usually be terminated without a hold-up situation. I will take up this point in the conclusion (chapter 10) by referring to game theory.

Although more rooted in sociology than economics, embeddedness theory has also been subject to the argument that it overlooks power in economic transactions. Nevertheless, the embeddedness approach in principle allows for modeling power. It emerges from two themes: the position of an actor in a network, and the degree to which an actor is autonomous from social ties (i.e. not overembedded). Regarding the first point, Burt (1992, 1997) models structural holes as positions that connect previously unconnected participants. Being in such a position renders an actor powerful vis-à-vis those who are unconnected to parties he is connected to. Although Burt rarely refers to power as a term and notion, he outlines the transactional and resource consequences of such disparities thoroughly.

Regarding the second point, Uzzi's (1997) notion of overembeddedness implies powerlessness, as it refers to the difficulties (or very high costs, to use economic terms) of making decisions autonomously from the influences that the ties involve. Being involved in few but strong trust relationships enables the trustees to take advantage, although they may be worse providers than someone else to whom the client has no tie. Overembeddedness thus represents a similarity to hold-up, with an important difference: overembeddedness involves a certain innocence or convenience, whereas being held up is an unfortunate situation that firms are fully aware of but cannot escape from. In other words, overembedded firms may be able to change provider or client but do not bother to do so, while held-up firms want to get out of the trap but are not able to.

With both the structural hole and the overembeddedness notion of power, we are back to the debate between transaction cost economics and the embeddedness approach. From the transaction cost perspective, Burt's (1992) structural hole analysis is methodologically very sophisticated, and, although pertaining more to sociology than economics, his analysis of advantages emerging from structural hole positions can, in principle, also be expressed in cost terms.

As Williamson points out in the above quote (see page 88), the key is the resource dependence of those in a less advantaged network position. The same is true for the overembeddedness notion of powerlessness. Due to personal relations and difficulties in comparing providers, clients are tempted to hire trusted consultants even if other consultancies might be much better qualified to conduct the task. The power of consultants emerges from strong ties to clients as entry barriers for competitors, but this does not preclude an operationalization in transaction cost terms either.

The autonomy of the embeddedness notion of power from transaction cost economics emerges from another point of view. Personal interaction is not limited to the immediate contracting situation, and there are regular conversations about tasks and opportunities even between projects. In such cases, consultants are able to influence the direction of an upcoming topic to their areas of competence. Ernst (2002: 109–19) has explored this mutual definition of tasks in detail. Consultants acquire follow-up projects through continuous conversations about their clients' business, trying to channel communication toward the consultants' strengths. Moreover, terminating a consulting contract and commissioning a new provider also involves a certain degree of internal embarrassment for the responsible client executive. Having chosen an inappropriate provider does not exactly foster one's status within the firm (Ernst 2002: 109–19). While it is certainly possible to express such mutual project definitions in transaction cost notions, for example in terms of the costs of getting second and third opinions, it is questionable whether this can capture the subtle nature of such communicative procedures. Transaction cost economics may be able to model and rationalize such situations *ex post*, but it has difficulties modeling the subtle influences that a client executive is exposed to in an array of information resources.

We can now look at the sources of power from the signaling and neoinstitutional perspectives. Here, power can be expressed as low signaling costs, and powerlessness involves high costs of signaling future productivity. For example, women and ethnic minorities in the job market for university graduates have higher costs of signaling future productivity than Caucasian men (Spence 1974). This stems from a variety of reasons, from taste-based discrimination (prejudices) to statistical discrimination (discrimination based on saving screening and selection costs rather than on actual attitude). Regarding the client–consultant relationship, signaling power emerges as the degree to which consultants operate as signaling devices of management quality, for example toward the capital market. This argument relies on an institutionalization of consultancy as a source of sophisticated analysis of business decisions, much as Spence (1974) relies on the institutionalization of renowned education as an indication of high future productivity. Consultants are powerful vis-à-vis those clients who have higher costs of signaling management quality – i.e. those who are under pressure from the capital market, want to get access to it, or are suspected of having made management mistakes in the past. Signaling theory conceptualizes as powerful those who can keep the signaling costs of other actors high. Consultants may be in such a position if clients have no alternative ways of indicating management quality.

The signaling approach also indicates the power differences between different kinds of consulting firms, for which it, again implicitly, relies on sociological neoinstitutionalism. From the latter perspective, power can be framed as different degrees of legitimacy. For example, the large international strategy consultancies represent rationality and analytical quality much more than less-known providers. The implicit function of consulting firms that emerges from sociological neoinstitutionalism, the certification of management concepts and decisions, applies to large strategy providers much more than to small or medium-sized consultancies. As a result, large consulting firms can not only charge higher fees (see chapter 3), they can also hire top graduates from renowned universities, which in turn allows them to charge higher fees (see the signaling circle, chapter 1 and conclusion).

Now, is there really an overembedded situation between clients and consultants, and does the elite status of top consultancies really render them unsubstitutable for clients? Although chapter 3 has pointed out that experienced-based, personal trust plays an enormous role in assignment decisions, this does not mean that a client has only one trusted advisor. A trusted consultant can certainly influence the opinions and plans of the client. Typically, however, a sophisticated client has strong ties to several senior consultants and will still be able to choose among them. A typical client, for example a senior executive of a large bank or automotive corporation, has had experience with very many consulting firms and has established strong ties to senior partners in several large consulting firms. Moreover, the certification function may render consultants very desirable from a signaling or neoinstitutional perspective, but the consulting market is competitive and there are several firms in the top tier that represent similar images of rationality and analytical quality. Let us now look at these sources of client power in greater detail.

Sources of client authority

Investment in consulting as discretionary spending

The consulting market is persistently portrayed as one in which consultants benefit from crisis or underperformance on the part of their clients. The myth says that consultants are healers of corporations in need of salvation, and that consultants are ready to provide all sorts of "downsizing" solutions to clients who would otherwise not know what to do (Sorge and van Witteloostuijn 2004). Translated into a hypothesis, this would mean that the consulting sector, or at least the strategy and organization segment of the market, benefits from economic decline and thus moves countercyclically to the economy. However, while cost savings definitely belong to the portfolio of all large strategy and organization consultancies and represent a considerable part of their revenue, the assumption that the consulting market operates countercyclically to the economy is erroneous.

Kennedy Information (2002: 3) compares the annual growth rates of management consultancy between 1970 and 2001 with the annual growth rates of the gross global product (GGP); see figure 4.1. The graph shows that the growth of consulting was particularly strong in those periods in which GGP grew strongly. In periods of global stagnation or slowdown, the growth of the consulting market slowed down as well. Both phenomena occur with a certain pipeline effect: as the economy slows, consulting growth continues for some period of time, indicating an emptying of the pipeline. If the economy resumes growing, clients start spending on outside consulting again only when the recovery is well under way (Kennedy Information 2002: 59).

Hence, management consultancy not only breathes with economic cycles, but it does so in a strongly reinforced, procyclical way: the highs of consulting growth are much higher than general economic highs, and the lows are even lower than general economic lows. A weak economy or a recession pulls consulting revenues down

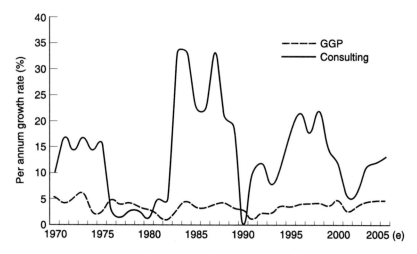

Figure 4.1. The consulting business cycle: per annum growth rates, 1970–2005
Source: Kennedy Information (2002: 3); 2002–2005 are estimates. Reprinted with permission.

forcefully, and a flourishing economy generates consulting revenues that far exceed the growth of the general economy. As Kennedy Information (2002: 3) points out, "The rise out of the trough and the drop back into the trough has, historically, been steep. [...] When in a trough, consulting spending lags overall growth, indicating that much of consulting work is truly a discretionary spend." Management consultancy, therefore, depends on and responds to blossoming or recovering client firms, rather than feeding on corporations in a crisis. Typically, therefore, investment in consultancy is discretionary spending, and, in conjunction with the choice of competing providers, the consultancy market represents a buyer's rather than a seller's market.

Kennedy Information (2002: 19) admits that there may be situations or periods in which management consulting shifts to a seller's market – for example, a particular craze for services in a given period. For the years between 1998 and 2001, in which concern over a possible 'year 2000 bug' boosted demand for IT consultancy and when e-commerce was considered the business channel of the future, Kennedy Information suggests that a seller's market emerged temporarily. As Kennedy Information further points out, however, this was only a short-lived situation, and does not represent the rule. Management consulting represents a buyer's market by default, and a seller's market only in temporary crazes for particular topics.

A study by Ashford (1998) confirms this. In a survey of London Business School alumni, he found that to the question "Why do clients call in consultants?" only 6 percent of clients and 9.5 percent of consultants ticked the box "Need to get out of crisis." Much higher was the score on answers such as "Desire to learn from others," "Facilitate internal processes," "Lack of skills in-house," "Need for change," or "Lack of time in-house" (Ashford 1998: 273). As far back as twenty years ago a regional study in Germany arrived at the conclusion that around two-thirds of consulting demand emerges as a result of low problem pressure on the client's side and only one-third arises from high problem pressure. Based on a survey of small and medium-sized industrial corporations in south-western Germany, Wirtz (1985) investigated the relationship between competitive pressure and the demand for consulting. His hypothesis was straightforward: the greater the economic burden on medium-sized enterprises the more they seek advice. Consistent with the results of Ashford (1998) and Kennedy Information (2002), Wirtz's data do *not* confirm the hypothesis. Wirtz finds that initiatives for problem solving emerge primarily in phases of growth and boom, or at least in phases of optimism among business owners and management. Clients take up novel or controversial ways of approaching tasks and business problems when the risks of procrastination are deemed higher than the risks of project failure – that is, in phases of optimism about economic performance. Consulting demand is – not exclusively but primarily – a matter of discovering and seizing opportunities.

Hence, a common image of management consultancy, that consultants have structural power because clients are in crisis, does not hold. While cost reduction methods definitely belong to consultancies' portfolios, crisis management is not the essence of the consulting market. Certainly, a common application for consultancy is to increase clients' capacities, a function which is more in demand in boom periods. However, consultancy is not about increasing routine capacity but about aperiodic analyses dissimilar to client routines (see chapter 2). Clients use consultants mostly in times of expanding the business, reorganizing it in phases of market expansion, testing opportunities in new or old markets, or experimenting with new technologies. Investments in consulting services are primarily discretionary spending, and this puts clients in the comfortable position of choice between several providers, without being in desperate need of advice.

Quality certainty through embeddedness effects

While clients' overembeddedness has been discussed above as a source of consulting power, the embeddedness approach in general does not suggest that the consultancy market is a seller's market. On the contrary, conceiving of it as a seller's market would ignore the market mechanisms outlined in chapter 3. In particular, it would overlook the overarching influence of word-of-mouth effects and the fact that existing satisfied clients generate around two-thirds of consulting revenues. Consultants operate in a web of personal relations and mutual obligations, and, as Glückler (2005) points out, even in so-called trust relations poor performance soon results in the loss of follow-up contracts and networked reputation (see chapter 3). That is, consulting growth hinges on client satisfaction, and assuming that this can be manipulated by information asymmetry and impression management seems to be based on a shaky premise: that clients are naïve, quality-imperceptive victims in the management arena.

The premise does not apply. For example, Larwood and Gattiker (1985) observe that the power relation between client and consultant is asymmetrical to the benefit of the client, since he has the choice between several providers (see also Richter 2004). Sturdy (1997) tries to redirect the dominant assumption of consulting power by outlining how business is extremely insecure for them. Fincham (1999) tries to steer a middle road and concludes that the consulting process contains no necessary structures or fixed dependencies, but that the balance of power "may be tipped one way or another by contingent factors" (349). But, as the above discussion suggests, consulting or client power is not just an empirical case-by-case question but a matter of clients' quality certainty, gained through experienced-based trust and word-of-mouth referrals.

Clients' increasing professionalism in managing consultants

Two German-language observers of the consultancy market, Zimmermann (2004) and Mohe (2004), point to the following aspects.

- Clients have much experience of consulting; many of them know all the large consulting firms and have a comparative perspective – and many executives are former consultants.
- Clients have considerable negotiation expertise; they know the capabilities of each consultancy and have substitutes for each.
- Expectations have risen, especially with regard to the implementation of solutions, global delivery, and technological competence.
- Clients have professionalized their sourcing processes; in ever more cases, procurement departments are involved in the choice of consultants.

Along the same lines, Richter (2004) points out that there has been an increase in the elasticity of demand, Wiemann (2004) holds that there has been a trend toward "consulting governance" within client firms, and Petmecky (2004) confirms that purchasing departments are increasingly involved in selection processes.

One point that Zimmermann (2004) and Mohe (2004) mention seems particularly important: many clients are former consultants. In Germany alone, tens of thousands of former consultants are now in executive positions at client firms, and this has certainly contributed to client sophistication. For example, four out of eight members of the management board of the German mail corporation Deutsche Post were formerly consultants at McKinsey. Interpreting this as a case of consulting power would mean asserting that these board members are still more loyal to their former employer than to their current one, which would be a grave allegation.

In such cases in which clients are former consultants, information asymmetry may be very low. Both consulting critics and transaction cost theorists assume by default that consultants possess more detailed information about their own capabilities than clients. The German-language work of Stegemeyer (2002) represents an interesting case. He conceptualizes management consulting as a market with considerable potential for consultants' opportunistic behavior to remain unnoticed by clients. Then he measures client satisfaction, and wonders why there is no substantial client dissatisfaction.

He briefly argues that the market may not quite be as anonymous as he had conceived (211), but then concludes that it must be consultants' "moral consciousness" and "consulting philosophy" that account for the fact that they do not behave opportunistically (211–15). This ignores the fact that clients can gain a considerable degree of quality certainty, especially through embeddedness effects (see chapter 3) and by employing former consultants. Stegemeyer's work represents an interesting example of how academics may have difficulties in understanding market mechanisms when following the pure lines of economic theory without being aware of embeddedness theory.

While the tendency for procurement departments to become more involved in selection processes is also indicative of a trend toward more arm's-length relationships between clients and consultants, the wide dissemination of former consulting personnel in client organizations accounts for the low level of information asymmetry between clients and consultants, adding to the quality certainty gained by embedded relations. Moreover, the involvement of the procurement department rarely goes as far as dictating to the responsible executive which consulting firm to choose. Rather, it improves his negotiation position regarding pricing and contract details, thereby strengthening client power over consultants.

Consultants' stress and the market mechanisms

As mentioned above, transaction cost economics and signaling theory differ in their views regarding the party that makes the effort to reduce information asymmetry. Signaling theory models this effort as coming from the party with more information, transaction cost economics the other way around. This is based on different assumptions about market power. Regarding job markets, signaling theory tends to assume a buyer's market and models the job seeker as the person with more information but little power. This corresponds to the consulting market, where even the large providers with high reputation make considerable efforts to signal quality (see chapter 9 for details). Transaction cost theory, in contrast, tends to assume a seller's market and models the effort as coming from the information seeker (typically the buyer is the information seeker). In the case of the consulting market this would be the client's side. If consultancy were a seller's

market then clients would make a major effort to reduce quality
uncertainty, not only by experience-based trust and word-of-mouth
referrals (chapter 3) but also by formulating a long and detailed
contract to protect themselves against hold-up, opportunistic action,
and moral hazard. However, there are no such elaborated contracts
in the consulting market. While contracts for IT outsourcing work
are usually very long and legally complicated (almost like M&A
contracts), contracts for consulting projects are usually short and
legally straightforward. Typically, it is the consultants rather than the
clients who submit a draft of the contract together with the consulting
proposal. Clients either accept the contract or do not, and the only
clause they make sure of is the ability to fire the consultants almost at
will. The reduction of uncertainty is almost completely a matter of
informal social institutions (chapter 3) rather than a matter of formal
contracting. Clients are not particularly afraid of hold-up situations or
consultants' opportunism.

In general, it is reasonable to assume that the well-known stress
under which consultants work is an indicator of clients' authority.
If strategy and organization consultancies had a strong market
position, they would be perfectly able to transfer their stress to clients.
Typically, however, it is consultants rather than client employees who
are to be found still working in the project room hours after client
employees have gone home. Long hours and the subordination of
private commitments to professional demands is a typical reaction
to performance pressure and the need to validate the client's trust.
In his self-ethnographic passages, ex-consultant Ashford (1998:
193–5; emphasis in original) puts it this way:

What ultimately I found a grind was not being able, ever, to plan my life
outside work in any confidence of honouring the commitments which I might
make. [...] If the client wanted me in Budapest the day after tomorrow,
Budapest is where I had to be. Too bad about the wedding anniversary or the
dinner party... When an old customer in Spain wanted a bit of follow-up
work, it was back to the airport ... Once you have done this a few times, you
begin to feel a complete heel. Essentially, then, consultancy *is* stressful but the
hours and the deadlines and the travelling are really just a reflection of the
client–consultant relationship which drives everything you do...

The situation will sound familiar to most consultants. Stress and
placing project requirements before private issues belong to the normal

life of a business advisor. Even large consulting firms seem to be substitutable in terms of their expertise, and competitors are always waiting for a project of the current advisor to fail. Building up specific capabilities and new consulting approaches is thus a key to staying at the competitive forefront.

The price mechanism outlined in chapter 3 provides another clue to consultants' stress. Engaging in a price competition would be very dangerous for strategy consultancies, because lowering their daily fees could do considerable damage to the signaling effect that high fees carry. The top-tier consultancies are, typically, powerful enough not to negotiate their daily fees, but not powerful enough to avoid negotiating the price of the total package. In order to comply with client wishes to lower the total sum, consultants have to agree to provide the same service in rather fewer consulting days. As a result, the consulting staff (project manager and below) have to carry the burden. They have to carry out the same analyses in fewer days than such a project would normally take. The enormous stress experienced by consultants – their long hours and frequent work over weekends – must be seen in this context: senior consultants are unable to lower their fees for signaling reasons, but the client is powerful enough to insist on a less expensive service. Senior consultants sell assignments for fewer days than initially planned, and the consultants lower down the hierarchy have to carry the can for it.

In summary, the market grants clients several sources of authority, and experience and word-of-mouth effects mitigate or even compensate for information asymmetry. Unless the last bill has been paid and no follow-up contract is in sight, consultants typically do not take any steps during an assignment without seeing the most important individual at the client firm in advance (McGivern 1983). This does not mean that a consultant needs to take any assignment. In fact, consultancy has recovered after three difficult years between 2001 and 2003 (FEACO 2006), and the top-tier consulting firms have to reject many assignment offers due to a lack of personnel. But having to decline assignments does not mean that consultants are powerful vis-à-vis clients. Firms such as McKinsey or Accenture are certainly not dependent on one individual project. However, individual senior consultants or partners of large consulting firms depend in their careers on individual assignments. At consulting firms, even large ones, any partner or senior consultant is generally responsible for only a very few clients. Any termination of a contract represents a considerable career blow, and could result in the individual having to leave the firm according to the "up or out" system (see chapter 9). There may be cases in which the consultant can provide a very specialized and unsubstitutable kind of advice, in which some client manager's career depends on successful cooperation with this particular consulting firm, or in which a consultant has better access to information within the client firm. This may tip the balance of power towards the consultant in individual, temporary situations. However, these sources of consultant power do not make up for the general character of a buyer's market and the ability of clients to choose between several trusted or recommended providers.

5 | Substitutes or supplements? Internal versus external consulting

Internal management consultancy emerged as an alternative to external consulting and grew considerably in the 1990s – parallel to but with a delay in relation to external consulting growth. Looking at the often considerable expenses for external consultants, many large firms searched for less expensive sources of organizational analysis and established internal consulting functions. In some cases, internal consulting firms were newly founded as additional units or subsidiaries. In these cases, new personnel were predominantly recruited from renowned external consulting firms, offering them equally interesting analytical tasks, less traveling, and less overtime work than in external consultancies. In other cases, internal units such as "Organization," "Corporate Development," or "Corporate Planning" were renamed as internal consultancy departments, expanded, and given more responsibility and tasks. In these cases, most of the personnel of the former department or staff function were carried over and only a few additional consultants were hired from outside.

The point of founding internal consultancies is not only to save costs. Two additional reasons come into play. First, an internal consulting firm, possibly founded as a subsidiary, is also meant to be a source of additional revenue. If the internal consultancy has overcapacities, their services can be offered on the market. Hence, internal consulting firms are often conceived of as competitors to external consulting firms, both for analytical work within the firm and – sometimes but not always – for contracts in the market. The second reason for founding internal consulting firms has been the emerging dissatisfaction with external consulting work. Clients felt that external consultants often provided abstract solutions that did not really fit with the concrete reality and possibilities of the client firm.

Today there are many different relationships between internal and external consultancies. Depending on the legal form of internal consultancy, the boundary between internal and external advice is not always clear-cut. For example, if an internal consulting firm is founded as a legally separate subsidiary and its services offered in the external market, then they are both internal and external advisors. Accordingly, the definitions of internal consultancy differ. For example, Niedereichholz defines internal consultancy as "consulting units which are submitted to the decisions of the superordinate corporate board even if they are legally separate and active in the external market" (Niedereichholz 2000: 14; author's translation). This loose definition can be contrasted with a tighter one by Oefinger (1986: 14), who defines internal consultancy as such only if the staff are employees of the advised company.

Not surprisingly, the business models of internal consulting firms differ considerably. Mohe (2002: 329–37) has systematized the possibilities. He distinguishes between types of internal consulting in terms of form of establishment, organizational integration, organizational structure, forms of billing to the client, size of the internal consultancy, types of clients, spatial expansion and coverage, market approach, and consulting approach. His list shows that the difference between internal and external consultancy is a matter of degree rather than kind. Speaking of internal consultancy as a fixed term, therefore, has its dangers, for the term does not represent a homogeneous business model. Nevertheless, establishing an internal consulting unit or subsidiary is motivated by the same idea: to provide a less expensive or more appropriate source of advice than external consultancies can offer.

On this basis, several authors (Allanson 1985; Hoyer 2000; Kelley 1979; Schmidt *et al.* 2000) have tried to point out the advantages of internal consulting. They suggest that it improves coordination and communication within corporations and fosters thinking in terms of markets rather than internal turfs, and it may collect, centralize, and disseminate knowledge in the corporation. Internal consultancy, moreover, may increase the firm's organizational innovativeness and problem-solving capacities by coordinating tasks between departments, and it can ensure that innovative knowledge remains within the firm and is not transferred to others (see Allanson 1985: 2, 22; Hoyer 2000: 62; Kelley 1979: 112; Schmidt *et al.* 2000: 260–3).

A central point is that internal consultants may be more familiar than externals with internal procedures and knowledge sources, power relations, and micropolitical issues and sensitivities. They may be better able to anticipate possible points of resistance and may be more likely to avoid a number of traps into which external consultants could fall. Internal consultancy may thus be appropriate for tasks that require more implicit, client-specific knowledge. In addition, internal consultancy is usually tasked with the implementation as well as the formulation of solutions. This view implicitly suggests that there can be a division of labor between internal and external consultancies, which can, again, be theorized from different theoretical perspectives.

Economic analysis of internal consultancy

Listing the functions of internal consultancy provides an overview of the possibilities for establishing and running such a consultancy, but does not yet offer a theory-based outline of when and why a particular kind of consulting is suitable. The transaction cost considerations in chapter 2 are a useful point of departure. The frequency of demand, the asset specificity of investments, the similarity of expected tasks, and the internal coordination costs represent the dimensions along which we can outline a theory-based comparison of when and why internal consultancy is more useful than external (see figure 2.3 in chapter 2). The central aspect is that establishing an internal consulting function makes sense only from a certain demand frequency onwards. For many firms, there has been a frequent rather than just an occasional demand for consultancy, and therefore incorporating this service has been a reasonable economic reaction. The costs for an internal consultant per day are lower than for external consultants, and some of the costs may even be considered as investments in management development because internal consultants are often promoted to executive positions in the firm after working for the internal consultancy.

As Theuvsen (1994: 71–3) outlines, the distinction between fixed and variable costs is essential in this respect. The costs for external consultancy are variable, as they vary in line with the number of projects, or, more precisely, with the number of consulting days. The costs for internal consultancy, by contrast, comprise a large proportion of the fixed costs for setting up the internal consultancy (hiring, offices, etc.) and maintaining it. Salaries must be paid permanently and do not vary with the number of consulting cases.

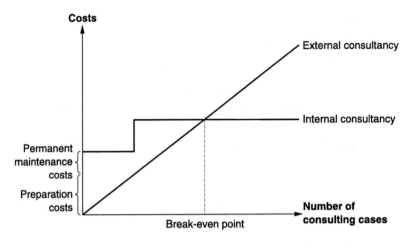

Figure 5.1. The cost-effectiveness of internal versus external consultancy
Source: Theuvsen (1994: 72), referring to Sauer (1991: 151).

Based on these considerations, Theuvsen presents a straightforward
break-even analysis; see figure 5.1.

Such a straightforward comparison, of course, assumes an equi-
valence of internal and external consultancy regarding consulting
quality and performance. This may be unrealistic, however. A corporation setting up an internal consultancy is interested in using its
capacities permanently in order to cover the fixed costs and render
it efficient. Here emerges the central dilemma: if an internal
consultancy is used permanently, then it is increasingly integrated
into the hierarchy and loses its difference from internal non-
consultancy solutions. In other words, the more cost-effective an
internal consultancy is when it is utilized by the client, the less
effective it will have become since it is progressively more involved in
everyday work.

The frequency of consulting tasks, therefore, is only one variable in
the equation, and other variables emerge as equally important –
especially the type of competence and utility of internal versus external
consultancy. Theuvsen (1994: 73–5) has provided important comparisons in this respect. He distinguishes between four factors: the
knowledge of the consultants, the absorption of know-how by
the client firm, the independence of consultants, and the flexibility of
using them.

Consultants' knowledge

Regarding knowledge, in the sense of educational and human resource qualifications, there are good reasons for assuming that external consultants can draw on a pool of more talented individuals. Based on signaling theory, it can be argued that individuals with higher future productivity have less costly access to the top-tier consulting firms, which are associated with elite status and attract particularly qualified graduates. Moreover, working in a top-tier consulting firm constitutes a very strong job market signal in its own right (Franck and Pudack 2000; Franck *et al.* 2004; Pudack 2004). Extending Spence's (1974) view, it can be assumed that many graduates will apply first to external management consulting firms, and take on a job in an internal consultancy only if they have not been offered a job in one of the top external ones. (This topic is discussed in greater detail in chapter 9.)

Nevertheless, the main point may well be not the amount of knowledge but the kind. Internal consultants accumulate their expertise primarily within the boundaries of one firm, whereas external consultants are exposed to the realities of, say, between two and five firms a year. As a result, the type of knowledge will differ substantially. Internal consultants are more familiar with the business issues in their particular industrial sector, while external consultants accumulate knowledge about tools and procedures that are applicable to more than one sector and region.

To this end, we can look at chapter 2 and Kehrer and Schade's (1995) analysis. They address the compatibility between task characteristics and human resource skills (whether of external consultants, internal consultants, or internal employees) in terms of information compatibility, especially in terms of the specificity of the task to client operations and the task complexity. With regard to the specificity, they argue that internal consultants possess a higher information compatibility, because they are more familiar with client operations. The more specific a task is to the client's operations the more likely it is that internal consultants will conduct the assignment more economically than external consultants. This is based on the assumption that the costs of collecting information regarding the issues in the client firm are lower for internal than external consultancy, and gaining access to and the trust of client employees is easier and thus less costly (see figure 5.2).

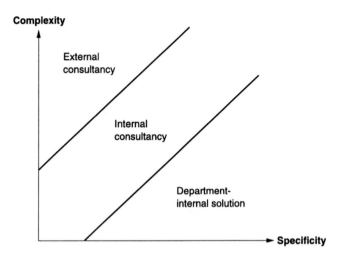

Figure 5.2. Task characteristics and make-or-(also)-buy solutions
Source: Kehrer and Schade (1995: 471; author's translation).

With regard to task complexity — i.e. the number and intricacy of
determinants — the opposite is the case. In this instance it is external
consultants who possess higher information compatibility, because
they are exposed more often to new situations and complex problems,
and they have greater capacity for gathering external information
and resources. External consultants are in a better position to collect
external information, transfer knowledge, and apply analytical tools
from other industrial sectors or regions.

   In terms of the structure of the future problem-solving demand,
Kehrer and Schade distinguish between the expected frequency of
demand and the similarity of the expected tasks (see figure 2.3 in
chapter 2). In both cases it is clear that, the higher the intensity of
demand and the similarity of the expected tasks, the more likely it
becomes that internal consultants will be more economical than
external ones. Hence, from this viewpoint, there is an optimal form of
consulting, or an optimal degree of externality, for each client task. A
client would have to figure out the details of each assignment and would
then be able to decide which type of consulting is more compatible.

Clients' know-how absorption and consultants' independence

As Theuvsen (1994: 75) also mentions, internal and external
consultancy differ not only in terms of knowledge types but also

in terms of the way the client firm acquires know-how in the consulting process. While external consultancies have privileged access to external knowledge sources, internal consultancy may have advantages arising from the internal distribution of knowledge. Again, depending on the required type, the client needs to work out the details of the task and then choose out of internal or external advice. If the prevailing opinion is that the knowledge is already in the firm and needs only to be crystallized, then internal consultancy may make more sense from an economic point of view. However, this ignores the more sociological aspect of legitimacy: internal knowledge often lacks the credibility to be taken seriously by top executives. Only if external sources of high repute spell out this internal knowledge does it acquire the legitimacy necessary to be treated seriously. This is an instance in which economic theory would have to develop an economics of certification (discussed in chapter 9 and the conclusion).

The question of the independence of internal versus external consultants is a critical one. Chapter 4 has mentioned that external consultants are often dependent on one particular client executive, the person "bringing you in." The general independence of the consulting sector, upon which principle it always claims to be based, becomes questionable if – in order to get a follow-up contract – the opinions and approaches of that person have priority over others'. Internal consultants, by contrast, may well not depend on a follow-up contract, but, of course, this does not necessarily render them more independent. On the contrary, their approach may be biased by an even more immediate power relation: administrative fiat, expressed, say, in overt orders as to how to analyze a problem, or subtle expectations with regard to storylines and results. Moreover, internal consultants also have an individual sponsor for each assignment. Typically, internal consultants want to have a career within the firm and are forced or persuaded in a subtle way to give priority to the views of those internal clients that influence their promotion prospects.

Flexibility

With regard to the flexibility of using consultants, one could argue, along the lines of Theuvsen (1994: 74), that the use of internal consultants is more flexible since they are available more readily than external consultants. The costs of producing a speedy analysis of a problem that arises suddenly may then be lower. However, this is based on a number of conditions that do not always apply. For example, it assumes that an internal consultancy has over-capacities, with the result that some internal consultants can take on the task straightaway. Otherwise, the internal consultancy would have to hire personnel, which involves higher transaction costs than hiring an outside consultant. Moreover, arguing that internal consultants are more readily at hand (and thus more economical for immediate problem solving) ignores the initial costs of setting up an internal consultancy (see the break-even analysis above). Whether the costs of searching for and selecting external consultants are higher than the up-front costs of internal consultancy (recruiting personnel, rental fees, and maintenance for offices and workplaces, etc.) is a matter of short-term versus long-term considerations. Furthermore, external consultants who enjoy already established relations of trust are often just as readily at hand as internal consultants.

Economic choice criteria between internal and external consultancy

To summarize the economic perspective on internal consultancy, let us assume that the internal consultancy already exists and that we can disregard the costs of setting it up, recruiting and training the people, and elaborating an organizational structure and cooperation guidelines within the firm. If the client company has a choice between experienced in-house consultants, acquainted with the procedures of the firm, and experienced external providers, based on cost considerations its choice criteria come down to the following ones.

- How critical is confidentiality? Are the costs of losing exclusive access to information higher than the gains of repute if it is not treated confidentially?
- Is there a gap in talent, education, and qualification between the experienced internal consultants and the experienced external consultants? In economic terms, do external firms have more qualified personnel; is the learning curve of external consultants steeper?

- Does the elaboration of the contract differ in cost terms? Do we have to engage in costly negotiations with external providers? Do we have to reckon with monitoring and legal costs to ensure that the external provider adheres to the terms? By contrast, when choosing an internal consultancy, what are the costs of fiat, administration, and monitoring?
- Which kind of knowledge is more appropriate — i.e. what is the nature of the task? To what extent does the task require comparative knowledge across firms, industries, or regions, or does it primarily concern the collection and leverage of internal knowledge? Expressed in economic terms: to what extent can an external consultancy use economies of scale and scope across external sectors to conduct the assignment?
- Can an external provider use procedures which have been proven useful in other sectors or regions and which the internal consulting firm could build up only at much greater costs, or does the task involve so many internal intricacies that any outside procedure would require a more costly way of making external consultants familiar with the internal particulars?
- Do we have to reckon with internal resistance or external legitimacy differences vis-à-vis the consulting assignment? Can internal or external consultants overcome these sources of resistance at lower cost?
- Do the authority relations and the potential for administrative fiat to which internal consultants are exposed render an unbiased solution more costly? Or are external consultants equally dependent on follow-up assignments, meaning that an unbiased solution from them will be equally expensive?
- Do we have to search for and select external consultants or do we have trust relations with qualified external providers that would render the search and selection costs low?
- Last but not least — the bare production costs. How high are the fees for external consultants per day and how many days would they charge us? Alternatively, how much do we have to transfer to the profit or cost center of the internal consultancy in order to get the task done?

These economic considerations provide a useful framework for looking at clients' options. All the same, this kind of analysis has its limits. Clients do not make their decisions about consulting issues in an ivory tower or in an arm's-length way. Even from a short-term perspective and disregarding the up-front costs, arguing that internal consultants are more readily at hand ignores the personal relations between clients and external consultants (chapter 3). In the face of long-term business relations, external consultants may be perfectly able to compete with in-house consultants in terms of availability and readiness. Theuvsen (1994: 74; author's translation) admits this when he writes: "The consultation of an external consultant requires comparatively intensive search and assessment costs, if there is no ongoing business relation with a consultant." Moreover, from the client's point of view a microscopic analysis regarding the similarity of expected tasks, specificity, and complexity may be unrealistic. We have to look at how the client firm reaches its decision as to internal or external consultancy options, for which, again, embeddedness theory and sociological neoinstitutionalism are useful.

Sociological analysis of internal consultancy

The transaction cost framework paints an ideal picture of a smooth sequence of events – i.e. client executives first discover an issue, secondly they define the task, and thirdly they select the appropriate form of consultancy. This may occasionally be the case, but in many instances it is unrealistic. Client executives are often in regular contact with external consultants and discover the topics to be worked on during their interaction with them. Client–consultant relationships are frequently stable even if there is no ongoing project. Often they even endure an executive's or consultant's change of employer. A client executive then hires the same consultant when working for a different firm, and executives sometimes hire consultants as individuals even if they have changed consulting firm or set up their own business. Vice versa, a change of senior executives often means a change of consultants, for the relationships often connect people rather than firms (Ernst 2002: 108–9).

As Ernst (115–19) further points out, close and lasting relationships lead to many conversations on topics that have the potential to be translated into consulting assignments. In many cases this predetermines which consulting firm gets the contract. From the first contact between client executive and consultants, the decision as to whether to use internal or external consultants is influenced by the quality of social relations — not only at the time of selecting a consultant but earlier, during the identification of issues, and throughout the further decision-making process. Only in rare cases are client decision-making committees completely separated from such pressures. Internal consultants are aware of these circumstances, as the following statements show.

Now, when I started here I talked to every member of the board and to every director for several hours — I am myself [director of internal consulting] one level below the board. I have a very good relationship with all my colleagues I rely on — I meet them regularly and exchange experiences. Absolutely crucial (director of internal consulting, large German corporation).

You place the people on whom you build up your network. Parallel to that, the former director of Division [X] was a co-founder of the internal consultancy. Now he is the director of another division and he is our direct contact to the CEO. And this way you have already defined your points in the corporation and placed your people, whom you can of course approach with project ideas, whom you can possibly also approach with problems, where you can direct certain information into the appropriate channels (senior internal consultant, large German corporation).

Internal consultants, therefore, build up strategic networks within the firm and regularly talk to executives in order to generate, identify, and define consulting issues. Personal relations and the ideas that are passed back and forth in this network of contacts influence the client's decision-making process, as well as the choice between external and internal consultants. Let us therefore look at what clients of external and internal consultancies say about this form of mutual task definition.

[T]hen the project is discussed with two or three optional consultants, for example, with McKinsey or the internal consultancy, because one knows each other, one knows whom to contact. Now, I would decide that on my own only if I knew all players, [but] who is in the position to know all of them? (client of both internal and external consultants).[1]

This statement illustrates that decision-making processes are not made in isolation, but that clients actively involve consultants at an early stage in the discussion of topics and upcoming tasks.

---

[1] I would like to thank Sebastian Wind, who conducted the interviews cited in this chapter in the context of his diploma thesis, which I initiated and supervised. The interviews were conducted in German; the selection and translations of the quotes are mine.

Moreover, and even more interestingly in the context of internal versus external consultancy, experienced-based trust relations of clients involve both internal and external consultants.

The connection [between know-how and trust] is that if all consultants [internal and external] are on the same level of know-how, then personal relationship plays an important role... As long as the [know-how] level is not the same, personal relations play only a subordinated role. Because these are two sides: that you can work with them, or work with these but not with those. This is crucial: if you know that you can't work with him, then you don't take him, no matter how good he is... (client of both internal and external consultants).

The client implies that a consultant's know-how and the quality of the personal relationship with him are two independent constructs. He claims that he first checks the consultant's know-how and then, after selecting a few with an equal level of know-how, he chooses the one with whom he can work best. This sounds like a perfectly reasonable selection strategy, one fully compatible with the transaction cost arguments outlined above. However, in the second half of the statement the client also indicates that the quality of the relationship takes priority over know-how, which represents a weak aspect of the economic approach. In general, clients are pretty frank about the importance of personal trust and networks, although most present them as decoupled from service quality.

Both external and internal consultants struggle to gain the attention of senior executives. Competition does not start after the client has identified a topic, but much earlier, and is centered on claiming the attention of client executives for topics and possible approaches. The decision for or against a particular internal or external consultant is, to a large extent, a result of this earlier process. The compatibility between consulting tasks and consulting skills is influenced by social tie quality.

Nevertheless, such market mechanisms leave a number of questions open. First, embeddedness theory is barely able to explain why internal consultancy emerged and became institutionalized in the 1980s (North America) and 1990s (Europe), even though internal analytical functions and external consultancy were already established.

Second, are there only economic reasons why external consultancy has continued to grow rapidly even though internal consultancy has become increasingly viable?

Regarding the first question, sociological neoinstitutionalists would argue that in the 1970s one or a few corporations may have acted as institutional entrepreneurs and founded internal analytical functions. Institutionalized under the term "internal consultancy," internal analytical know-how could circulate as a concept even though analytical in-house functions such as corporate development or corporate planning already existed. Corporate executives could adopt the practice, on the basis either of an authentic belief in its usefulness or of the mimetic process of "What others do is probably not too bad and we should do it too."

As discussed at the beginning of this chapter, different internal consultancies operate on the basis of dissimilar business models. They can be organized as independent subsidiaries or as departments embedded in the corporate hierarchy; as centralized headquarters functions or as decentralized, local staff; as profit centers billing market prices or as free internal services. The organizational forms of internal consultancies are heterogeneous, and yet these diverse forms of internal analysis and support are all today known as "internal consultancy." Thus a process has taken place that early institutionalists are completely familiar with: a decoupling of the label from the actual procedures (Meyer and Rowan 1977). Establishing an internal consultancy signals to those outside that the firm takes a responsible attitude to its own organization and cost structure, for internal consultancies are mostly less expensive than external ones. It also signals that the firm is not content with "on paper only" advice but has a strong focus on implementation, which in turn signals readiness for change and organizational adaptability. Hence, the establishment of an internal consultancy may not be (simply) an economic solution to the limits of external consultancy, it may also − or alternatively − be an adaptive but less deliberate solution to problems of legitimacy. It may be that the most important outcome of founding an internal consultancy is not to be found in the efficiency of analyses but in the matching of other firms according to institutionalized standards of good management.

Internal consultancy as competition and supplement to external advice

Regarding the question of whether internal consultancy represents a supplement or competition to external consultancy, we can also look at signaling theory. Relatively independent from their products or services, the internal procedures and management quality of corporations are to a large extent unobservable by stakeholders and shareholders. The establishment of an internal consultancy signals due diligence in internal operations. It symbolizes a commitment to analytical competence and continuous improvements without the large expenses entailed in external advice, and corporate executives can present themselves as responsible leaders who engage both in constant auditing of the work flow and in keeping an eye on the budget. Establishing an internal consultancy is an efficient signal if it successfully differentiates the well-managed from the less well-managed firms. The latter point marks the difference from sociological neoinstitutionalism, which does not assume an efficient outcome for such signaling processes.

However, to a much greater extent than internal consultancies, the large external providers are associated with a top-rate workforce and with innovative solutions, on account of their outside perspective. As Meyer (1996, 2002) points out, externality and otherness comprise their advantage. If analyses have been conducted by subordinates of top executives, as happens with internal consultancy, then they may be regarded as no more than a few minor suggestions by a bunch of junior employees. If the very same analyses and results are presented by a prestigious strategy consultancy, they carry the stamp of thoroughness, rationality, and expertise, achieved by an intellectual elite. Internal consultants and clients have much to say about this, as the following quotes illustrate.

I am sure that if an international McKinsey partner or two or three meet the management board and say, "Believe us, it is such and such," then this has an enormous weight... Based on...I'd say, the "historical data" about McKinsey, there is definitely additional worth there (senior internal consultant, large German corporation).

Sometimes there are topics, for example also reorganization topics, where you say I want to have an external stamp on that. [...] Now, meanwhile, we're that open here in the firm that we say: "No, no, we think you could do that but we need the [particular consulting firm stamp] on that (client of internal and external consultancy in Germany).

Internal consultants are fully aware that there are certain instances when top management prefer external consultants from prestigious providers. These cases are usually ones that involve major shifts of resources and power. Senior executives are surprisingly open about this topic: they acknowledge that internal consultants could perform the analyses and yet they prefer external consultants to do them, for "political" reasons. Only external consultancy holds the symbolic capital that certifies contested decisions. A division of labor between internal and external consultancy emerges with respect to the hierarchical levels and the importance of consulting projects. Prestigious external providers dominate the "hard core" of substantial reorganizations; internal consultants take care of softer issues further down the hierarchy.

Clients' awareness of the certification function of external consultancy again builds a bridge to cost considerations. As mentioned in chapter 1, sociological neoinstitutionalism has difficulties in integrating strategic action in the context of known norms. What emerges is an economics of certification, in which the decision to legitimize business resolutions involves costs (Franck *et al.* 2004; see chapter 9 and the conclusion). The fees for external consultants, and the transaction costs incurred in hiring them, can then be viewed as investments in management certification. If an internal consultancy already exists and a firm still decides to call in external advice, they have clearly opted for the more costly solution. The fact that they can afford this is a signal of good management and a stable financial situation. If this pays off in the capital market then it was an efficient signaling process, and the signaling circle outlined in chapter 1 closes. This argument leads back to the point mentioned at the beginning of this chapter. Since working for a large external consultancy firm represents an important job market signal, talented graduates will seek such employment in preference to a job with an internal consultancy. As a result, external consultancies may well consist of more talented personnel than internal consultancies. Chapter 9 discusses this mechanism in greater detail.

PART II

The drivers of managing a consulting firm

6 | *Diversified services or niche focus? Strategies of consulting firms*

Until the 1990s the top-tier strategy consultancies typified what was generally understood as management consulting. Their businesses had grown on two fields of advice: corporate strategy and internal organization/operations management. While they continued to expand until the economic slowdown hit many Western economies in 2001, they grew alongside the information technology developments of the 1980s and 1990s. During this period IT consulting emerged as a central and lucrative segment of the consulting market. In principle, the large accounting firms and the strategy consulting firms both had the opportunity to step into this segment. Only the accounting firms did so, however, and they recorded growth rates that exceeded those of the strategy consultancies (for details, see Suddaby and Greenwood 2001). From the mid-1990s to 2002 IT consulting accounted for the largest share of the consulting market. It is only since 2002 that IT consulting and operations management consulting have comprised roughly equal shares of the sector (FEACO 2005: 8), though operations management also involves a lot of IT-related topics.

In the field of strategic management, the difference between economics and sociology is reflected in the economics of strategy on the one hand and the "strategy as practice" approach on the other. The book by Besanko *et al.* (2000) represents the classic text for the economics of strategy. They build on the works of Chandler (1962) and Porter (1980) and provide the economic underpinning for firm boundaries, market analysis, and strategic positioning. By contrast, the more sociological strategy as practice approach (www.strategy-as-practice.org; de Wit and Meyer 2004) looks at the processes underlying the making of strategic decisions in organizations, and at how actual firm behavior deviates from strategies that would be ideal according to economic theory.

This chapter uses the strategic decision concerning horizontal firm boundaries as an example: whether or not to diversify into the segment of IT consulting. To strategy consulting firms, this was the central question of the 1980s and 1990s, and it still leads to debates and governance changes in these firms. Both economic and sociological accounts are relevant to the question as to why it was accounting firms rather than strategy consulting firms that tapped into the fastest-growing segment.

From the economic viewpoint, the question of whether professional service firms should diversify into IT consulting is a classic matter of the horizontal boundaries of the firm (Besanko *et al.* 2000: 71–108). Services exhibit economies of scale when the costs per unit decline over a range of output – for example, by way of learning effects, by spreading fixed costs over increasing output, or by adopting technology that pays off its up-front investment above a certain production level. Economies of scope emerge when the costs of producing a variety of services in one firm are lower than producing them in two or more firms. This can be due to transferring learning effects between different services or sharing fixed costs (Besanko *et al.* 2000: 72–4). From this perspective we need to look at whether accounting firms or strategy consulting firms are better able to economize on scale or scope when providing IT consultancy. To sociologists, the question is whether economies of scale and scope suffice to explain the behavior of the market participants or whether other theories need to complement or correct the picture. Before engaging in this discussion, however, the shifts in the consulting market toward IT consulting need to be outlined.

The shift in the consulting market in the 1990s

The emergence of IT outsourcing and consulting

The point of departure for IT-related consulting services was the need for corporations to save costs by outsourcing IT services. Due to economies of scale, external providers focusing on IT services could offer these services at lower costs. In the 1980s the large accounting firms recognized this business opportunity and met the demand by taking over activities that had formerly been performed by clients' in-house IT departments. The large accounting firms were well equipped to do this, based on their accounting-related experience with large-scale data processing. Due to auditing requirements and acceptability, accountants and auditors often do not have to look at individual accounting entries but do need to check the functioning of the software. Hence, IT had become a critical factor in auditing acceptability, and accounting and auditing are more related to IT consulting than strategy consulting. Moreover, as Czerniawska (1999: 96–7, 119, 144) points out, the established trust relationship of accounting firms with clients had helped them to recognize the demand for IT and to appreciate the first-mover advantages in the upcoming outsourcing market.

Large IT providers such as IBM, Hewlett Packard and Siemens have also expanded into consulting, because it offers higher margins than their businesses. As Kennedy Information (2002: 47) observes,

When IBM reorganized to incorporate its Business Innovation Services consulting division into its International Global Services Group in 1999, it marked a deliberate strategic move away from hardware and software sales into the services arena. The move has paid off, as IBM Business Innovation Services bumped Accenture to become the largest consultancy in the world, boasting over $10 billion in sales for 2000.

McKenna (2006: 20–5) points out that IBM's move into IT consulting had previously been barred by antitrust regulation. Since the 1950s the US Department of Justice had prohibited IBM from offering advice on the purchase and integration of information technology. McKenna argues that this affected IBM's move into IT consulting until 1991, which allowed firms such as Arthur Andersen to occupy this segment.

The introduction of enterprise resource planning systems

In the early to mid-1990s another development affected knowledge-intensive services: the emergence of enterprise resource planning systems and the decision by large and medium-sized corporations to implement them on a large scale. ERP systems provide a company-wide IT architecture that facilitates the comprehensive control of data and information through packaged configurations for different functions. The demand for these systems, and – in this context – for ERP-related consulting services, grew rapidly during the 1990s, and the big accounting firms' consulting branches quickly concentrated on this strongly growing segment. Not only have ERP systems generated demand for the implementation of this software, they have also triggered a number of different advice services in order to restructure and prepare client organizations for these systems.

The demand for implementation

Also in the 1990s, client expectations underwent a noticeable change. While consultancy had traditionally been seen as external staff for the analysis and elaboration of concepts, straightforward suggestions for improvements were no longer satisfactory for clients (Ashford 1998; Czerniawska 1999). As a former executive director of the British Management Consultancies Association (MCA) points out, it has been "apparent that clients want their 'advisors' to take a much more hands-on role; strategy firms, for example, are constantly exposed over their perceived reluctance to be involved in the implementation of their recommendations" (O'Rorke 1999: 168).

The increasing overlap of service types

As part of their work on the installation of ERP systems, management consultancies quite naturally came to deal with organizational issues. The boundary between IT advice and organizational restructuring became blurred, and firms needed to provide both types of service. As a managing partner of Accenture UK points out: "Andersen Consulting was dominated by IT implementation work. But what we started to realize was that, although we could win specific battles, we could not win the war: in order to be able to deliver results to clients we needed to be able to put other processes around IT − change management, business strategy, analysis of core competencies, and so on" (Hall 1999: 154).

Furthermore, the market for strategy consulting was no longer restricted to strategy consultancies, since the accounting firms/IT consultancies used their powerful position to compete with the strategy providers in their home territory. As Kennedy Information (2002: 82) reports:

Approaching the strategy/technology weave from the other end of the spectrum is Deloitte Consulting, with plans to enlarge its strategy practice. "We're seeing more and more opportunity to provide strategy-oriented services to our clients," says Stephen Sprinkle, global director of strategy, innovation, and eminence at the firm. "At the same time, clients are starting to really value the practicality of implementation and the whole organizational change experience in developing their strategy."

Suddaby and Greenwood (2001: 945–6) point out that these firms "have transformed themselves from accounting firms to consulting firms and, ultimately, to multidisciplinary business service providers." IT-related consulting providers have tapped into the strategy market, and the Big Four's revenue grew at over twice the rate of those of McKinsey or Booz Allen and Hamilton (Suddaby and Greenwood 2001: 947). Although public reputation still distinguishes consulting firms between areas of core competence in strategy or information technology, strategic and organizational issues often overlap with IT-related questions.

Changing financial requirements

In order to take over outsourced operations from client firms, consultancies had to undertake programs of change that required extraordinary investments. Large-scale projects, especially those that involve outsourcing activities, require immense capacities in terms of human resources and physical assets, as well as technical and estate-related capacities. As the former worldwide managing partner of Andersen Consulting has pointed out, merely *proposing* large-scale projects sometimes requires not only up to twelve months of planning but also around $1 million in capital (Measelle 1999: 195). Likewise, the UK chairman of KPMG Consulting has explained it this way: "Outsourcing – especially IT outsourcing – requires a very high level of prior investment in the supporting infrastructure. Because of the lead-time involved in such investments, late entrants will find it difficult to catch up with the established players, except, perhaps, through acquisition" (Oliver 1999: 195).

These developments called for financial resources that the traditional partnership structure could no longer provide. To obtain equity, KPMG filed for an initial public offering (IPO) in the United States in 2000. In April 2001 Accenture followed this example and raised

$1.7 billion through the initial offering of 12 percent of the company
(James 2001: 35). In early 2002 PwC Consulting also declared its
intention to float the company in an IPO, but in June of the same year
it announced a merger with IBM. While IPOs certainly raise a number
of new problems for consulting firms (James 2001: 37–8), which have
today partially reversed this process, the central advantage is that
capital-intensive projects become feasible (see chapter 8 for more
details about the governance structure of consulting firms and their
relation to capital).

Richter and Lingelbach (2004, 2005) have conducted empirical
work in this area. They tested the likelihood that consulting firms
would adopt outside ownership based on capital requirements,
business risks, firm size (number of staff), and the standardization of
services. Their data set of 151 consulting firms confirms that the
likelihood of adopting outside ownership grows with these four
factors. The trend toward outside ownership, however, is cushioned or
may even be reversed because of the lower costs of monitoring staff
performance. Richter and Lingelbach (2005: 12) argue, "Employees
[of consulting firms] have ample scope for behaving opportunistically,
as monitoring their behavior and performance is difficult. Assigning
ownership rights to employees can help mitigate these costs. At the
same time, assigning ownership rights to a narrowly defined group
of senior employees as partners helps limit the governance costs that
are associated with this assignment."

The economic explanation

To summarize these developments, the 1980s and 1990s saw major
growth in the IT segment of the consulting market, with former
accounting firms rather than strategy consulting firms entering it.
Neither the Enron scandal nor the ensuing discussion about conflicts
of interest between accounting and consulting has changed this
development; nor has the economic slowdown from 2001, which hit
IT consulting harder than strategy advice.

Certainly, the rapid growth of the IT segment of the consulting
market is related to the outsourcing business. IT firms that also provided consulting services often took over entire IT departments from
their clients, which led to massive growth rates for these firms

even though no traditional services were involved. From the outset the accounting firms were better able to respond to this outsourcing wave because of their sheer size. The larger a firm the easier it is to incorporate additional employees – and the outsourcing business sometimes involves transfers of several hundred employees.

Nevertheless, there is another economic explanation as to why it was accounting rather than strategy consulting firms that entered the IT consulting market. As far as economies of scale and scope are concerned, firms with a *diversified* portfolio – that is, those that offer a large variety of services – have a competitive advantage over less diversified firms, for three reasons.

The first reason has already been mentioned above: because of auditing requirements and accountability, IT consulting is more closely related to accounting and auditing than to strategy consulting. Accountants and auditors often do not have to look at individual accounting entries, but just to check the functioning of the software. This means that IT becomes a critical factor in auditing accountability, and accounting and auditing firms need to have IT know-how. The second reason is that large firms such as accounting firms can share resources between services – for example, overhead capacities (research, personnel, administration, etc.). And, third, due to information asymmetries, clients' information costs are lower when they buy a service from a provider with which they have had a previous transaction. The more diversified the provider's portfolio the more services clients can choose without high information acquisition costs. Clients transfer evaluative information from one kind of service to another when performed by the same firm.

Nayyar (1990) and Nayyar and Kazanjian (1993) have outlined the last reason – related diversification – in detail. Related diversification may be beneficial for service firms even without any resource-sharing economies of scope. The buyer–provider relationship represents a firm-specific investment on the part of the buyer and involves switching costs. "Customers who have favorable impressions of current service providers will tend to favor such providers when making purchase decisions about other services that these providers may offer" (Nayyar 1990: 516). To Nayyar (1990) and Nayyar and Kazanjian (1993), related diversification means that reputation can only legitimately be transferred between services that can potentially be provided by similar human resources. They argue as follows:

A reputable retailer does not necessarily appear to possess the requisite skills and competence to provide a wide array of specialized financial services, just as even a reputable management consulting firm does not appear to have the skills required to provide accounting services (Nayyar 1990: 517).

Firms with favorable reputations may benefit from the presence of information asymmetries in many situations. For example, public accounting firms often provide management consulting services to buyers of their auditing services (Nayyar and Kazanjian 1993: 737).

This is a reasonable explanation as to why firms need to diversify into *related* services, but it does not fully explain why accounting firms rather than strategy consulting firms can economize on information asymmetry. Accountants may be legitimate providers of consulting services, but in terms of reputation the strategy providers have nothing to hide. On the contrary, their reputation is probably higher than that of accounting firms. However, because of auditing accountability and the auditors' necessary competence in information technology, strategy consultants are not perceived as being related to IT and less able to transfer their reputation to the other segment.

Coming back to economies of scale and scope, an additional mechanism comes into play. When the accounting firms decided to step into the IT consulting market in the 1980s, they were already large firms – much larger than the strategy consulting firms were. Economies of scale apply in several contexts. First, in terms of marketing and project acquisition, larger providers have lower costs of sending messages per potential client and/or they have a higher advertising reach (Besanko *et al.* 2000: 84–6). Marketing efforts involve high fixed costs, and the larger the firm the more fixed costs can be spread across potential clients. Hence, tapping into the IT consulting market was somewhat less expensive for accounting firms than for strategy consultancies. In the same vein, in a market where trust and credence are crucial, the potential for acquisitions may present a competitive advantage for accessing new clients. If tapping into the IT consulting segment involves the acquisition of small or medium-sized providers, it is, again, the larger accounting firms that were in an advantageous position, because they were better able to engage in acquisitions. Finally, much as it was foreseeable that IT consulting involves large investments (see above), larger providers of other services were more likely to engage in these capital risks because the fixed costs involved in such investments are spread over a greater output. In general, as Besanko *et al.* (2000) point out, the purchasing function benefits from economies of scale because firms offer discounts for volume purchasers. It is less costly for a seller to sell to a single buyer because he saves the costs of writing a contract, setting up a production run, and delivering the product. Moreover, sellers offer discounts to large purchasers because they want to ensure a steady flow of business (Besanko *et al.* 2000: 84).

There is one more factor that is relevant here, which concerns the internal structure of service firms. In comparison to accounting firms, strategy consulting firms have considerably fewer junior consultants per partner or senior consultant (so-called "leverage"; Maister 1982, 1993). Maister (1993) explains these differences by distinguishing between "procedural work" (e.g. IT implementation) and "brains" work (e.g. strategy consulting). Procedural work requires a staff structure with more operating consultants at lower ranks; brains work requires a slimmer project staff structure with more senior people advising the project group. The differences can be sketched as follows.

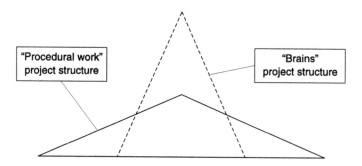

Figure 6.1. Project structures of "procedural" versus "brains" consulting
Source: Maister (1993: 6–7).

In the "brains" project structure, relatively few consultants at lower levels (e.g. three) work in a project that is supported and supervised by more senior consultants, partners, and directors. In the "procedural work" project structure, by contrast, a relatively large number of junior consultants (e.g. fifteen) work on a project that has few senior staff. This is economical if the project involves a lot of operational rather than conceptual work, such as the programming or implementation of software. In "brains" projects, it is analytical competence rather than operational work that is to the fore, and the financial leverage effect is represented in premium fees per consultant and day. Hence, as Kipping (2002) also points out, strategy consulting firms cannot lower their daily fees to a level that would be competitive with the accounting firms. The latter have more consulting staff per partner, which leads to a comparable profit per partner in spite of the lower revenue per consultant. Strategy consulting firms would have to adopt a different fee structure in an IT consulting division, which would require internal divisionalization (see the discussion below in this chapter).

Sociological accounts

Do these economic considerations suffice as explanations of why accounting firms rather than strategy firms entered the IT consulting segment? Size certainly mattered, but strategy consultancies, although smaller than accounting firms, were at that time in a phase of enormous growth, and worked with comfortable margins that might have allowed them to take some of the risks of investing in IT advice.

The strategy as practice approach comprises a wide array of decision-making practices, and it would be fascinating to see the microsociological events around such decision-making processes. However, rather than looking inside the decision-making bodies of consulting firms, we can look at more structural aspects that other sociological accounts have brought about. Embeddedness-based research on status similarity (Podolny 1994; Chung *et al.* 2000) suggests that service firms enter into most transactions with firms of the same status. Applying these insights to the consulting market would lead to the hypothesis that large service firms work primarily with client firms of high status. Empirically, if we use size as an (imperfect) indicator of status, we can observe that large corporations hire primarily large consulting firms, while small and medium-sized consulting firms work mostly for medium-sized clients (Barchewitz and Armbrüster 2004: 95–6).

Podolny's (1994) and Chung *et al.*'s (2000) research can be complemented with neoinstitutional insights. Service firms of high status have to protect their status keenly in an imagined ranking of reputation in order to secure deals with high-status clients. Applied to the consulting market, the household names of strategy consulting firms account for their distinction from lower market segments and secure deals with top-tier client firms. Chapter 3 pointed out that public reputation categorizes the consulting market into at least two classes of firms: a stratum of highly prestigious consulting firms on the one hand, and a stratum of less prestigious ones on the other. The strategy providers, with their high degree of public reputation, enjoy a brand name because of, rather than in spite of, their high fees. Strategy consultancies earn an average of $400,000 to $500,000 per year per consultant, while IT implementation firms may earn around $100,000 (Harrison 1999: 210). The elitist element of the highly prestigious firms enabled them to attract high-potential graduates and to charge above-average fees for their services, since high fees serve as a signal of value in the absence of more tangible criteria for measuring performance.

Information technology, by contrast, was associated with unfashionable, "nerdy" individuals who work in the basements of corporate buildings, rather than on the floor of the management board, and with technical issues that are too operational for strategic questions. To strategy consulting firms, entering into the growing IT segment would have meant tapping into a market of lower fees, which in turn would have meant a devaluation of their elitist image, with potential consequences for both recruitment and public reputation. For accounting firms, by contrast, tapping into IT consulting has never been connected with lower fees, hence their market entry did not endanger their status. Later on, accounting firms/IT consultancies had an incentive to enter the strategy and organization segment because it helped them enhance their image, and thus their clientele and recruitment basis. Thus, the social market mechanisms suggested by embeddedness theory and sociological neoinstitutionalism help in the understanding of these strategic decisions.

In the mid- and late 1990s some strategy consultancies did diversify into the IT consulting market. For example, in 1997 McKinsey founded the Business Technology Office (BTO) as a competence center. Today the BTO has about 500 consultants worldwide, which is very few in comparison to the IT consulting firms. This is because the BTO represents a competence center as a complement to the strategy and organization business, rather than as a fully fledged competitor in the IT advice segment. The IT sector is a lower-price segment and competing in this market would entail engaging in price-based competition. Even during the economic slowdown between 2001 and 2003 price reductions were a very slippery slope for the strategy firms (MCI 2002c), while accounting firms/IT consultancies did engage in price-based competition (MCI 2002g: 10). Gil Gidron, partner with Accenture and FEACO chairman, put it this way: "I understand the competitive pressures when supply exceeds demand. But we are seeing a lot of margin deterioration. In a service industry, once you work for a client at one [price] level, it's hard to get out of it. This is a very sensitive issue. We have to be very careful about the precedents we set. We need to balance the short and long term" (MCI 2002g: 10).

In summary, for strategy consultancies price-based competition is not an advisable strategy (see chapter 3). IT implementation is a more tangible type of service and the relationship between price and quality is closer. Lowering fee levels in order to engage in price competition with IT consultancies might be counterproductive, as the signaling effect of the high price would be lost and the public reputation of the firms would suffer. With these arguments, signaling theory reemerges as an economic explanation. Consulting fees signal quality efficiently if the performance of expensive advice is better than services for lower fees. This mechanism works if the most talented students look for jobs primarily in the top-tier consulting firms and accept job offers from IT consultancies only if the top firms have rejected them (or as a matter of self-selection, if the graduates do not consider getting such jobs and do not apply to the top firms at all). As mentioned in chapter 1, for consulting firms of lower reputation that cannot charge such high fees it would be more costly to hire the same graduates, as they cannot pass on the higher personnel costs to clients in the same way. To strategy consulting firms, lowering fees in order to compete in the IT sector, or for any other reason, would mean distorting the signaling circle.

Strategy consultancies and the IT segment: three generic strategies

Standard strategic theory offers three channels of competitive advantage: price, quality, and niche occupation (Porter 1985). They usually imply a choice between differentiation and cost strategies, or between superior value creation and more efficient production. Moreover, engaging in strategic alliances or joint ventures emerges as an additional strategic choice (Besanko *et al.* 2000: 185–93). On this basis, if full entry into the IT consulting segment is not advisable for strategy providers, there are still three theoretical options to react to the IT challenge: staying in the niche of strategy consulting, divisionalizing such that one division can compete in the IT segment, or engaging in alliances to team up with IT providers. Strategy consulting firms have chosen the first two strategies.

The niche strategy

Apart from cautiously enriching their supply structure through IT consulting, the strategy firms could stick to the niche of high-end strategy consulting and thus keep charging premuim fees in a market segment that they keep separate from others. This is reasonable for two related reasons. First, entering the IT segment would mean entering into price competition (see above). Second, IT consulting represents an experience rather than credence good. The outcome of IT consulting is more easily measurable and thus more coupled to the price. Strategy providers may then be less able to avoid price competition even in the strategy and organization segment.

As a result, most strategy consulting firms pursue this policy; but it has its risks. All firms in this segment have traditionally focused not only on strategy but also on internal operations and organization. However, be it the supply chain, production procedures, marketing and distribution, or access to financial resources, today none of them can be treated independently of information technology. Any high-end advice is connected to the evolution of information technology, and IT competencies are needed for strategy firms to be able to keep up with the pace of technical developments. Focusing on purely strategic questions, whatever these may be, would render the market niche smaller and smaller, especially given that IT consultancies tap into strategy advice. It is, therefore, questionable whether the strategy consultancies can successfully enter the IT advice market half-heartedly while otherwise sticking to strategy and organization. As a result, some strategy consulting firms have built up IT knowledge in internal units as competence centers (McKinsey's BTO being the most prominent one), but without fully committing to large-scale IT consulting and outsourcing.

Using this approach of pursuing a niche strategy and building up IT expertise only on a supplementary basis, strategy and organization consultancy has continued to grow (apart from the 2001–2003 stagnation), although the IT segment has grown more rapidly. The crisis in which Kipping (2002) perceives the strategy providers to be may be attributable to the general economic crisis, but not to a general decline of strategy providers. The growth of the strategy segment seems sufficiently robust to ensure flourishing revenues. However, the question is the extent to which accounting firms/IT consultancies enter the market for strategic advice. As long as the signaling mechanism results in a supply of superior personnel (many applicants accept job offers from IT consulting firms only after having been rejected by strategy firms), the distinction will remain. Strategy consulting keeps flourishing on the signaling circle, and it is an open question as to whether accounting firms/IT consultancies will be able to disrupt it.

The divisionalization strategy

When entering the IT segment, another approach for strategy consultancies would be to build a firm of independent divisions in order to prevent spillovers between them and to avoid negative reputation effects. Booz Allen and Hamilton and The Boston Consulting Group pursue this strategy. Booz Allen consists of two separate divisions: Worldwide Commercial Business and Worldwide Technology Business. They serve more or less separate markets; the former offers strategy and organizational advice to corporations in competition with other strategy consulting firms; the latter provides IT-related services and competes with accounting firms/IT consultancies. The German office of The Boston Consulting Group has founded a subsidiary, Platinion GmbH, as its IT consulting arm. Both face the problem of whether or not to differentiate fees between the two divisions.

A divisionalization according to service types may also enable strategy consulting firms to step into the market for management development, training, and coaching. However, the same problem occurs as for IT consultancy. The management development market, too, requires a different human resource base from that which the strategy consultancies currently possess. The current pool of personnel comprises mostly MBAs, economists, and graduates from natural sciences such as physics, biology, etc. Even if strategy firms often mention that they have some philosophy or theology graduates, there is no systematic recruitment in these disciplines. Strategy consultancies attract predominantly those human resources that can handle quantitative approaches, and it is questionable whether these firms can enter the training and coaching market this way. Hiring management trainers and coaches with other academic backgrounds and views about how to approach business problems may lead to an internal heterogeneity that could eventually force them to abandon the one-firm principle (see chapter 8).

This kind of diversification is known as the "one-stop shop" business model for consulting firms. While it is successful at Booz Allen and Hamilton, it would require massive changes for most of the other strategy providers. In principle, a consulting firm such as McKinsey could form separate divisions, such as McKinsey Strategy and Organization (the classical McKinsey), McKinsey IT and e-commerce (the current BTO, which could then expand into IT consulting), McKinsey Mergers and Acquisitions (to compete with the advice services of investment banks), McKinsey Coaching and Development (to cover the training and coaching market), and McKinsey Venture Capital and Private Equity. Consultants could become permanent members of one particular division and then specialize in that area.

However, such massive changes would run counter to the existing one-firm principle and homogeneity tenets of strategy consultancies, and constitute a source of considerable tension within these firms. The one-firm concept has been an important factor in the worldwide expansion of these largely US-based strategy firms during the postwar period (Kipping 1999; Maister 1993), and it is very difficult for them to strike a balance between the demands of an increasingly specializing market and their own internal logic (cf. Bartlett 1998). Similar educational backgrounds, a uniform promotion policy, and a worldwide organizational culture have prevented the partnership governance systems from disintegrating (see chapter 8). An increasing diversification of recruitment and consulting approaches or the multi-divisional form suggested above would threaten this homogeneity. IT specialists, strategy consultants, and management trainers/coaches would represent a much-diversified workforce, which could not be integrated into a uniform organizational culture. The different backgrounds and working styles would hardly fit under a single promotion and compensation policy and would increase the likelihood of spinoffs. The danger would be that the main value offered to clients, the quantitative analytical approach to business questions conducted by individuals with the same value system, would lose its foothold, and the firm as a whole might lose relative market shares even in its home territory of operative analyses and strategic advice.

The alliance and network strategy

Considering the technology-driven shift of market structure on the one hand and the core competencies of strategy firms on the other, another option would be to engage in cooperative networks or joint ventures with firms of other knowledge types, such as IT consultancies. Powell (1990) has explicitly suggested network forms of organization in cases where the need is to exchange know-how and cope with the demand for speed. Research on joint ventures and alliances (Hamel 1991; Hagedoorn and Schakenraad 1994; Mowery *et al.* 1996; Powell *et al.* 1996; Appleyard 1996; Simonin 1997; Dyer and Nobeoka 2000; Koput and Powell 2000) has shown that establishing network ties to companies that offer complementary types of service is a promising strategy for accessing knowledge and developing new fields of business. Dyer and Nobeoka (2000: 345) have found that networks with partner firms "(1) motivate members to participate and openly share valuable knowledge (while preventing undesirable spillovers to competitors), (2) prevent free riders, and (3) reduce the costs associated with finding and accessing different types of valuable knowledge." A network of firms such as a strategy consultancy, an IT consultancy, and a management development institute might provide all the knowledge types required by a client without the danger of over-stretching the internal logic of the strategy firms. This way, the value of the strategy consultancies' appeal to clients could be enhanced by an integrated service that strategy consultancies cannot provide on their own.

Although the above-mentioned studies on inter-firm collaborations have been undertaken in industries other than management consulting, they present examples and evidence of successful collaborations among firms with different types of knowledge. These studies share the notion that learning capabilities need to be extended beyond firm boundaries. In other knowledge-intensive fields, such as biotechnology and semiconductors, firms are not only actively expanding the volume and scope of collaborations but also broadening the kinds of partners with whom they cooperate (Powell *et al.* 1996; Koput and Powell 2000; Appleyard 1996). Koput and Powell (2000) find that the larger, older, and more successful firms in the biotech sector are the more they cooperate with other firms, and the larger the variety of cooperation partners. Inter-firm cooperation, they conclude, is not only a transitional stage to success and maturity but, rather, a significant organizational practice, which "represents neither dependency nor specialization but an alternative way of accessing knowledge and resources" (Koput and Powell 2000: 2). Strategic alliances may foster knowledge transfer and promote knowledge creation on the basis of complementary competencies with other knowledge-intensive firms.

However, there are three key differences between the consultancy and the biotech sectors, although both are knowledge-intensive. First, biotechnology is extremely research-intensive, while consultancy is customer-driven. Second, biotechnology brings about tangible products, whereas the results of consulting services are mostly intangible. And, third, in biotechnology there is relatively little market stratification, while consultancy is a strongly stratified market. If a sector is research-intensive it means that the bottleneck of success is access to knowledge rather than to clients. The clientele grows automatically for all cooperating firms if the research cooperation is successful. By contrast, in management consultancy the bottleneck of success is access to clients, which renders cooperation among consulting firms a contradiction to the ambitions of individual providers. The tangibility of products in biotechnology means that inputs and outputs are attributable to individual providers, hence there is an enhanced ability to detect shirking between cooperating parties. In consultancy, the opposite is the case. Intangible products render the information costs of monitoring cooperation partners high, which discourages or even prevents cooperation. Finally, the egalitarian and non-stratified nature of the biotechnology market means that cooperation can be focused on complementary knowledge, while the stratified nature of the consulting market renders an association with other firms more complicated in terms of status differences.

These differences explain why there is much more cooperation in the biotechnology market than among consulting firms. As a result, the biotechnology market is a perfect case for the application of embeddedness theory, while management consultancy is more complicated. How should alliances between consulting firms look like in practice? If two firms, for example a strategy firm and an IT consulting firm, jointly acquire a project that involves both types of advice, how do they allocate the fees? If they were to build joint teams of strategy and IT consultants then they would certainly learn from each other, but the costs of monitoring joint inputs would be extremely high. Moreover, the mutual learning processes would render the firms a competitor to each other in each firm's original field. And if learning from each other is not really wanted then a client might as well hire firms that do not cooperate. Moreover, for a strategy provider to be associated with an IT consulting firm would raise the above problems of reputation and signaling. Accordingly, over the past years no strategy provider has pursued the alliance strategy, and even among small and medium-sized consulting firms cooperation has remained very limited.

Discussion

In the 1980s and 1990s technological developments caused major changes in the consulting market structure. Strategy consultancies stood at a crossroads. Advice on strategy and organization could no longer be provided without engaging with information technology; competing in the IT advice segment was a slippery slope in terms of reputation and signaling effects; and IT advisors sought to – and continue to – step into the strategy segment. Nevertheless, the rumors of the death of strategy consulting were exaggerated. Strategy consultancy has remained a thriving sector by embracing IT know-how as competence centers (McKinsey), as a separate division (Booz Allen and Hamilton), or as a subsidiary (The Boston

Consulting Group). They have established IT expertise as a limited offer to clients, without competing in large-scale IT projects with accounting/IT consultancies. The interplay of strategy and technology has been and continues to be the central strategic issue in the consulting business. Kipping's (2002) provocative hypothesis on the fading of strategy consultancies from the market cannot be disproved at this point, but strategy consulting has reemerged out of the 2001–2003 crisis with strong growth rates (FEACO 2006).

Coming back to the theory debate, the economic approach has suggested that large, diversified service firms are theoretically in a better position than niche players. This is because they can economize on information asymmetry and exploit the effects of economies of scope. However, the discussion of the consulting market and its events over the past fifteen years has also shown that size is only one variable in the equation. The one-stop shop idea of multiple service firms has not become the sole strategy of choice but only one out of several possibilities. Sociological theories help to explain why a uniquely successful way for consulting firms does not exist. The reputation effects following the Enron scandals, especially the fall of Arthur Andersen, have shown that related diversification can also have negative effects for firms: when a brand name is spoiled then the firm as a whole is endangered. Sociological neoinstitutionalism explains that firm behavior is often oriented at societal customs, and in the aftermath of the Enron scandals Arthur Andersen became institutionalized as an icon of insincerity. Moreover, economies of scope effects certainly exist, between strategy and IT consulting as well, but they cannot bridge the status difference between these two segments. With few exceptions, strategy consulting firms have stayed away from the IT segment, although they have integrated IT know-how into the firm structure.

Nevertheless, economics does have a strong argument as to why Arthur Andersen was abandoned by its clients: game theory. In a game of three or more players, with two or more offerors of trust (here: clients) and one or more decision-makers on trust (here: consultants), a client reasonably decides not to offer trust if an accounting and consulting firm has not honored trust to another client (Axelrod 1984; Fudenberg and Tirole 1991; Kreps 1991). While clients may fully trust individual advisors of the firms in question, the withdrawal of cooperation by third parties leads them to abandon their service provider. (This point is taken up in the conclusion.)

The circumstances of individual firms, independent of their association with IT or strategy consulting, and the market developments between 2001 and 2003, put Kipping's (2002) hypothesis of a declining strategy segment into perspective. The corporate scandals and their consequences for the consulting market have shown that reputation effects have a massive influence on market structure. In fact, for a brief period between 2001 and 2003 these unexpected events dwarfed the technology-based changes. McKinsey was one of the major service providers for Enron in the 1990s and praised the company as a role model. Astonishingly, the firm got away with little damage to its reputation, but the large accounting firms have undergone major changes since then.

Moreover, even within individual market segments, different firms have had very contrasting fortunes, which dwarf the differences between market segments. Accenture, for example, achieved record results in spite of the general economic slowdown in 2001, whereas Cap Gemini Ernst and Young Consulting was shaken by the 2001 crisis (MCI 2002a: 1; 2002e: 2) and PwC Consulting was sold (MCI 2002f: 1). Also, Monitor experienced a 9 percent growth in revenues, whereas McKinsey and the BCG lost 3 and 5 percent respectively in 2001 (MCI 2002d: 12). As the managing director of a UK consultancy commented, "It's more complicated than that – the performance of the Four is dramatically different. The same is true of the 'beautiful' players – some are doing well, some very poorly" (MCI 2002b).

Finally, the entry of hardware/software providers into management consulting has threatened the accounting firms/IT consultancies more than the strategy consultancies. While a few years ago the selling of AT Kearney to EDS (reversed in November 2005) was considered the most important sign of the times, IBM's market entry showed that IT consultancies are not immune to market threats (MCI 2002f: 1). In a conglomerate of IT provider and IT consultancy, a strategy branch may become a foreign body and be considered out of place, which may lead to a new round of spinoffs and further strengthen the position of strategy consulting. The management buyout of AT Kearney from EDS in November 2005 illustrates this. Economies of scope effects seem to be smaller than assumed, and clients bridge information asymmetry by means other than just transferring quality expectations within one firm. As discussed in chapters 3 and 4, experienced-based trust and word-of-mouth effects are the central market mechanisms, and clients are more sophisticated users of consultancy than simply to transfer quality expectations within a diversified service firm.

7 | Fostering reputation and growth? Marketing consulting services

Service marketing and the market mechanisms

For some reason, the debate between economics and sociology has not touched the field of marketing very much. While a few scholars refer to institutional economics and others to the embeddedness approach, marketing has understood itself traditionally as a practitioner-oriented field in which theoretical debates give way to empirical research. From both economic and sociological viewpoints, the intangible nature and initial quality uncertainty of consulting services as experience or credence goods are the points of departure. As a matter of marketing, consultants must convey their sincerity and output quality, which places emphasis on the institutions of trust, reputation, and word-of-mouth effects (Greiner and Metzger 1983: 41−55). From an economic viewpoint, the question emerges of how these institutions can be worked on at low cost, and how information about service quality can be conveyed economically.

Among other considerations, the sheer size of a consulting firm may matter in this respect. As Besanko *et al.* (2000: 84−6) point out, larger providers have lower average costs of sending messages per potential client. Marketing efforts involve high fixed costs, and the larger the firm the more fixed costs can be spread across potential clients. Nevertheless, chapter 3 has shown that trust and word-of-mouth effects emerge primarily on the basis of client satisfaction. Only the delivery of high service quality can retain existing clients and lead to referrals to new clients. Are marketing efforts therefore appropriate at all, or are they redundant to service delivery, or even detrimental, since they may lead to irritation on the client side?

If experience-based trust, public reputation, and word-of-mouth effects are the central mechanisms that connect supply and demand, then from a marketing viewpoint the goal of consulting firms must be to score high on all three mechanisms. Public reputation allows consulting firms to be contacted by unconnected clients, experience-based trust enables them to retain existing clients, and word-of-mouth effects make it possible for them to acquire contracts from clients' business partners. The question is whether it is not just consulting performance and client satisfaction that foster these three mechanisms, but whether the "score" in these three respects can be reinforced by the employment of marketing instruments.

Research on services marketing is often concerned with two issues: the practice of customer relationship marketing, and the application of the SERVQUAL instrument to a number of contexts such as financial services, health services, information technology services, etc. (see, e.g., Durvasula *et al.* 1999; Palmer and O'Neill 2003; Eriksson *et al.* 1999). The SERVQUAL instrument consists of more than twenty pairs of statements to measure service attributes such as speed, accuracy, product features, accessibility, and flexibility. The literature on customer relationship management focuses on tools for client loyalty. Reputation, branding, word-of-mouth effects, and customer loyalty have been subject to many empirical studies (e.g., over the past few years in the *Journal of Services Marketing* alone: Mangold *et al.* 1999; Coulter and Coulter 2002; Johnson and Zinkhan 1998; Hausman 2003; Gounaris and Venetis 2002; Svensson 2002; Mackay 2001; Mitra *et al.* 1999; Lee and Cunningham 2001). However, the specific literature on the marketing of consulting services (Karlson and Crisp 1988; Shenson 1990; Connor and Davidson 1997) is practitioner-oriented and not represented in academic, empirical studies.

A recent survey of consulting firms regarding their marketing efforts, carried out by Barchewitz and Armbrüster (2004), has explored and identified the marketing and project acquisition tools of consulting firms and related them to firm size, consulting segment, and firm growth. It was conducted in cooperation with the German association of management consultancies (Bundesverband deutscher Unternehmensberater – BDU), and based on a BDU data-base; a list of 1,500 consulting firms was compiled using regional distribution as the only nonrandom selection criterion. Additionally, in order to ensure a response from the biggest market players to enable statistical comparisons between market strata, the twenty largest IT and strategy consulting companies were added to the list. As suggested in the literature on services marketing, the survey questionnaire distinguished between instruments to retain current clients and instruments to attract new ones. A range of thirty-six marketing measures, from simple website presentation via media cooperation to speeches at client industry gatherings, was derived from the literature. The questionnaire asked the extent to which consulting firms made use of them and considered them effective. The survey generated a return from 180 consulting companies, consisting of 23 percent strategy, 14 percent IT, 18 percent human resources, 37 percent organizational, and 8 percent financial consultants. More than a half of the participating companies had been founded within the last ten years, confirming the high entry rate mentioned in chapter 3.

Four components of marketing measures

In order to get an overview of the main components of marketing instruments, a principal component analysis over thirty-six marketing instruments was conducted (for the methodological details, see Barchewitz and Armbrüster 2004: 129–40). Table 7.1 presents the components and the marketing instruments with factor loadings greater than 0.4.

These four dimensions represent reliable factors (Cronbach's Alpha greater than 0.7) and can be broadly interpreted as focusing either on public reputation or on client proximity and interactivity. Publication-based marketing significantly influences public reputation through a large number of potential readers and public availability, but it is

Table 7.1. Components and loading items of marketing measures

Component	Loading items
Direct marketing	Mass or direct mailing, telemarketing, mailing for certain products or to certain industries
Event-based marketing	Speeches, presentations, talks (e.g. at conferences or fairs), seminars and workshops (for potential and current clients)
Publication-based marketing	Professional journals, professional books, publication of research reports, media cooperation
Online marketing	Websites (for potential and current clients), mailing lists, brochures

Source: Barchewitz and Armbrüster (2004: 139).

low on client interactivity since the reader is unknown to the consulting firm. Direct marketing includes all types of marketing activities directed at individual persons, and is therefore high on interactivity but low on public reputation. Event-based marketing is high on both dimensions as the participants at presentations or workshops are known or can be personally met there, and the announcement of or invitations to these events, as well as potential media coverage, support public visibility. Finally, online marketing is low on both dimensions since the interactivity of most consulting firms' websites is still very limited, and the effect of online marketing on public reputation is certainly much lower than, for example, publication-based marketing.

The four components thus represent different ways of fostering two key issues that can potentially be influenced by marketing instruments: public visibility to gain reputation, and connectedness to promote interactivity and trust. The third and central channel outlined above, word-of-mouth effects, could not be identified as a component of firms' marketing efforts; only event-based marketing could be interpreted in this direction (see the discussion at the end of this chapter). Figure 7.1 displays the four components on these two dimensions.

Four clusters of consulting firms

The next step was to identify groups of consulting firms that exhibit similar approaches to the marketing of their services (Barchewitz and Armbrüster 2004: 141–7). Cluster analyses seek to identify groups of cases (here: consulting firms) with similar characteristics. We conducted a cluster analysis on the basis of the four components identified above, first using the single-linkage procedure to exclude outliers (five firms with abnormal factor loadings were identified and excluded), and then the Ward method to recognize clusters (for the details of these procedures, see Backhaus *et al.* 1994: 263–300). Four clusters have been identified; table 7.2 presents the average loadings of the clusters on the above four components.

Cluster A consists of consulting firms which mainly employ direct marketing measures, and have an average level of event-based marketing and low reliance on online and publication-based marketing; hence companies in this cluster can be called "Direct marketers."

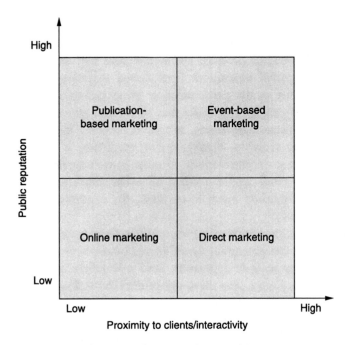

Figure 7.1. Approaches to marketing in the consulting sector
Source: Barchewitz and Armbrüster (2004: 140).

*Table 7.2. Loadings of marketing clusters on the
individual components*

Cluster	Components				Label given (based
	Direct marketing	*Event-based marketing*	*Publication-based marketing*	*Online marketing*	*on the scores on the components)*
A	0.89	0.01	−0.50	−0.85	"Direct marketers"
B	−0.67	−0.63	−0.57	0.02	"Marketing refusers"
C	−0.15	1.90	−0.17	0.52	"Marketing champions"
D	0.03	−0.09	0.85	0.29	"Publicists"

Source: Barchewitz and Armbrüster (2004: 141).

Companies in cluster B can be labeled "Marketing refusers," since they do not make use of any instrument except for online marketing to an average extent. Cluster C includes consultancies with a high level of marketing activities on two components, event-based and online marketing. As this involves both dimensions – reputation and connectedness – they can in our context be called "Marketing champions." Finally, firms in cluster D can be named "Publicists," since they make above-average use of publications but employ other marketing tools only to an average extent.

These four clusters can be positioned in the above matrix with the axes "Proximity to clients/interactivity" and "Public reputation." In order to distinguish between the effectiveness of the four components in terms of public visibility and client connectedness, and to position the clusters in the figure, the x and y values of the average component loadings of the four clusters for those marketing types with a high attribute on the respective axis were multiplied by factor 2. This leads to an intuitive image of "Marketing refusers" positioned in the bottom left corner and "Marketing champions" in the top right corner. As the two dimensions are not completely uncorrelated – i.e. items loading high on one component exhibit (small) loadings on others – all clusters are positioned around a line from the bottom left to top right of the matrix. The "Publicists" are to be found above this line, since they focus more on public reputation, whereas the "Direct marketers" are positioned below this line, as they maximize proximity to clients and interactivity. Figure 7.2 illustrates this.

To analyze the identified clusters further, descriptive statistics have been employed with respect to the dimensions: consulting segment, firm size, and growth rate. They exhibit the following associations.

- Strategy consultants are strongly represented in the "Marketing champions" and "Publicists" clusters and under-represented in the two other clusters.
- IT consulting firms are over-represented in the "Direct marketers" cluster but under-represented in the "Publicists" cluster.
- Human resource consultancies figure prominently in the "Marketing champions" cluster and are relatively close to average in all the other clusters.

Figure 7.2. Marketing types in the consulting market
Source: Barchewitz and Armbrüster (2004: 142).

- Organizational consulting firms are over-represented in the "Publicists" cluster and under-represented in the cluster of "Marketing champions."
- Finally, financial consultants make up the bulk of the "Marketing refusers" clusters and constitute the segment with the lowest level of marketing activities.

These results correspond largely to the market mechanisms outlined in chapter 3. Strategy consulting firms, and to an extent organizational consultancies, are most active in terms of publications because of the stratified nature of the market in which they operate, resulting in a need to emphasize public visibility and status. IT consultancies, by contrast, have a more tangible output than strategy and organization consultancies, hence they do not build on public visibility and publications. Financial consultants, too, have a measurable output, which may explain their refusal to engage in marketing activities.

The number of firms is the smallest in the "Marketing champions" cluster and highest in the "Marketing refusers" cluster. This shows that explicit marketing strategies are not very popular among consulting firms, and/or that, given the social market institutions outlined above, the pursuit of marketing is not considered particularly relevant for success. (The discussion at the end of this chapter takes up this point.)

As far as firm size is concerned, small consulting firms are strongly represented in the "Direct marketers" and "Marketing refusers" clusters. This confirms the above economic argument that marketing involves a lot of fixed costs, which small firms cannot spread across clients as much as large firms can. A central result in this context is that large and medium-sized consulting firms do not significantly differ in terms of their marketing behavior. Most of them are in the cluster of "Publicists" (relative to the other clusters). This indicates that medium-sized firms regard public visibility as a central factor of firm growth, much as large consulting firms consider publications a means of public visibility.

To observe the relationship between marketing behavior and firm growth, data on annual revenues in 1997 and 2002 could be gathered from about 70 percent of the responding firms (127 out of 180 consulting firms). The interesting result here is that, in terms of marketing behavior, there is no significant difference between firms of high and low growth (chi-square $= 5.876$; df $= 6$; p $= 0.44$). Even omitting the row for medium growth and comparing only the slow-growing and fast-growing firms does not lead to a significant result (chi-square $= 3.176$; df $= 3$; p $= 0.37$). Table 7.3 presents the data in detail.

While there may be a connection between firm growth and the proportion of firms in the "Marketing champions" cluster, the number of cases in this cluster is too low to obtain an interpretable result. Other observations include the fact that consulting firms with slow growth are strongly represented in the "Publicists" cluster. This may indicate that those firms that do not obtain referrals on the basis of client satisfaction attempt to boost their public visibility as a means of acquiring new clients. However, it appears that this focus on publications does not make up for the lack of word-of-mouth effects. Another interpretation might be that consultants in firms with slow growth have more time "on the beach" (a consulting term for

Table 7.3. Marketing cluster distribution per firm growth, 1997–2002

					Four clusters, Ward method		
		"Direct marketers"	"Marketing refusers"	"Marketing champions"	"Publicists"	Total
Slow growth	Count	6	13	2	19	40
	% within "Slow growth"	15%	33%	5%	47%	100%
	% within cluster	22%	33%	15%	40%	32%
Medium growth	Count	10	13	4	10	37
	% within "Medium growth"	27%	35%	11%	27%	100%
	% within cluster	37%	33%	31%	21%	29%
Fast growth	Count	11	13	7	19	50
	% within "Fast growth"	22%	26%	14%	38%	100%
	% within cluster	41%	33%	54%	40%	39%
TOTAL	Count	27	39	13	48	127
	% within "Total"	21%	31%	10%	38%	100%
	% within cluster	100%	100%	100%	100%	100%

Source: Barchewitz and Armbrüster (2004: 145).

NB: Chi-square = 5.876; df = 6; p = 0.44. About 70 percent (127 out of 180) of the firms in the sample met the two conditions of already operating in 1997 and disclosing data on firm growth.

doing internal work because of a lack of projects), and thus have time to write publications. In any event, the fact that the growth figures refer to the annual revenues of 1997 and 2002 presents a considerable limit in its own right. During this period the consulting market underwent a rollercoaster ride, which renders individual growth figures very volatile and difficult to interpret.

In summary, there is little reason to assume that the growth of consulting firms depends directly on marketing strategies. This is a very interesting result and feeds back on the market mechanisms outlined in chapter 3. Assuming that the lack of statistical significance in this regard is not a consequence of the number of firms in the sample, the following interpretation suggests itself: in the face of social market institutions such as trust, reputation, and word-of-mouth effects, marketing has very limited impact on the success or otherwise of consultancies.

Discussion

Apart from this possibly unexpected result for experts on service marketing, the empirical analysis has delivered a number of results that can easily be interpreted, and others that are more difficult to account for. Some of the more easily interpretable outcomes include the results that the cluster of "Marketing champions" is the smallest in terms of the number of firms, and that there is a very high number of "Marketing refusers." They indicate that many consulting firms are of the opinion that marketing efforts make little difference. Indeed, clients may be thin-skinned with regard to the marketing instruments of consulting firms, and may easily associate them with bothersome sales promotion. Moreover, some consulting firms may operate in a fairly stable environment. For example, small consultancies may operate in a similar fashion to an outsourced client department, and work for fixed clients for years rather than strive to expand their business. The group of small consulting firms may possibly comprise quasi-employees of larger firms and may be able to renounce the use of any marketing instruments. This interpretation would be compatible with the result that small consulting firms are over-represented in the clusters of "Direct marketers" and "Marketing refusers."

Results that are more difficult to interpret include the following. First, large and medium-sized consulting firms do not differ very much in terms of their marketing approach, not even with regard to publications and public visibility. In a sense, this is surprising, since it is only large rather than medium-sized firms that are associated with public visibility. However, the result may be an artifact of the empirical threshold between large and medium-sized consulting firms, which we set at forty-nine consultants. If the line had been drawn in the range of, say, 200 consultants, then a difference between large and medium-sized consultancies might have emerged. However, there would have been too few cases in the group of large consultancies to allow for meaningful comparisons.

Another important result is the fact that there are no significant differences between small and large consulting firms in terms of recommendations and intermediation by clients. Regardless of the size of the firm the word-of-mouth mechanism seems absolutely central, and the fact that this mechanism operates independently of firm size confirms the conceptual considerations in chapter 3. The analysis has ascertained two directions for marketing strategies: public-reputation-oriented and connectedness/trust-oriented. However, marketing centered on word-of-mouth effects has not emerged as an explicit category even though questions along these lines were part of the questionnaire. Only event-based marketing serves as a means of fostering word-of-mouth recommendations. Word-of-mouth effects are certainly the most difficult to influence by means of marketing (Grönroos 2000; Kotler *et al.* 2002; Lovelock 2000). The crudest way, of course, is to ask a satisfied client directly whether he or she could recommend the consulting firm to other firms as potential clients. While this may seem a somewhat strenuous approach, clients may not be fully aware of the word-of-mouth mechanism of the consulting market, and, if the trust relation between client and consultant is deep enough, the client may regard a referral as a return of a favor. A more sophisticated approach for small to medium-sized consulting firms would be to bundle any marketing efforts with a consulting firm that offers complementary but noncompeting services. An alliance of cooperating firms could organize events with speeches and pre-sentations and invite the current clients of all the firms. This way, cross-referrals between clients of complementary firms would be made possible independently of actual cooperation in projects.

The result that is certainly the most interesting is that no signi-ficant relationship between marketing behavior and firm growth was ascertained. The fact that connectedness-oriented and reputation-oriented marketing approaches have been identified reinforces the assumption that word-of-mouth effects are the crucial factor for growth. Consultants appear to assume that marketing instruments do not help very much in influencing this important effect. Rather, they seem to assume that only service quality and client satisfaction − not marketing instruments − can foster referrals. In fact, refraining from marketing belongs to the professional ethos of many consultants, especially when they believe that their service performance speaks for itself.

As a result of this professional ethos, the large strategy consulting firms in particular consider commercials or poster advertising to be a matter for the lower segments of the market. The only, and most intensive, kind of marketing they allow themselves are discussions with clients, about their current challenges and possible consulting themes, and the recruitment events at top universities and business schools. The vigilant observer may have noticed that advertisements on consulting service quality − as, for example, at airports or in business magazines − stem from IT consulting or accounting firms, not from strategy consultancies. Nevertheless, strategy consulting firms do advertise in business magazines and at airports, but in a different way: they are directed at potential applicants and seek to render the firm attractive as an employer rather than as a service provider. For example, even in 2002, when most strategy consulting firms had to reduce their staff, they advertised for applications even though at that time they were barely hiring anybody. This very subtle type of marketing can be explained by signaling theory, as is outlined in chapter 9.

8 | The economics and sociology of knowledge distribution: organizational structure and governance

Chapter 2 outlined the reasons why consulting firms exist as independent firms. The core of the argument has been that consulting firms can realize economies of scale if they focus on tasks that require a particular type of knowledge: analytical knowledge to solve problems which occur infrequently or aperiodically in an individual client organization but frequently across firms, industries, or regions. Economizing on knowledge by clients means hiring consultants for tasks which involve high coordination costs (such as coordination between different domains or regions), which are dissimilar to client operations and to each other, and which involve low asset specificity, such as analytical capabilities that do not require investments in physical assets.

Moreover, chapter 2 also outlined the economic changes that have occurred since the 1980s. Production, service, and financial processes are both increasingly dispersed geographically and based on a higher degree of abstraction than a few decades ago. Technological progress, less expensive means of communication, and decreasing costs of transport and logistics have made it increasingly possible to produce components at the most inexpensive place and assemble them at another site. The intra-industry trade index and foreign direct investment rose slowly until the 1970s, but then picked up pace in the 1980s, continuing in the 1990s. The globalization of production and services, which has been under way for many years, has increased in the past twenty years.

To client firms, this globalization of production and services means that new kinds of analytical tasks and abstractions need to be performed. Information on different regions or countries and their conditions of production needs to be gathered, partners for cooperation, acquisition, or merger in other countries or regions need to be found and evaluated, the value chain needs to be reorganized and adjusted to the new possibilities of dispersed production,

152

and new ways of logistical integration need to be analyzed and put into practice. Moreover, these requirements and ventures need to be financed in a financial market that has also undergone a leap toward globality and abstraction. This process involves successions of aperiodical or one-off changes that are dissimilar to each other and thus likely to be outsourced to external providers (see chapter 2).

Consulting firms have specialized in those tasks that represent precisely this series of dissimilar one-off changes: those that require the gathering of information from a variety of dispersed sources and that are dissimilar for individual client firms. The transaction cost argument about the existence of consulting firms thus translates into firm-internal matters of organizational design, governance and knowledge management. The specialization of consulting firms in tasks of the above kind involves considerable challenges in this regard. How do you design an organization which needs to collect information more rapidly than a client firm, which can gather data and knowledge from a variety of international sources, and which can economize on tasks that are dissimilar to each other but recurrent across industries, regions, or countries?

Part of the answer is to have a global firm in which the capacity to exchange information and knowledge across countries, functions, and professional backgrounds can be institutionalized in the organizational structure. As Moore and Birkinshaw (1998: 82) put it, "Competitive advantage is gained not through the sharing of activities but through the transfer of intangible assets from country to country... Top management's task is to develop, leverage, and disseminate knowledge on a worldwide basis, and to foster an environment in which intercountry learning can occur." The organizational structure must facilitate the exchange of methods and tools across countries, regions, and competence centers within the consulting firm; it needs to facilitate consultants' familiarization with new tasks in little time; and it needs to foster learning across corporate functions in order to economize on clients' internal coordination costs. At the same time – and this represents an additional challenge – personal trust and network ties to clients represent a crucial competitive advantage; therefore, the organizational structure must also focus on the customer and allow for systematic customer relationship management. The large international consulting firms seek to achieve this primarily through the following elements of organizational design.

- A governance structure with flexible decision-making bodies.
- Binding the higher organizational structure to client firms (from senior project manager level to senior partner).
- Project organization and a "pool concept" of staffing (from consultant to project manager level).
- Job rotation and cross-staffing across countries, functions, and client industries.
- A well-funded research department to provide publicly available or fee-based information quickly.
- The institutionalization of competence centers (also called "practices," "practice groups," or "expert groups").
- The "one-firm" concept.

The governance structure

With regard to decision-making bodies, consulting firms are mostly partnerships or corporations that are run like partnerships. Typically, it is only internal managers (partners), not outsiders, who hold shares. In some consulting firms partners are called partners, in others principals, directors, or senior executives. If a partner decides to leave, typically he or she must sell the shares to the remaining partners. The partnership structure may be tiered, which means that there are at least two levels of ownership (junior and senior partners). To advance from a lower to a higher level of ownership is subject to the "up or out" system (see chapter 9 for details). Among those of the same partnership level, profits may be shared equally, while incentives for bringing in clients and revenue may render the shareout unequal. Typically, compensation decisions are made by a financial committee of senior partners. Such committees often use formulas that compensate according to time billed, business brought in, and – sometimes – public stature (Farrell and Scotchmer 1988: 294).

In economic terms, partnerships are advantageous for their peer pressure and mutual monitoring, which reduces or precludes opportunism among partners (Kandel and Lazear 1992; Armour and Whincop 2004). If liability is not limited, individual owners of the firm care greatly who the other owners are. Firms such as McKinsey are incorporated firms with limited liability of individual owners, but firm contracts bind owners to sell shares only to other owners when leaving, thus keeping an informal partnership system in a closely held business (a close corporation; for legal differences between the United States and Europe, see McCahery *et al.* 2004).

Partnerships have no reason to publish their profits, compensation schemes, governance structure, or employee turnover. This secrecy typically leads to rumours among outsiders, employees, and interested business students. When partnerships decide to adopt a corporate structure, they need to disclose financial and other significant information concerning securities being offered for public sale. In the United States this is based on the Securities Act of 1933, the Securities Exchange Act of 1934, and the Sarbanes–Oxley Act of 2002. Company data are then accessible on the website of the Securities and Exchange Commission. Over the past five years several firms chose to transfer to a corporate structure (see chapter 6). This was because, under limited liability, shareholders can buy and sell shares without the approval of other owners. As Pejovich (1997: 184) points out in his economic analysis of governance forms, this translates into a substantial reduction of transaction costs when raising large amounts of capital. Outside capital has become important for those consulting firms which need expensive equipment with a high turnover rate – for example, for IT outsourcing contracts. Strategy and organization consultancies have typically remained partnerships or close corporations.

Most consulting firms that are, or are led like, partnerships have a worldwide managing director with an executive function similar to but with fewer rights than a CEO. In a partnership, this person is typically appointed by and accountable to a board of partners. Maister (1993: 293–4) outlines this structure as follows.

The ultimate "approval" body in a professional firm is, of course, the partnership, which reserves the right to approve major policy decisions on such matters as mergers, new partners, and the like. However, among the largest firms, a distinction is made between a "decision-making" role and an "approval" role for the partnership. Sheer numbers (and, increasingly, geography) prevent the partners, en masse, debating every policy decision. In consequence, most large professional firms *elect* a board of partners whose task it is to examine policy issues and either decide or present decisions to the partnership for ratification.

This board of partners corresponds closely to the corporate model of a board of directors representing the interests of the "shareholders" (in this case, partners). Like a corporate board, a primary function of this body is to oversee and monitor the activities of the executive (the managing partner) to ensure that the shareholders' interests are being served. Some professional firm boards meet monthly, but, as with corporate boards, a more common pattern is three or four times a year.

It should be added that many consulting firms do not have a single board of partners but several boards, all concerned with different issues. For example, one board may be in charge of partner compensation, another one in charge of promotions to the junior or senior partner level, a third decides about new services or competence center development, while a fourth settles growth issues, such as expanding into new countries, or opening or closing offices. Often the senior partners of a particular country office are empowered to establish a new board at any time if a particular topic comes up. In this regard, local autonomy prevails over international coordination. Especially in high-revenue countries such as the United States and the large western European countries, the country offices may form domestic committees for matters that are specific to their country.

The point of the flexible formation of boards and the rotation of membership can be related to the need for a rapid flow of information and speedy decision-making processes in order to economize on dissimilar tasks in comparison to clients. Most consulting firms seek to be as unbureaucratic as possible in order to facilitate fast and flexible decision-making. Any senior partner may be a member of one committee one year and of another committee the next year, or of no committee at all.[1]

---

[1] This flexibility comes with some hazards. The governance structure of a partnership is, typically, not transparent, not only for outsiders but also for employed consultants. Often consultants up to senior project manager level do not even know which committees exist at the level of senior partners or what these are responsible for. This unbureaucratic decision-making policy may sometimes come dangerously close to being arbitrary. Individual senior partners are, in principle, free to lead their turf – say three to four junior partners and around 100 consultants and administrative staff – in the way they want, which sometimes leads to an almost feudal system of unlimited senior partner power.

The research units that large consulting firms host represent another element of the governance structure. They can typically be found in the larger offices in the big business cities. Due to the constant need for immediate information on firms, markets, and industries, large management consulting firms economize on scale and scope by pooling their search functions for publicly available or fee-based information in these research units. They have virtually unlimited financial means to access databases or the electronic archives of news magazines, business press archives or specialized industry journals, private information providers, national bureaus of statistics, etc. If a consultant needs information on a particular firm, industrial sector, market segment, or country, then the research unit will usually be able to provide the information within twenty-four hours.

Project organization and the pool concept of staffing

One of the well-known elements of a consulting firm's organizational structure is its project-based operation and pool concept of staffing. Consulting projects typically last between two and six months (in strategy, organization, finance, and human resources; in IT consulting the durations are often longer), and individual consultants are allocated to several consecutive projects every year so as to gain experience in a range of industries and corporate functions. While senior consultants typically focus on particular industries, such as automotive, banking, or consumer goods (if the flow of orders from one industry permits this), staffing departments seek to reallocate junior staff between sectors and functions in order to foster information exchange between projects.

Individual consultants thus work on about three different projects per year, and often for three different project managers, rather than for a fixed supervisor over a long period of time. Consultants up to the project manager level are typically considered as a pool of human resources. Senior consultants and a staffing department allocate individual consultants to projects. Ideally, they bring together consultants with different professional backgrounds (e.g. engineers and MBAs) and different industry experiences. This policy seeks to promote an exchange of approaches to business questions and a firm-wide dissemination of knowledge.

Above the project manager level, by contrast, a higher degree of human resource continuity is needed. This is because the people who win project contracts need to develop and maintain close relations with individual client managers and to be well placed in the network of business contacts among client firms (see chapter 3). Hence the pool concept applies only to junior levels, since for these ranks continuity is less relevant and the exchange of information and development of consulting experience across industries and functions is of greater importance.

So far, the governance system has been outlined in economic terms. Do more sociological approaches have anything to add or correct? The communities of practice approach (Brown and Duguid 1996, 1998) is relevant in this context. As outlined in chapter 1, this approach implicitly applies embeddedness theory to the firm-internal context, without looking at the limits to efficiency that embeddedness effects often bring about. For example, Bogenrieder and Nooteboom (2004: 302; emphasis omitted) have outlined the role of project teams in management consulting firms as follows.

The team members reported that they learned a lot from each other, especially tacit knowledge. For example, the team used a certain tool that all members had learned to use during official courses organized by [a particular consulting firm]. One team member reported that the tool, which was used by the team, is now much clearer than before the project... Asked why he now understands this tool much better, he said that he has now really experienced how this tool is applied.

The team also developed new methods for implementing changes in the client organization. Asked for the reasons why the project members were inclined to try new methods, the answer was that they developed these methods together and they have committed themselves (mutual absorptive capacity) in intensive ties.

Adapting the embeddedness notions of strong and weak ties to firm-internal learning processes, Bogenrieder and Nooteboom allot the role of strong ties to project teams that cooperate for a limited period of time. When a project terminates, the team typically disintegrates as the individual consultants are allocated to other projects. As opposed to the communities of practice approach, however, the positive effect seems to result precisely from the continuous formation of new project teams. The strong and weak ties resulting from previous cooperation can be used subsequently for exchanging information about analytical tools or project approaches.

In an empirical investigation of the determinants of successful projects, Lechler and Gemünden (1998) ascertain two factors as the main determinants of project success: the influence of clients' top management, and the quality of team cooperation. Top management nurtures project success by delegating responsibility to the project manager, appointing the team members, and allowing a high degree of participation (Lechler and Gemünden 1998: 443). The quality of team cooperation has a direct effect on project success through the degree of participation, better information and communication processes, and improved planning and project management (444).

The latter point in particular, teamwork quality, has been subject to further studies (Högl and Gemünden 2001; Högl *et al.* 2004). Högl and Gemünden, for example, operationalize teamwork quality as internal flow of communication, coordination of different contributions from different functional areas, balance of member contributions, mutual support, team member effort, and social cohesion of the team. They show that teamwork quality strongly influences the success of innovative projects such as R&D and new ventures, defined as project effectiveness and efficiency as well as work satisfaction and learning by individual members.

In a follow-up study, Högl *et al.* take another step toward a comprehensive understanding of team performance. They conducted a longitudinal analysis of teamwork quality and team performance. Most interestingly, they included inter-team coordination as a variable, which corresponds to the notion of weak ties in embeddedness theory. Based on a large-scale survey, Högl *et al.* are able to show that both teamwork quality and inter-team coordination, especially at the beginning of the project, are strongly related with overall performance and adherence to schedule. Inter-team coordination (weak ties) proved as important for project success as teamwork quality (strong ties).

Consulting firms typically combine the project team organization and the pool concept of staffing with extensive cross-staffing – as far as the network ties between senior consultants and the preferences of senior project managers allow. That is, cross-staffing has its limits. Senior project managers seek to allocate their trusted colleagues to particular topics and often overrule the plans of the staffing departments to bring together consultants of different backgrounds.

Although cross-staffing is an important factor in the internal dissemination of knowledge, and thus a key to the transaction cost difference between client and consulting firms, the strong and weak ties between consultants often overrule the economic purpose of cross-staffing. Successful teams often prefer to continue in the same constellation for as many projects as possible, even though this undermines the objective of human resource interchange.

On the other hand, the constant reallocation of staff to projects involves high internal costs for the project members in getting accustomed to each other and forming teams. Tearing apart successful teams means increasing the costs of coordination and cooperation. Moreover, even at the lower ranks of the consulting hierarchy, client–consultant relations may emerge in such a way that clients demand the same consultants for consecutive projects. Under the conditions of a buyer's market (chapter 4), such demands must normally be met (Richter 2004). Furthermore, cross-staffing across borders involves considerable transaction costs. Language barriers between countries hamper cross-staffing to non-English-speaking countries, as consultants must speak the client's native language. Hence, the extent of cross-border staffing is usually limited and unbalanced between countries. Within these limits, however, consulting firms try to staff projects in such a way that different consulting histories meet, but this effort is often restricted, or even reversed, by the force of extending cooperation within strong ties.

Competence centers, the one-firm concept, and organizational culture

The central structural element that complements the project organization and cross-staffing is the matrix structure of competence centers that large consulting firms have established. A competence center – also called a "practice" or "practice group" – comprises a group of people who are concerned with similar client industries or functions. They represent a form of inter-team coordination in the sense of Högl *et al.* (2004), as they collect and disseminate the experiences of various project teams working on related topics. One dimension of the matrix structure typically comprises competence centers on client industries (such as automotive, consumer goods, financial services, utilities, pharmaceutical/medical, or public administration).

The other dimension concerns client functions, such as strategy, marketing, organization and change management, finance, or IT. Typically, each consultant belongs to two or three competence centers, depending on the previous projects conducted (on the economics of matrix structures, see Besanko *et al.* 2000: 556−60).

Competence centers are normally run by a senior or junior partner and meet, for example, once a month. Since consultants do not want to lose a day that is chargeable to a client, the meetings of the competence centers often take place on Fridays, which are mostly not charged to clients anyway, or in the early morning at an airport hotel or conference room. As Moore and Birkinshaw (1998: 84) point out, these meetings have a twofold function: they leverage knowledge and transfer it. The transfer effect results from the coming together of members of different projects, client industries, and functions, while the leverage effect results from the fact that the interaction within a meeting about a particular topic raises tacit knowledge to a more explicit level (Nonaka 1994; Nonaka and Takeuchi 1995). This enables the creation of labels and accounts for a theorization of business cases or industry events. As pointed out in chapter 1, on the basis of sociological neoinstitutionalism, the flow of information between units along network ties is accompanied or even preceded by a process of theorizing and interpreting individual events. Only after a particular theorization has occurred, and after it has been given a label, can the knowledge and information about relevant incidents flow between units. As Werr (2002) points out, structuring individual experiences is the essence of raising knowledge in consulting firms, and this structuring occurs, among other ways, through the interaction of consultants in competence centers. These are the places in which individual events are interpreted and distilled into broader theories, which can then be presented to clients or other competence centers.

Competence centers thus represent inter-team coordinators (Högl *et al.* 2004) and knowledge brokers within a consulting firm. They emerged from the insight that informal, personal ties between consultants are not sufficient for the systematic dissemination of knowledge within the firm. Competence centers represent the attempt to formalize informal ties and to leverage and disseminate knowledge more systematically than informal ties would allow. From this perspective, competence centers serve two functions: they formalize the exchange of experiences on related topics beyond strong and weak ties within the firm, and seek to compensate for the negative effects of firm-internal embeddedness.

The crucial difference between this competence-center-based way of organizing and disseminating knowledge and a traditional, hierarchy-based way is that, in the latter, experiences and knowledge must be transported up the hierarchy before they can be disseminated to other parts of the firm. In the competence-center-based firm, the horizontal exchange of experiences and approaches adds to the hierarchical way. Nevertheless, competence centers are not free from hierarchy. They are often founded by a senior partner, who then determines topics and the agenda. Moore and Birkinshaw (1998) distinguish between three different types of competence centers: charisma-based, focused, and virtual. A charisma-based competence center is centered around a particular senior partner, who is often also its founder. A focused center is based around a single area of knowledge, and a virtual center represents recurrent meetings of larger groups of consultants across several countries.

Anand *et al.* (2004) have conducted empirical research on the emergence and development of new competence centers. They show that founding new competence centers in management consulting firms revolves around four issues:

- organizational support, in the sense of access to resources and developing junior consultants;
- the development of a differentiated knowledge base, to build on diversified sources of knowledge across functions;
- the career mobility of individual consultants, in terms of individual ambition and organizational growth objectives; and
- internal turf creation, in which partners have to define and mark their territory within the firm and fight battles with other competence centers to carve out their particular standing in the market.

With their last point, Anand *et al.* highlight a political issue concerning the development and leadership of competence centers: individual senior partners want to build their own empire in the firm. Indeed, herein lies the biggest danger in the establishment of competence centers: that they become little more than platforms for individual directors to build their territories on and assemble servile consultants around them. What is intended to be the pivotal element of knowledge dissemination within the firm may decay and become the submissive worshiping of individual "prima donnas" and their consulting approaches.

In his chapter entitled "How practice leaders add value," Maister (1993) shows that he has recognized this danger, and warns against it.

To be successful, the coach [practice leader] must also be able to suppress his or her own ego needs, since the very nature of the job is to make other people feel successful and important. The job of the manager is to build a team, not an empire. The best leaders of professionals are quick to give credit to others, and to play down their own role in successes – a behavior trait that many superb professionals have to work to acquire at some personal psychological cost (219).

He goes on to write (220): "In many firms, regrettably, being appointed as a practice leader is some form of 'reward.' The position goes to the most eminent, or the most senior, or the best business-getter among the partners. None of these criteria is appropriate. Practice leadership should be seen as a role or a responsibility, not a title, a promotion, or a reward."

The one-firm concept and organizational culture

A central feature of strategy consulting firms is the so-called "one-firm" approach to governance. This principle means that (a) the terms, organizational units, and hierarchical levels are the same worldwide, (b) all technology-based resources such as the intranet or the knowledge management structure are firm-wide systems without internal boundaries, and (c), as far as country-based flexibility allows, the decision-making bodies are firm-wide and international. The one-firm principle typically expands to issues such as firm-wide boot camps for new employees, in which all the new intake of a particular period worldwide meet and get to know each other. It includes a homogeneous way of addressing colleagues across hierarchical levels (only by first name, independent of the hierarchical level and up to the worldwide managing director) and establishes the principle of contacting colleagues across countries based on a "reply within twenty-four hours" policy.

The last point in particular represents a difference from other, more traditional organizations. In international consulting firms, the intranet introduces all internal experts on particular topics (e.g. on statistical analysis of a certain type, employee satisfaction surveys, or market analyses for automotive firms). If a question on such a topic emerges, then a consultant looks for internal experts on the intranet and contacts them by telephone. Typically, the contacted person is required to reply within twenty-four hours, which enables a firm-wide, international exchange of knowledge irrespective of national boundaries.

Competence centers and a cross-staffing policy also represent the one-firm principle. While competence centers are usually held at the national level, since worldwide meetings of marketing, banking, or supply chain management experts would be too costly, the intranet facilitates a constant exchange of topics between equivalent competence centers across national boundaries. Moreover, possibly the most important element of the one-firm principle is the firm-wide organizational culture, or, at least, the attempt to achieve a firm culture that emphasizes consistency in an internationally homogeneous firm culture.

In economic terms, organizational culture has four functions: it simplifies the processing of information and reduces employee uncertainty; it lowers the costs of monitoring employees; it facilitates cooperation by substituting explicit communication; and it reduces internal bargaining costs (Jones 1983; Kreps 1990; Crémer 1993; Besanko *et al.* 2000: 596−600; Hermalin 2000). In other words, formal contracts are in many situations more costly than informal, culture-based organization, or even defective. Repeated games facilitate cooperation in a less costly way than contractually, and the informal contract of culture is better equipped to deal with unforeseen contingencies than formal ones (Kreps 1990).

Crémer (1993) decomposes corporate culture into a common language or coding, a shared knowledge of certain facts, and a shared knowledge of rules of behavior. All three of them are recognizable in strategy consultancies. There are firm-wide terms regarding the features of governance (hierarchical levels, competence areas, etc.), and there is a recognizable emphasis on a firm-wide culture. This is to facilitate the cooperation of consultants across national boundaries, functions, and professional backgrounds. A relatively homogeneous culture accounts for a regulation of action, for a smaller likelihood that conflicts will arise from different ways of interacting, and for lower costs of controlling or supervising consulting staff. The resulting cooperation within the firm can, in principle, also be induced by formal contracts, but such contracts would incur massive transaction costs. (The downside of such cultures in management consultancy is discussed in chapter 9 in the context of personnel selection and social homogenization effects.)

Another effect, rarely recognized by economists, is the signaling effect of the one-firm culture to the environment – i.e. to existing and prospective clients. A relatively homogeneous way of dressing and interacting, and thus the limitation of individuality, signals neutrality, objectivity, and rationality. The one-firm principle signals that the firm as a whole "stands for" something. It is not just an arbitrary pool of individuals but represents a particular way of tackling business problems. For this argument we assume that the costs of producing this signal are lower for top-tier consulting firms. This is realistic, because the culture fosters a consultant's identity as belonging to an elitist club, and it enhances the self-selection of those who will be proud to work for the firm.

Knowledge management

The management of knowledge faces a number of challenges for consulting firms. Client expectations about the provision of information and solutions in a minimum of billable time are high, and consultants' stress during project work is notorious. Clients are frequently unaware of how much time it takes to collect data, analyze them, and formulate remedies. The information and data gathered are often ambiguous and solutions do not immediately suggest themselves. Approaches must be thoroughly compared to other models and possibilities before a considered conclusion can be presented to the client. At the same time, clients expect all consultants involved in a project to be experts in their industry and domain, which often not only is impossible, due to the limited pool of human resources, but also contradicts the logic of management consulting, which economizes on the transfer of information across industries and functional specializations.

An additional challenge is that consultants often work four days a week at the client's site rather than in the consultancy's office. This means that personal interaction is bounded to the other members of the particular project, and contact with fellow consultants must be maintained over the phone, by email, or by IT-based knowledge management systems that consultants can access via the internet. Intensive inter-team coordination in the sense of Högl *et al.* (2004) is required, but it is difficult to achieve. Not surprisingly, therefore, the IT-based knowledge management system, consisting of a sophisticated intranet, groupware, and a document management system, plays a critical role in the internal dissemination of knowledge. This, however, creates the following additional problems.

- Consultants have little incentive to contribute their project knowledge to the system, because formulating and uploading it costs time that is not necessarily billable to projects, and because making one's expertise available to others undermines one's expert power in the firm. Information hiding would be a typical reaction if no other incentives operate.
- The presentation of expertise such that it is readily available in a downloadable document requires skills of formulation and codification. Much of the knowledge acquired in a project is tacit rather than explicit, and can hardly be codified and stored in a written document. Documented, written knowledge is often not directly applicable and needs to be supplemented by more tacit knowledge about specific cases.
- Double-loop learning (Argyris and Schön 1978) about what went wrong in a project requires contemplation, reflection, and supervision – and therefore time, which the hectic project work often does not allow.
- Technologies, tools, and practices change quickly and have a high turnover. An IT-based knowledge management system must constantly be updated and actively managed.

Werr (1999: 286–93) outlines the challenges to internal knowledge management as the problem of combining the three pillars of a consulting firm's knowledge: experience, methods, and consulting cases. Experience represents the tacit knowledge of individual consultants, which is difficult to articulate. Methods represent the ways of approaching a business problem; they are articulate and readily available to every consultant, but open to varying interpretations in that they necessarily abstract from individual clients. Cases consist of former projects for which the procedures and solutions are stored in the knowledge management system; they represent a specific and articulate kind of knowledge in that they describe individual client situations in a codified form of sentences, figures, and statistical analyses. Nevertheless, for the new case of the current project former cases do not suffice, but have to be enriched by methods and individual experience in order to render the specific business problem operational. Werr sketches these circumstances as follows.

Werr's (1999, 2002) analyses point out the central challenge for consulting firms: to disseminate and combine the partly tacit and partly explicit knowledge of experienced consultants, transfer it to new consultants, and render it available and applicable across countries,

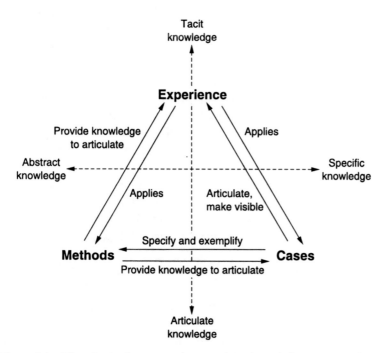

Figure 8.1. Three basic elements in the consulting knowledge system and their interrelations
Source: Werr (1999: 288).

industrial sectors, and functional specializations. Hansen *et al.* (1999) draw a central distinction in this context: between codified and personalized knowledge management. Having looked at various management consulting firms they find that different firms rely on dissimilar means of knowledge distribution. Some firms focus on information technology and try carefully to codify and store knowledge in databases, mostly groupware and document management systems. In other consulting firms, either knowledge units are closely tied to the people who developed them and shared principally in person-to-person interaction, or the IT-based knowledge management system is primarily used to locate the knowledge carrier in the firm. Hansen *et al.* juxtapose the two knowledge management strategies as in table 8.1.

The process of knowledge codification typically goes as follows. An existing document prepared in the course of a project – the final report to the client, for example – is removed from client-sensitive information and either presented in the knowledge management system as a general approach to a project of this kind or divided into different sections that contain individual pieces that can be used for other purposes. Examples of such pieces would be questionnaires, interview guides, work schedules, benchmark data, market analyses, or particular statistical procedures. Contract formulations and value propositions (estimates of client's gains or saved costs) help to clarify bids and project proposals. These pieces of information or data are then saved under several keywords in the knowledge management system and suggested for download if a user searches for one of the terms. Based on the title and abstract of the document, users can download the file and obtain at least an inspiration for a project, or even fully elaborated tools, such as questionnaires or interview guides that need only to be adjusted to the current client firm.

In any case, the authors, co-authors, and project members are listed in the document, so that users can contact them and obtain additional, possibly more tacit, information through a telephone call or personal interaction. In some cases the documents can be readily used without any further contact between author and user, in other cases the document emerges as useful and instructive only after an author has been contacted. Often, assigned consultants are in charge of codifying and synthesizing the documents for a particular competence center.

Table 8.1. Two types of knowledge management

	Codification	Personalization
Type of knowledge management	Provide high-quality, reliable, and fast information-systems implementation by reusing codified knowledge.	Provide creative, analytically rigorous advice on high-level strategic problems by channeling individual expertise.
Competitive strategy:		
Economic model	**Reuse economics** Invest once in a knowledge asset; reuse it many times. Use large teams with a high ratio of associates to partners. Focus on generating large overall revenues.	**Expert economics** Charge high fees for highly customized solutions to unique problems. Use small teams with a low ratio of associates to partners. Focus on maintaining high profit margins.
Knowledge management strategy	**People-to-documents** Develop an electronic document system that codifies, stores, disseminates, and allows the reuse of knowledge.	**Person-to-person** Develop networks for linking people so that tacit knowledge can be shared.
Information technology	Invest heavily in IT; the goal is to connect people with reusable codified knowledge.	Invest moderately in IT; the goal is to facilitate conversations and the exchange of tacit knowledge.
Human resources	Hire new college graduates who are well suited to the reuse of knowledge and the implementation of solutions. Train people in groups and through computer-based distance learning. Reward people for using and contributing to document databases.	Hire MBAs who like problem solving and can tolerate ambiguity. Train people through one-on-one mentoring. Reward people for sharing knowledge directly with others.
Examples	Andersen Consulting [now: Accenture], Ernst and Young Strategy Consulting [now: Cap Gemini Ernst and Young].	McKinsey, Bain, The Boston Consulting Group.

Source: Hansen *et al.* (1999: 109).

Sarvary (1999: 99) explains the economics of establishing such a large knowledge management center.

Clearly, huge efficiency gains can be achieved by compiling the insights. However, a much deeper understanding can be achieved if after initial compilation someone looks at those insights and further synthesizes them. It is generally the case that insights are not independent but are reflections of a few causal patterns. Although individual insights are also useful for decision making, there are important synergies between them. [...]

In sum, much higher efficiency gains and, more importantly, qualitative improvements in knowledge creation can be gained if the synthesis, the integration of the firm's experience, is done centrally... This is why KM [knowledge management] is much more than simply storing handouts on a database with good search capabilities.

From this perspective a pure personalization strategy is inefficient, yet, interestingly, Hansen *et al.* (1999: 108) find that the large strategy consulting firms emphasize their reliance on personalization. "They focus on dialogue between individuals, not knowledge objects in a database. Knowledge that has not been codified – and probably couldn't be – is transferred in brainstorming sessions and one-on-one conversations. Consultants collectively arrive at deeper insights by going back and forth on problems they need to solve." In their comparative study of knowledge management in an accounting firm and a consulting firm, Morris and Empson (1998) arrive at the same result. Codification and leverage is one form, others rely less on codified analytical models. "Codification strategies work on the assumption that knowledge is appropriable and that knowledge holders are aware of what they know; but some knowledge may be so utterly reflexive and automatic that it is used without being recognised" (Morris and Empson 1998: 622).

Nevertheless, the duality of the two ways of managing knowledge may exaggerate the differences. As Hansen *et al.* (1999: 109) argue themselves, firms that they identify as pursuing a personalization approach to knowledge management still use the document base extensively. Not only is a purely personalized approach to knowledge management less efficient the larger the firm is but, due to the high personnel turnover, knowledge would be completely lost every time a consultant leaves the firm. As Sarvary (1999: 100) adds, without a knowledge management system the quality of the firm's service would suffer substantially because decisions would be based on anecdotes provided by a few senior consultants rather than on a more thorough understanding and theorization based on a variety of sources.

The most important point is that the document base is the central institution for identifying the internal expert on a topic. What is meant as a side effect of the document management system, the disclosure of the authors' names, is a central element of the knowledge retrieval and transfer process. Identifying and selecting colleagues who have worked on similar or related topics, and talking to them in person or on the telephone, is a central element of the knowledge management process. The document base represents an electronic equivalent to a structural hole position (Burt 1992) that connects previously unconnected participants within the firm.

Levine's (2004) study is instructive in this context. Based on embeddedness-inspired research on knowledge management in a consulting firm, he ascertains a third category beyond strong and weak ties: "performative ties." These enable an exchange of information between previously unconnected participants on the basis of referrals through the document retrieval system. As he observes,

A performative tie involves two or more individuals that became linked following a process of wide search. While they have no transaction history nor expect to develop one, the transaction is carried out in a mode of generalized exchange, which allows it to take place *as if* the actors were embedded in a trustful dyadic relationship... Similarly, a performative tie is both created and accessed at the same time. Performative ties appear as ties only when they are activated – there is no prior indication of a tie, direct or indirect, between the nodes involved... Because as short-lived as the transaction may be, the sides behave as if they had an established social tie between them, and behave not as a faceless economic agent should behave in a setting of market transaction... The term communicates both the ad-hoc nature of the transaction and the trusting behavior involved (Levine 2004: 19–20; emphasis in original).

Because two members of the same profit-oriented firm share a common interest by default, care is in order so as not to confuse intraorganizational action without ties, on the one hand, with market behavior in interorganizational matters on the other. Nevertheless, Levine's analysis makes clear that even those consultancies that

Hansen *et al.* (1999) portray as personalized knowledge firms cannot do without a sophisticated, managed, and constantly updated knowledge management and document retrieval system. As Levine (2004: 14) observes, "Rather than a library of codified knowledge, KMS [knowledge management systems] served more as a collection of pointers, which identified individuals who may be in possession of relevant knowledge. Knowledge seekers used the information contained in the KMS to filter through the list of potential knowledge carriers and decide which ones to contact."

Another two observations by Levine are interesting here. First, the authors of relevant documents have often already left the firm. However, this does not mean that the "performative tie" cannot be used. Rather, the person's details are in the alumni database of the firm and can still be contacted. If the information seeker strictly keeps the confidentiality of the issue, then the alumni can still be asked for elucidations of the subject or for referrals to other persons in the consulting firm. The second interesting embeddedness effect that Levine has observed is that "performative ties" operate as much on the basis of status similarity as interorganizational ties. A knowledge seeker, when having identified the individuals to be contacted in the firm, first chooses those who have the same or a similar hierarchical level in the firm. That is, for example, a senior consultant first pursues those performative ties to other senior consultants or project managers, but only secondarily to partners or directors. Vice versa, a partner will first contact another partner before he or she resorts to the lower ranks of the hierarchy. If consultants need to contact an unacquainted knowledge carrier of a very different status, they prefer to do this via an acquainted consultant of the same or similar status to the knowledge carrier. Thus we have another interesting embeddedness effect in which the nature of social ties reduces efficiency.

From a neoinstitutional perspective, the cases and information stored in the knowledge management system or provided by the research department help to abstract from the particular matter of the client firm and leverage it to a more theoretical dimension. The reuse of old cases or applications of similar approaches to different firms can lead to isomorphic solutions, as outlined by DiMaggio and Powell (1983). However, this is not a necessary consequence. As Sarvary (1999: 100) points out, with a good knowledge management system, consultants gain time for customized problem-solving because they spend less time searching for information.

Active management of knowledge and incentives to knowledge contributions

An IT-based document management system requires active content management and continuous updating. For consulting firms, this is a costly issue. Every change of a telephone number or email address, move between offices, or change of status must be noted and entered into the system in order to guarantee immediate contact. The document storage and retrieval system in particular is based on active content management. The individual contributions must not only be saved under keywords or potential search terms but also be categorized in topics about which knowledge packs can be assembled for industry or competence center meetings. These keywords, potential search terms, and topics are typically suggested by the author but are often cross-checked by knowledge managers or competence center leaders. Knowledge managers belong to the administrative staff of consulting firms and thus represent overhead costs. Typically, each download of a document or request to knowledge managers or to the research department is billed to the project for which the enquiring consultant works. This allocates the overhead costs to the individual projects and transfers overhead costs to project expenses.

The collection of documents to knowledge packs is often based not only on the judgments of competence center leaders but also on download analyses by knowledge managers. The number of downloads per time is the key to categorizing documents according to importance, and the analyses of search terms allows for distinctions between "hot" and "cold" topics. Hot topics can be brought to the attention of all users, much as the rankings of documents, topics, and search terms are provided to users. If documents have not been downloaded over a certain period of time (for example, two years) then they will be deleted. All documents are linked to the names of their authors, and the knowledge management system can be accessed not only from consulting offices but through the internet from clients' sites, airports, and hotels.

One issue, however, is critical: the low incentivization for consultants to contribute documents to the knowledge base rather than only retrieve them (Reimus 1997: 10; Dunford 2000: 297–9). Without any incentive system consultants would hold back their knowledge, since owning a topic renders them experts and thus irreplaceable in the firm. Contributing knowledge to the system renders them replaceable; information hiding would be a normal reaction of an opportunistic agent. Dunford (2000: 298) notes: "There is a market for knowledge in organizations, therefore it is not surprising that some potential 'knowledge sellers' believe that they benefit more from hoarding their knowledge than from sharing it. In some situations sharing knowledge is seen as giving away power and influence." In addition to these issues of power and information hiding, preparing a document for storage in the knowledge management system takes time and effort, and the project work is hectic.

However, the fact that the documents are linked with the names of their authors accounts for visibility in the firm, representing an incentive to make contributions. This mechanism is not too different from the academic system of citation and reputation. Within the firm, individual consultants are associated with particular approaches *because* (rather than although) they have published them in the knowledge base. Consultants gain internal reputation and are increasingly contacted by other consultants the more documents they have uploaded into the system.

Nonetheless, this mechanism in isolation would probably not be sufficiently motivating. More important is that, in strategy consulting firms, the contributions to the knowledge management system are an integral part of the performance appraisal system. Typically, contributions to the knowledge base can be counted simply as the number of entered documents over time. However, this would represent an incentive to split a report into as many subunits as possible. Hence the knowledge managers, in cooperation with competence center leaders, must assess whether a document can be considered an independent piece of information or not, which increases the need for the active management of the system. Another way to assess contributions is to count how often documents by a particular author have been downloaded. High-quality documents are more frequently downloaded by colleagues than less important contributions. Hence, in a manner similar to citation statistics in academia, the number of downloads is a rough indicator of document quality. Certainly, this system has its imperfections. Counting the number of downloads per document leads to an incentive to save a report under as many keywords as possible. Thus colleagues download a document believing that it is closely related to the search term, although in fact it is not. A balance between indicators must be found that reflects the quality of the contribution as accurately as possible.

Hansen and Haas (2001) have conducted empirical research in this area. They show that, due to the connection to performance appraisal, the knowledge management system has evolved to become the central forum of competition for firm-internal attention. Hansen and Haas's point of departure is that users of knowledge management systems have limited time and attention to search for relevant documents. Since searching by keyword often either fails to lead to the desired outcome or results in too many documents, many users resort to a sequential search behavior and first consult a subset of credible suppliers. Hence, consultants use the reputation of individual suppliers as an important piece of first-hand information on the quality and usefulness of documents. If document suppliers compete for the limited attention of users looking for the same knowledge content, they are engaging in publishing strategies that can be described along two dimensions: (a) topic concentration versus a generalist strategy of covering many different topics, and (b) the degree of document selectivity – that is, the extent to which a document is edited. The resulting four strategies can be outlined in a two-by-two matrix.

Table 8.2. Consultants' firm-internal publishing strategies to gain attention

		Document selectivity	
		Low	*High*
Topic concentration	High	Mixed	Less is more
	Low	More is more	Mixed

Source: Hansen and Haas (2001: 5).

Hansen and Haas ascertain that, in crowded segments of knowledge contribution (where contents are relevant for a large number of projects, such as business process reengineering), most attention is allocated to very selective and concentrated documents, and thus to suppliers pursuing the "less is more" strategy. In uncrowded segments (where topics are relevant for a low number of projects), by contrast, more attention is allocated to suppliers who contribute less selective and less concentrated documents – that is, to suppliers pursuing the "more is more" strategy. Hansen and Haas have thus highlighted an intriguing paradox: the less information a supplier offers the more attention and reputation he or she can gain.

These results show that a whole culture on document writing and supply has emerged in management consulting firms, with individuals pursuing different strategies and developing skills on how to behave in this internal market for attention. This has not always been the case. Bartlett (1998: 4–5) notes on the history of McKinsey:

Although big ideas had occasionally been written up as articles for publication in newspapers, magazines or journals like *Harvard Business Review*, there was still a deep-seated suspicion of anything that smacked of packaging ideas or creating proprietary concepts. This reluctance to document concepts had long constrained the internal transfer of ideas and the vast majority of internally developed knowledge was never captured.

This began to change with the launching of the *McKinsey Staff Paper* series in 1978, and by the early 1980s the firm was actively encouraging its consultants to publish their key findings... But books, articles, and staff papers required major time investments, and only a small minority of consultants made the effort to write them... Believing that the firm's organizational infrastructure needed a major overhaul, in 1987 Gluck [then worldwide managing director of McKinsey] launched a Knowledge Management Project.

From this knowledge management project today's managed document storage and retrieval system emerged, and the way consultants approach projects has changed considerably since then. While competition for attention in consulting firms has always been strong, the knowledge management system emerged in the 1990s as a new forum in which to carry out this internal competition.

The foundation of the *McKinsey Quarterly* in 1964 and its expansion in the 1990s is another aspect of knowledge management and attention effects. The firm recognized the signaling effect that published documents have, and the *McKinsey Quarterly* is an application of these signaling mechanisms to the outside market. The fact that a firm has its own journal, and that consulting firms with lower margins would have higher costs of producing a journal, signals consulting quality. The journal raises attention among clients for particular topics and signals the reputation of McKinsey as an elitist firm. Today the internal knowledge management system and the *McKinsey Quarterly* are related, because articles in the *McKinsey Quarterly* are often extended versions of contributions to the internal knowledge base.

In summary, knowledge management systems have become an integral and central part of consulting work, and the effects are manifold. (a) They embody economical ways of disseminating knowledge within the firm; (b) they shape the way consultants compete internally and trigger an entire culture of knowledge contributions; (c) they facilitate personal contacts to consultants who have worked on similar topics, while embeddedness effects such as status similarity reduce the tendency to a free exchange; and (d) they epitomize the signaling of consulting quality to the business environment by providing material for a quasi-academic journal.

9 | *Gaining talent and signaling quality: human resource management*

To consulting firms, human resource management (HRM) is vital for two reasons. First, they need personnel who are capable of performing cognitive abstractions and mathematical procedures of varying complexity. And, second, in a market of experience and credence goods, the quality of human resources signals consulting quality. The fact that the leading consulting firms comprise some of the most sought-after organizations for graduates from prestigious business schools and universities to work in is central to their business. Graduates and members of the business environment not only view these firms as springboards for senior managerial positions but also associate them with an elite status. Being hired by a leading consulting firm considerably enhances the self-esteem of graduates, who have often stuck at their studies for several years in order to gain placement in such a firm. This, in turn, nurtures the reputation of these firms in the management arena, and the procedures of personnel selection are a constitutive element in this cycle.

This chapter introduces and seeks to explain personnel selection and promotion policies in consulting firms. As far as the selection of personnel is concerned, I argue that the main outcomes are the signaling effect to the business environment and the social homogenization effect within the firm. As far as promotion procedures are concerned, I first review the economic literature on "up or out" tournaments and rat races, and then use the example of female consultants to introduce embeddedness-related and neoinstitutional mechanisms of promotion.

Personnel selection

The focus on personnel selection procedures is particularly instructive because, in management consulting, senior consultants supervise projects but junior consultants perform them. While common sense would suggest that an advisor is more experienced than the person receiving the advice, management consulting operates on the basis of the paradox that young and managerially less experienced consulting personnel advise senior client managers, who often have many years of experience in their particular industry. As chapter 2 has pointed out, this can be explained by transaction costs: consultants focus on tasks that are different from clients' routines, and they have developed methods and tools for analyses that rarely occur in individual client firms but can be used across client industries and regions.

Until the economic slowdown hit the consulting sector in 2001 competition for talented graduates was very intense, and in 2003 it again became very strong. A look at business magazines up to 2001 shows that the consulting sector spoke in terms of a "war for talents" (Chambers *et al.* 1998; Michaels *et al.* 2001) in order to indicate that they were making considerable efforts to attract and hire qualified personnel. Consulting firms continue to invest a lot of money in recruitment events at leading universities and business schools, and in the selection of applicants.

Procedures for personnel selection are based on an organization's intention to gain information about the behavioral and attitudinal characteristics of the candidates. As such, they reflect an organization's assumptions regarding the personal requirements for and the nature of the business. Moreover, research on recruitment and selection has broadened its view from the traditional psychometric model to an emerging social process approach (Townley 1989, 1994; Iles and Salaman 1995; Ramsay and Scholarios 1999). Rather than analyzing selection procedures in terms of reliability and validity, the social process approach treats selection procedures as interactive processes with a number of considerable effects on those selected, those rejected, and those who select.

The leading consulting firms build their personnel selection policies on different grounds from those in other industries and service sectors. In industries such as banking, insurance, retail trade, or in any sector that recruits university graduates, it has become common practice to select graduates at assessment centers of varying degrees of sophistication with a considerable variety of tests and exercises. These industries have adopted those methods that the discourse in organizational psychology and human resource management advocates. Management consultancies, by contrast, especially the leading firms, rely on a different tool: the case study interview – a job interview in which an abbreviated form of a business case study is posed to the candidate. Nearly all top-tier consulting firms rely on this tool. Some firms also include normal job interviews, and a few additionally employ psychometric tests or group exercises for testing social or communicative competence (Armbrüster and Schmolze 1999).

The fact that the management consulting sector relies on this tool and has not adopted the methods that the HRM discourse suggests may indicate that there is a specific way of thinking within this industry regarding the capabilities a future consultant must have and regarding the way these talents can be found and selected. Hence, looking at the social processes the case study method may trigger – and their potential consequences – may lead to interesting insights into the consulting sector.

Job interview preparation booklets (Wet Feet Press 1996; Wharton MBA Consulting Club 1997; Asher and Lerner 1999) that are available in internet-based bookshops build the empirical basis for these analyses. These booklets are widely used by graduates considering a career in consulting. They collect the experiences of applicants who have undergone consultancy selection procedures and then forwarded the cases they had to solve in their job interviews to the editors. Hence they provide information about cases that consultancies have used in actual job interviews, and they offer extensive and reliable information on the contents of this selection process.

What renders these booklets particularly interesting is the fact that they provide not only case studies but also the expected solutions, or ways of approaching the cases, as demanded by the interviewer. Accordingly, they also provide information about the selectors' expectations and thus allow for insights that are otherwise very difficult to access. They make it possible to look not only at the ideas and attitudes behind the case studies but also, since the selection procedure is supposed to simulate real-life consulting cases, at the selectors' beliefs regarding the nature of management consulting. Hence, this analysis of selection methods focuses both on the message such procedures communicate to the external environment of leading management consultancies and on the subjectivities of the selectors and those selected. As Townley (1993) suggests, the predictive validity of the selection procedure may be less interesting than the social processes they prompt. This does not downplay the functional usefulness of the selection procedures, but serves to show that actual and symbolic rationality are intertwined.

The role of case studies in personnel selection

The origins of this selection tool are the cases used for teaching purposes by Harvard Business School (HBS) and other business schools. McKinsey started to hire from HBS when it founded management consulting as an activity to be performed by business school graduates rather than experienced consultants (Bhide 1994, 1995). The cases used for teaching purposes usually involve written information presented on many pages and require a few hours' or even days' work to elaborate a solution. For practical reasons, the cases used for personnel selection in management consulting are much briefer. Here, the information to be processed is condensed into units that a candidate can discuss with the interviewer in no more than half an hour's time, since candidates have to undergo a series of two to nine case study interviews varying from firm to firm (Armbrüster and Schmolze 1999). The case questions usually belong to one of the following categories (see, e.g., Wet Feet Press 1996: 13; Wharton MBA Consulting Club 1997: 2; Asher and Lerner 1999: 2–3):

- market size cases, or "guesstimates";
- business cases (e.g., strategy, operations, logistics, distribution); or
- brainteasers.

In market size questions the interviewer asks the applicant to estimate, for example, the number of paint stores in the United States, the number of manhole covers in Chicago, or the market for personal computers in fifteen years (see, e.g., Wet Feet Press 1996). When dealing with a business case question, the interviewee commonly receives a brief introduction to the company and a strategic proposal originating from its management. The interviewee is then asked to develop a business strategy. Examples of these types of case studies are: "A bank is thinking about going into the brokerage business. Should it?"; or "A large, diversified petrochemical company wants to fend off a hostile acquisition bid. What should it do?" (Wet Feet Press 1996: 16). Business operation questions usually describe a business problem that includes high costs, low production, or slumping sales, culminating in a request for suggestions or ideas for improvements. Brainteasers are such questions as: "If you have a drawer with eight white socks and thirteen black socks, what is the smallest number you would have to pull out without looking in order to be sure that you have a matching pair?" (Armbrüster and Schmolze 1999).

The structure of such cases is largely the same. Case studies used for the purposes of personnel selection are abbreviated versions of typical HBS cases. While HBS cases usually provide long introductions in which the company and industry history and structure are described, the personnel selection versions of case studies are mostly void of such information, and present information that must be transformed into quantitative analyses. The candidate is expected to make assumptions in order to have a basis for calculations. The interviewer assesses the candidate's ability to generate questions about the critical business issues, to make realistic assumptions, and to deal with the numbers given (Armbrüster and Schmolze 1999).

While at first glance some of the business cases seem similar to problems that a consultant may encounter in real-life assignments, the solutions provided in the booklets indicate particular assumptions about the information needed for solving a business problem and disclose some expectations about appropriate information processing (the original article underlying this section – see preface and acknowledgments – analyzes specific examples of case studies in greater detail). While guesstimate cases may have some validity regarding making realistic assumptions and quickly dealing with numbers, it is questionable whether the kind and format of information on which the candidate needs to solve the case simulate a realistic task during a consulting assignment. The actual problem in a consulting assignment, to gather reliable data and information, is screened out in such a case interview. If the assumptions that the candidate must make in the case interview refer to publicly available information, a consultant in a large consultancy would ask the research department of the firm to locate the relevant data (see chapter 8). If the consultant could gather the required information only within the client firm, the consultant needs significantly different skills in order to obtain it.

From a methodological viewpoint, the most remarkable features of the abbreviated case studies as simulations of business questions are (a) the kind of information given to the interviewee – that is, the pre-selection of what is regarded as important; and (b) the format of the information – that is, the expression of information in numbers and figures. The candidate receives little or no information about the history of the company, its present situation, or the internal development of say, the question as to whether the company should enter the market for phone cards. Such case studies abstract from the interdependence of sales and profits, on the one hand, and the company history and current opinions about directions and possibilities on the other.

If the critical discourse on consultancy, such as Jackall (1988: 144; see chapter 1), is right in saying that the real issues that consultants face are the political and social structures of corporations rather than the problems defined within them, and if Bloomfield and Danieli (1995) are not wrong to say that the technical skills of consultants are indissoluble from sociopolitical skills, then the business questions are connected to individuals and their opinions and positions within the company. In view of this the case interview must be regarded as decontextualized – i.e. removed from those circumstances that account for the problem and for the problem definition as it is presented to the consultant. This holds up the image that the consultant is an objective arbiter who deals only with objective information and eventually arrives at rational solutions.

While some kind of decontextualization might be useful, or even necessary, for storing a consulting approach on an internal knowledge system (see chapter 8), consulting work does not start only after all this information has been gathered. On the contrary, often the core work of consultants is to gain data and information from circumstances in which data are at least ambiguous and equivocal, if not subject to interest-driven distortion. The calculation process advocates an operations research approach to business questions, and treats organizational processes as neutral specifics rather than consequences of previous actions that have taken place within a certain institutional environment, under particular power constellations, and based on interactive and communicative rituals (Angell 1989).

Validity of and doubts about the case study method

Stewart (1991) has looked at the function of the HBS case studies for teaching and learning purposes. She focuses on their narrative structure and argues that their value in comparison to conventional business teaching lies in their ability to illustrate the problem for a specific application of theoretical principles, to socialize the learner into the situation of a particular problem-solver, and to familiarize the learner with specific instances in which intellectual and emotional involvement are required.

However, given the character of case studies as abbreviated business cases, it seems barely possible that this tool can validly test whether applicants possess the necessary social competence to cope with managerial, personal, and micropolitical difficulties as they often occur in consulting projects. While the case study interview certainly also involves social interaction between selector and applicant, the discourse in organizational psychology and human resource management suggests very different methods to detect quantitative skills, social competence, etc. Among them are cognitive ability tests, personality scales, work sample tests, or interactive group exercises under the observation of trained assessors (see Andersen and Herriott 1997; Robertson 1996; Smith and George 1994; Levy-Leboyer 1992; Muchinsky 1986). The management consulting sector does not use such methods, but relies almost exclusively on the case study (Armbrüster and Schmolze 1999). In contrast to the general trend toward psychometric testing and assessment center techniques, the consulting sector sticks with a tool that became an established practice in this service sector back in the 1950s. The methods used in the leading consulting firms thus stand in opposition to the variety of methods used elsewhere nowadays that can draw on ample examinations of validity and reliability. It is surprising, therefore, that it is precisely that service sector which has the reputation of recruiting an intellectual elite which employs selection methods that must be considered less sophisticated than those prevalent in other industries.

There is yet another difference between management consulting and other sectors in the context of personnel selection. In recruitment and examination procedures, many large organizations rely on trained members of a human resource department or on external expertise from human resource consultants, often with backgrounds in organizational psychology. The management consulting sector, by contrast, does not have recourse to such experts but relies on its own consultants. Those consultants responsible for personnel selection have received training only on one-day or half-day courses (if at all) and must be considered laypersons in this respect (Armbrüster and

Schmolze 1999). A consulting industry culture has emerged, in which firms trust their consultants even in fields that are not their specialty (personnel selection). Yet the effects that these selection procedures prompt may occur entirely independently of this question of validity.

The signaling effect of personnel selection

According to Bhide (1994, 1995), Marvin Bower envisaged a professional model that demanded innovative "brain power" rather than business experience from management consultants. It was assumed that graduates from leading business schools had the "intellectual superiority" that Bower's concept of consulting required. The highly selective recruitment provided the consulting industry with a considerable touch of intellectual elitism, and this conveys a strong message to the business community independent of the procedure's validity or reliability. The selection process as an initiation ritual combines consultants' belief in its validity with a signal of quality to the business environment.

Franck and Pudack (2000), Franck *et al.* (2001) and Pudack (2004) discuss the hidden economic effect of the procedure's selectivity in terms of signaling theory. Since the quality of consulting services is difficult to determine, management consultancies need to signal the quality of their services by substitutive means, among which is a highly selective hiring process. According to this logic, management consulting firms must primarily generate a long list of applicants, because the more applicants there are the higher the rejection rate. A high rejection rate signals selectivity, and thus consulting quality, to the business community. In this sense, the high investments of top-tier consultancies in recruitment events at leading business schools aim not only at attracting the most qualified applicants but also at generating the maximum number of applicants, in order to achieve a high rejection rate as a signal of quality (Pudack 2004; Franck and Pudack 2000; Franck *et al.* 2001).

Long lists of applicants have, according to Franck and Pudack (2000), another interesting effect: a self-selection process takes place among potential applicants, since a long list of applicants attracts and challenges highly qualified graduates in particular. In this case, the selection of high-performance personnel would result from the self-selection of applicants, and thus from the signaling effect of meritocracy rather than from the selection procedure itself. Most importantly, for consulting firms with lower output quality, attracting and hiring graduates from the most prestigious business schools would be somewhat more expensive.

Based on the above insights into the selection procedures, we can integrate into the insights of Franck and Pudack (2000), Franck *et al.* (2001) and Pudack (2004) the fact that it is not just the generation of long lists of applicants, and thus the high rejection rates, that signal quality but the selection procedure itself. As a tool that is used only in management consulting, the case study serves as a signifier of otherness and analytical skills. Irrespective of its validity with regard to a consultant's actual job, the selection procedure is associated with elitism and symbolizes special business training and competence. Moreover, it is not only the selectivity and the association of the procedure with the HBS that operate as symbols but also the contents of the case studies themselves. Turning business questions into calculation processes symbolizes rationality, in the sense of data-driven objectivity, and presents the solution as scientific, apolitical, and trustworthy (Porter 1995). The symbolic effect of the selection procedure is thus based on both the selectivity and the kind of rationality it represents.

Signaling theory has another contribution to make: viewing the recruitment and selection procedures as a central marketing tool, especially for fostering public reputation. As discussed in chapter 7, the marketing means of consulting firms are fairly limited. Where public reputation, experience-based trust and networked reputation determine assignment decisions, marketing tools are in danger of being perceived as somewhat artificial by clients. However, both the selectivity and the kind of recruitment represent a central tool for fostering public reputation. Only accounting firms and IT consultancies also advertise in business magazines and at airports in terms of consulting quality. Strategy consultancies do not do that. Their advertisements are directed at personnel recruitment and their posters at airports and in business magazines call for applications. Interestingly, even in 2002, when most strategy consulting firms had to reduce their staff, they advertised for applications even though they were hiring virtually nobody then. The reason is that graduates form only one target group for these advertisements. The other target group is client executives, who are supported in their belief that the strategy consulting firms accept only the very top graduates. Even in 2002 the advertisements for recruits sought to create the impression that the strategy consulting firms were hiring personnel due to full order books.

To understand these mechanisms in management consultancy, it is useful to recall Suchman's (1995) proposal of three mechanisms on which legitimization strategies are based: pragmatic, moral, and cognitive. The leading consulting firms' selection procedures meet all three of them. They symbolize pragmatism, in that the case studies are associated with pragmatic problem-solving and closeness to real business questions (rather than with "dry academic theory" or "psychological" assessment centers). They stand for morality, in that the calculation process represents the virtues of neutrality and objectivity. And they symbolize cognition, in that they meet the cognitive structure of a business environment in which those aspects that are not purely technical are labeled "politics," with the potential to jeopardize an otherwise objective solution. If strategy consulting firms were to use different recruitment methods, they would jeopardize these symbolic sources of legitimacy. The procedure of personnel selection provides quality certainty to the client in that it signals not only the selectivity of the process but also the reliance on mathematical procedures and data-driven objectivity.

The social homogenization effect of personnel selection

Given the significance of human resources for management consultancies, the consulting firms' renunciation of experts in the field of personnel selection is an interesting fact in itself. While the human resource principles that have come into practice in many corporations within the last few decades may be on a questionable track from a Foucaultian perspective (Townley 1993, 1994), they are generally regarded as advanced and valuable for corporate performance. The consulting industry seems to hold an explicit or implicit assumption that only consultants themselves and only the tool of case studies, rather than human resource experts and assessment centers, can assess the desired capabilities of a consultant. The case study method therefore hints at a unique pattern of industry culture and cognitive commonalities.

Referring to Foucault-based organization theory is appropriate in this context, as it has brought about analyses that indicate ways in which industry culture and selection procedures influence patterns of thinking or the identities of participants. To Foucault, the disciplinization of individuals and their behavior can generally be conducted in two ways: through subjecting them to observation, measurement, and assessment, or through tying them to an identity and subjectivity by "technologies of the self." Townley (1993, 1994) has employed these notions to analyze modern concepts of human resource management. She argues that HRM procedures account not only for the former effect, of disciplinary practices, but also for the latter, of identity formation through self-disciplinization (see also in this context Alvesson 2000 and Covaleski *et al.* 1998). Bergström (1998) and Bergström *et al.* (2004) have presented important findings in this context. Bergström conducted a series of interviews with candidates of leading management consultancies after the selection procedure. He finds that recruitment is not a one-sided process of transmission of corporate norms and values, "but rather a construction of how reality should be understood and by offering jobs to those candidates who accept that construction of reality, looking upon their employment as a result of their own decision" (Bergström 1998: 17). Consulting firms hire those individuals who best correspond to the expected form of information processing and frameworks set by the interviewers. Bergström points out that applicants receive offers only if they have complied with the frame-work of the selection tools.

The consultancy expects the candidate to comply with the decon-textualization of the issue and to solve the case based on the quantified information given. Those candidates will be selected who readily submit to these expectations and, as Bergström (1998) shows, not only exhibit the identity which considers the firm's expectations justified and legitimate but also see their own expectations met during the selection procedure. The fact that belonging to a leading management company is socially highly desirable for business graduates promotes these effects. The symbolism attached to the selection procedure conveys the pride of belonging to the company. The selection method channels the candidates' ambitions and self-esteem into assessment expectations, and they decide in favor of the company as a result of their own choice and determination. In this sense, the case-study-based selection procedure is not a test of aptitude, skill, or talent but, rather, of attitude, identity, and subjectivity.

Grey (1994) has pointed out how "career" as a project of the self can constitute work discipline and define a life according to the demands of the organization. Based on extensive interviews with staff at leading accounting firms, he distinguishes between those employees who internalize the demand for enthusiasm so that it becomes part of their identity and those for whom the project of career motivates performance without any need for enthusiasm. With respect to personnel selection, Grey (1994: 485) concludes that "the selection procedure indicates that successful applicants are already constituted as certain sorts of subjects, whether 'actually' as they appear, or willing to present themselves as if they were." Hence, as in other types of professional service firms, personnel selection has emerged as a definer of identity rather than merely a detector of aptitude and talent.

Discussion

Jackall (1988: 144) has found in his research that consultants are perfectly capable of recognizing the real issues as political and social ones. Questions such as: "Who can we approach in the client organization to gain relevant information?," "How can we approach this person in this situation?," "How can we identify the underlying issues or conflicts of this situation?," or "How can we mediate conflicts in this case?" are issues that a consultant learns to deal with in the course of his or her career. Most consultants are perfectly aware of the micropolitical circumstances in client organizations and their own micropolitical role. A consultant can barely acquire trust or generate word-of-mouth effects unless not only the results but also the interaction between the client and the consultant satisfy the client (McGivern 1983; Mitchell 1994; Clark 1995; Bloomfield and Danieli 1995; Sturdy 1997; Fincham 1999). The criticism that consultants lack the necessary social skills for tackling these issues may be misguided.

The selection procedures, however, are far from being able to assess these skills. Certainly, the case studies also involve social interaction between interviewer and interviewee, and to an extent facilitate an examination of the candidate's social and communicative competence. However, as the discourse on assessment centers in the HRM literature suggests, there are many more sophisticated means available for these purposes. Consulting firms do not make use of these tools but instead rely on untrained laypersons and unstructured means to assess those forms of competence that the social interaction in a client environment demands. It is perfectly possible that the leading consulting firms hire candidates with additional social and communicative skills. However, this is due more to the signaling effect and self-selection than a systematic outcome of the selection procedure. Since case-study-based selection is *regarded* as valid by consultants and the business environment, potential clients attribute intellectual elitism to it.

The link between these signaling mechanisms and sociological neo-institutionalism is interesting. Earlier neoinstitutional theory (Meyer and Rowan 1977; DiMaggio and Powell 1983) suggested that organizations should adopt practices that were regarded as rational in their environment. Following this argument, one would assume that top-tier consultancies need to adopt sophisticated assessment center techniques, since the discourse in organizational psychology and human resource management suggests this. However, they do not. Rather, they develop organizational isomorphism around a different technique, the case study, which signals a different kind of rationality to the outside world. To put it the other way around: if a leading consultancy hired a group of organizational psychologists to improve the validity of the selection procedure by adjusting it to a more realistic image of the consulting process, then the business environment could perceive this as a "psychologism" and a deviation from successful practices. The signaling effect could diminish. The new selection procedure may not have the reputation of selecting intellectual superiority and may eventually lead to a lower demand for this particular consulting firm.

Careers and promotion: the economic account

To consulting firms, promotion procedures are essential because many talented consultants consider working in management consultancy a springboard for further career steps rather than a career in itself. As a result, and reinforced by consultants' workload, personnel turnover is high in many consulting firms. For example, in Accenture's preliminary registration document, submitted to the Securities and Exchange Commission in April 2001 to file for their IPO, Accenture revealed a personnel turnover rate of 22 percent in 2000, excluding involuntary layoffs.

Promotion procedures are a central element of human resource management to give incentives and reduce personnel turnover. Moreover, the higher the hierarchical level the closer the contact between consultants and clients' management boards. In a market characterized by personal trust, networks, and word-of-mouth effects, mistaken promotions and inadequate senior consultants or partners may quickly cause clients to change provider and lead to negative word-of-mouth effects. Most of the large international consulting firms follow the so-called "up or out" policy; that is, consultants either get promoted with their cohort or have to leave the firm.

The up or out policy corresponds to a rank order tournament in sport. Strategy consulting firms generate internal lists of those who are about to be promoted (based on cohorts according to seniority) and decide who will be promoted first. If consultants miss the two or three time slots for promotion by performing worse than others of the same cohort, they will be asked to leave. An economic reason for implementing such rank order tournaments is that relative performance is easier to measure than absolute performance (Lazear and Rosen 1981). The standards as to what consultants can achieve in a given period of time are uncertain. There is no absolute standard of good versus average contributions. However, the relative performance of consultants is easier to assess, and in strategy consulting firms consultants are evaluated not only by their superiors but also by peers (in a few firms also by subordinates). Hence up or out rules also save the costs of carrying out performance evaluations, because these assessments would have to be much more detailed than if the up or out rules were not in place (Milgrom and Roberts 1992: 382).

In a different vein, Kahn and Huberman (1988) argue that, without an up or out policy, firms would have an incentive to justify a low retention wage and thus to claim that an employee exhibits low productivity. This would result in a low incentive for the employee to invest in firm-specific capital. An up or out contract, by contrast, would eliminate the firm's incentive to claim that the employee is of low productivity, and the employee has a strong incentive to invest in firm-specific capital. Waldman (1990) adds an important analysis based on signaling theory. The retention decision serves as a signal of an employee's productivity and thus helps reduce the information asymmetry between firms about employee performance. This results in an incentive for employees to invest in *general* human capital, for not only the direct employer but also other firms gain information about performance through the signaling effect that a retention decision entails. Kahn and Huberman's prior argument, therefore, is not limited to investment in specific human capital but extends to the general human capital case.

From a signaling viewpoint is must be added that the up or out tournament itself, in an environment in which client firms have not adopted this promotion policy, is an important signal of consulting quality. The retained consultants, so the environment assumes, represent an elite's elite. In addition, a self-selection mechanism applies. Those consultants who do not think to have a chance in the up or out competition will soon seek employment in other firms.

This signaling mechanism may even be stronger than the selection mechanism itself (similar to personnel selection; see above). Up or out policies are usually handled in a much less rigid way than the term suggests. Due to self-selection, very few consultants really need to be asked to leave, and, even in these rare cases, they are aided by placement services and usually given infinite time to find new employment. But, regardless of how rigidly or how liberally it is handled internally, it signals and fosters the image of a meritocracy. The signaling mechanism works because, for consulting firms of lower status, up or out rules would have damaging consequences. Lower-status consulting firms do not have an ample supply of applicants, and losing employees because they are not up to promotion would mean to lose the returns they bring in at the lower level. Asking those consultants to leave who perform well at a junior level but are not qualified for a higher level would be very costly for these firms.

The difficulties in measuring absolute performance in combination with the rank order tournament in consulting firms leads to the so-called "rat race" phenomenon (Akerlof 1976). Management consultants often work eighty hours a week or more, which means they stay at work until late many nights a week, sacrificing their social lives and sometimes jeopardizing their health (see chapter 4). The extra output of the long hours might be low, but, since performance output is difficult to measure, input in the form of long hours represents a proxy performance indicator that consultants can influence. The incentive to engage in a rat race is particularly high at the beginning of a career, because this is the time of greatest performance uncertainty. The longer a consultant works in the firm the more certainty his or her environment gains about his or her output (and the more the performance can be measured by the revenue it brings in), and the less he or she needs to supplement the evaluation by the input of long hours (Milgrom and Roberts 1992: 372).

While junior consultants are involved in the rat race, promotion to partner level ultimately depends on a measurable variable: the revenue that a senior consultant brings in. As pointed out in chapter 3, trust relations to clients, involvement in networks, and being referred between clients are central mechanisms in this context. This raises the questions of whether particular kinds of consultants are more likely than others to perform in this network kind of business.

The educational background has become less important in this context. While MBAs or economists still represent the majority of management consultants, the top consultancies in particular have increasingly hired physicists or life scientists. Once they have entered a consulting firm the educational background becomes unimportant from a practical point of view, and the performance evaluations within the firm take center stage. The predictive validity of the educational background for the speed or ultimate level of promotion is low. For example, the current head of McKinsey's German office holds a doctoral degree in physics.

However, another variable does continue to have a certain predictive validity for careers in consultancy: gender. As in many other business sectors, women have considerable difficulties in getting promoted, especially to the partner level. Hördt (2002) was able to gather personnel data from ten strategy consulting firms in Germany. She concludes that the number of female consultants at the lowest hierarchical levels (business analyst to consultant) varies between nearly 0 percent and 40 percent (mean 20 percent), while it varies at the highest levels (senior project manager to senior partner) between 0 percent and 10 percent, with a mean of 2.5 percent.

Economic models of discrimination typically refer to either taste-based or statistical discrimination. Starting with Becker's (1957) doctoral dissertation, taste-based discrimination in the labor market means that employers choose not to employ (or pay less to) a particular group as a matter of taste, without productivity differences between groups. Becker's analysis shows that, if the number of prejudiced employers is sufficiently large, a wage difference between the appreciated and the unappreciated groups arises and persists. In such a partial equilibrium, minority employees must compensate employers either by being more productive or by accepting a lower salary for equivalent productivity. By contrast, in a full equilibrium in which the number of non-discriminating employers is large enough, non-prejudiced employers will have a competitive advantage and discrimination will diminish. Prejudiced employers may still not employ minorities or women, but the competitive advantage of non-discriminating employers compensates for wage differentials. In other words, in Becker's model, discrimination is considered irrational and is expected to be eliminated by market forces. If there are no actual productivity gaps between groups then a functioning market is considered the best remedy against discrimination.

Statistical discrimination (Phelps 1972; Arrow 1973) occurs when employers use observable characteristics, such as gender or race, to infer unobservable ones, such as the future productivity of job applicants. Firms have limited information about the skills and future performance of job applicants, which is why they draw on (perceived or actual) group-specific means of productivity (e.g. gender or an ethnic group) as signals of applicant productivity. Group-specific means of productivity may, for example, occur on the basis of educational differences. Unlike taste-based discrimination, statistical discrimination is not diminished by market forces (Phelps 1972; Arrow 1973). Rather, it is a result of employers' rational efforts to minimize the information costs of hiring decisions, rather than a result of taste or mass conspiracy.

Spence's (1974) signaling model of discrimination argues that employer prejudices generate self-fulfilling prophecies that reinforce stereotypes. For example, if one group (such as an ethnic minority) thinks that the returns on educational investments are lower than for other groups, the members of this group invest less in education. Employees of the disadvantaged group have to bear the costs of signaling future productivity. This reduces the incentives for the members of the group to pursue such a career and to make educational investments in this direction. This way the beliefs of the employer and the resulting signaling costs become self-fulfilling.

This can easily be applied to management consultancy. If women think that they have greater difficulties in becoming partners in a consultancy firm, they invest less in a consulting career, which may feed back on their performance. The fact that they have greater career difficulties than their male colleagues may also be a result of market forces and represent a case of customer discrimination (Holzer and Ihlanfeldt 1998). If clients expect to see a male consultant, or if client networks are male-dominated, then female consultants may have greater career difficulties even though there is no taste-based discrimination or mass conspiracy in consulting firms. Rather, statistical discrimination may apply, because, in a male client context, female consultants may objectively bring in less revenue than their male colleagues. This is because it is more difficult to connect with and create trust in people of the other gender. Thus, in the consulting market we may have a case of taste-based *or* statistical discrimination by clients, resulting in statistical discrimination by consulting firms. Indeed, from a sociological viewpoint, there may well be two reasons for women's career difficulties in consultancy: an embeddedness-related and a neoinstitutional one.

Sociological accounts of career differences

Embeddedness effects and the careers of female consultants

The gender literature on management and organizations refers not only to patriarchy (the dominance of older men) but also to "fratriarchy" (the dominance of male networks) or "homosociality" (Williams 1991; Mills and Tancred 1992; Karsten 1993; Alvesson and Due Billing 1998; Danieli *et al.* 2003). In a fratriarchy, the exclusion of women is based on a rejection of the values and behavior ascribed to women. Men's accustomed manners and interaction create certainty and security among other men, while types of behavior that men perceive as typically female are considered less productive (Wajcman 1998; Rees 2004).

Clients, especially top executives, are mostly men, and, based on the insights of gender research, they are more at ease with male consultants. Female consultants do not deal with peer effects and homosociality in the same way and thus have greater difficulties in establishing trust relations or being involved in networks. The social interaction between the genders is more difficult and laden with more uncertainties than among men. Consultants express it as follows:

Perhaps both [men and women] have the problem of not finding the right level of communication [with the other gender], I'd say. They [male clients] are more accustomed to talk about their business with men. [...] It really is the case that interaction [with women] is more awkward, and you recognize it in the little details that interaction is a bit bumpy (male consultant).[1]

It's their own language that they speak at that [client executive] level, even in terms of gestures. [...] I'd say, if you look at these levels, there are no female CEOs, as far as I know, and if they [male CEOs] are your contacts at the partner or director level then you are again on your own as a woman (female consultant).

Familiar behavior patterns and clear-cut interaction among people of the same gender are preferred to interaction between the genders. Shared ways of communicating and accustomed patterns of behavior facilitate cooperation and create a feeling of commonality and certainty. Analytical tasks may then be passed on to those who act in the same way and are similar to those in charge, for familiar behavior is considered more competent behavior (Wajcman 1998; Rees 2004). For women, then, a big challenge is the "comfort factor" of men. Male clients must feel comfortable and at ease in the presence of highly qualified women.

In addition, female consultants have greater difficulties with meeting clients in a nonbusiness way, for in senior positions client–consultant relations often extend to dinners and semi-private interactions. Women cannot readily initiate such activity, because male clients may misinterpret this as an advance with a sexual element. The following statements illustrate this:

There [at levels at which acquisition is the central issue] you talk to people about their business and often over dinner or whatever. [...] [A]nd in this phase I'd say it is again the case that women perhaps have a slightly harder time, because it's just not commonplace to ask a client, "How about having dinner tonight?" or something like that (female consultant).

---

[1] I would like to thank Judith Eichner, who conducted the interviews cited in this section in the context of her diploma thesis, which I initiated and supervised. She gained access to female consultants in a way that would have been difficult for me as a man. The interviews were conducted in German; translations, interpretations, and the selection of quotes are mine.

And when I observe [a male consulting colleague and friend] ... it is perhaps a bit more easy and relaxed between his client and him, and they really go out then and have a drink together or get drunk together. I would never do that (female consultant).

Thus, a female consultant cannot easily meet a male client for dinner or for a beer because there is always the worry that the intention behind the meeting might be misunderstood. She has to find alternative solutions for nurturing her network, such as meetings for breakfast or visiting the theater along with the respective partner (this was a suggestion from a female consultant). But, even then, such meetings cannot be expected to be as casual and informal as between men. Even if a female consultant is objectively better in terms of analytical or industry expertise, a male colleague may find it easier to win contracts. Again, therefore, embeddedness effects limit economic efficiency.

Sociological neoinstitutionalism and the careers of female consultants

Based on sociological neoinstitutionalism, another component comes into play: the signaling effect of rationality and emotion-free professionalism to clients and the business community. Both the actual analyses by consulting firms and their aura of expertise and rationality represent important assets. For consulting firms this means that their individual consultants must symbolize and embody this aura. Neutrality, unemotionality, and professionalism are conveyed, among others, through a homogeneous appearance, and women are potentially considered as unusual in this context (Karsten 1993; Alvesson and Due Billing 1998; Danieli *et al.* 2003).

When the question on gender differences is posed, female as well as male consultants commonly emphasize that clients reckon with male consultants and that women have a more difficult task in this respect. Typical statements in this context are the following ones:

You arrive at a client and he has a certain expectation. He mostly expects a man (female consultant).

I'd say, it is just as difficult for them [women in consultancy] as it is for clients – they really expect men. Now, the image tends always to be a bit like: "Now the tough consultants are coming," and, when a woman comes along, then this is certainly... [gesture; pause]. I have noticed that several times (male consultant).

When the consultants arrive and there are some women in the team, the client is to some extent surprised and skeptical, their performance is more critically observed, and the tolerance of error may be smaller. Jay Berry (1995, 1996), one of the few consultants who has been a director at more than one large strategy consulting firm in the United States, has made the same observations, and claims that the difficulties of female consultants are multiplied. "Not only does she have to overcome those barriers within her own firm, but also she must overcome them in the client's with whom her firm works" (Berry 1996: 35). And Larwood and Gattiker (1985: 12) observe: "Clients generally prefer to work with male consultants and feel they will obtain better advice from a male. The males are expected to gain rapport more readily with others, and their thoughts are believed more likely to be accepted." For the promotion mechanisms under consideration here, we can discern that the association of rationality with men and of intuition with women – independent of whether they apply or not – can be detrimental for women in consultancy. The market demands rationality and objectivity, and men are more associated with these institutions.

Ignoring the self-selection that accounts for much of the fact that there is a smaller percentage of women than men in consultancy, at the beginning of a career the difficulties of women are less apparent. In the first two years, when spreadsheet calculations and analytical accomplishments take center stage, there may be no noticeable differences between the genders. Female consultants may even have advantages in gathering information at the client firm, as clients may consider them less threatening and be more open to them than to men. However, the higher the level in the consulting firm the more project acquisition rather than data analysis comes to the fore, and female consultants are increasingly exposed to client images of rationality and objectivity. A male consultant puts it most provocatively:

If at some point she reaches that stage [senior project manager], just below the partner level, then the criterion is "sales." And if she doesn't sell anything, then she doesn't sell anything. [...] And if this is because the client would rather have a man as a contact person, then we are at a different level. [...] When at the end of the day she is not well received by the client, this is simply a disadvantage, and then she gets fired (male consultant).

This consultant is talking about customer discrimination, but the forceful tone of his statement indicates that statistical discrimination may also apply. Whether the reason be an objective, external lack of acceptance (which the consultant suggests) or an internal prejudice that "women just can't sell" (which can be read between the lines of his statement), in both cases women have to bear the consequences.

Discussion

When highly qualified women with analytical expertise and consulting experience do not get promoted as rapidly as men and leave the firm, this should in principle be a matter of concern for consulting firms. The official position of management consultancies is that women are more than welcome. The lower proportion of female consultants at the entry level can to an extent be attributed to the lower number of female applicants. It would appear that self-selection takes place when university graduates apply, and women may tend to consider a career in consultancy to be less compatible with their professional and private plans. In the last few years in particular the top consulting firms have increasingly tried to recruit female graduates. Large strategy firms have published recruitment advertisements and explicitly invited female graduates to apply. In these ads, women are promised fascinating work content and excellent promotion prospects. The official position of consulting firms is that the criteria of performance evaluation are gender-independent, and that those women who leave the firm before reaching middle or top consulting positions have either underperformed in the up or out system or are leaving for private reasons. However, this either underestimates or ignores the effects of statistical discrimination and customer discrimination outlined above, resulting in self-selection by women before a consulting career is chosen or before engaging in the competition for partnership.

Nevertheless, as long as male consultants have objective advantages in gaining clients and generating revenue, for reasons of taste-based or statistical customer discrimination, the lack of women in top positions is economically not worrisome for consultancies. Consulting firms are profit-oriented and must promote those who are best able to develop a clientele. If women are structurally disadvantaged in terms of representing rationality and in terms of networking, then convincing clients that women can do an equally good consulting job would involve high costs. Statistical discrimination of women is the consequence.

This does not exculpate consulting firms from equal opportunities and affirmative action policies, but it does mean that, in the given societal environment, upholding these policies is costly. Window dressing, as sociological neoinstitutionalism suggests, is the logical consequence. If "being on the safe side" regarding project acquisition means sending men to the client then consulting firms will do that. Aigner and Cain (1977) have analyzed employers' risk aversion from an economics of discrimination viewpoint. In consulting firms, the risk of not winning a contract because a client is less comfortable with women, is one that cannot be taken. Whether client uneasiness with women is actual or presumed, in either case women would have to disprove the assumptions and experience higher signaling costs.

In summary, the careers of female consultants can be divided into two phases, with an approximate separation at the project manager level. Up to that point, promotions are largely equal between men and women. Analytical work predominates and performance evaluations operate accordingly. However, around the project manager level there is a glass ceiling. Representing the consulting firm to the outside entails being exposed to assumptions and perceptions in client industries. A woman will probably not be passed over in partnership decisions if her sales figures demonstrate her performance. But achieving growth figures is more difficult for women than it is for men, or possible only in client industries or corporate functions that employ more women. In other words – and this is the essence of statistical discrimination – consulting firms act rationally when they do not promote women in the same way as men, and female consultants act rationally if they leave the firm before engaging in a promotion tournament in which they have structurally worse opportunities.

Client industries in which there is usually a higher proportion of women are consumer goods and media; and typical functions are human resource management and marketing. A testable hypothesis, then, would be that female consultants are over-represented in consulting projects of this kind. Data to test this hypothesis are mostly confidential and hard to obtain. Industries in which women are under-represented and have a harder time are the automotive and automotive supply industry, the building industry, finance, energy and utilities, steel, and the chemical industry. Thus, management consulting firms are likely to reproduce this labor segregation between men and women. The question as to why there is no outcry from consulting firms about the lack of women in top consulting positions has economic reasons based on sociological phenomena.

PART III

Conclusions

10 | *The knowledge economy, management consultancy, and the multitheoretical approach*

The knowledge economy and management consultancy

The economic shifts of the past thirty years have been considerable. What Drucker (1969), Bell (1973), Gouldner (1979), Stanback (1979) and Stanback *et al.* (1981) realized around the 1970s, namely the rise of the knowledge economy and the trend toward service work, has grown even more since the 1980s and 1990s. In the industrialized countries, the growth rates of exports and FDI have dwarfed that of GDP (see chapter 2). In conjunction with the development of information technology and the decreasing costs of communication and transport, this means that the conditions of production have changed drastically between the 1970s and today. Moreover, the growth of intra-industry trade indicates that, in comparison to the 1970s, today the production of a good is preceded by a much higher magnitude of trade. Parts and half-finished products are manufactured at many more locations than thirty years ago. This change of production conditions has been paralleled by the increased mobility of finance, the liberalization of markets, and the privatization of formerly public institutions. These developments have forced industry, trade, and financial institutions to review their strategy, organization, and IT in increasingly shorter cycles. Those services that economize on scale and scope regarding aperiodical or one-off changes for client firms have capitalized on these changes and benefitted accordingly (chapter 2). Knowledge in the form of information-gathering techniques, cognitive abstractions, and analytical procedures became the currency of growth, and the first signs and predictions around the 1970s turned out to be anticipatory and clear-sighted (for more recent analyses, see Stehr 1994; Cortada 1998; Neef 1998; Neef *et al.* 1998; and Stehr and Meja 2005).

At the same time, these developments signified another change. While knowledge has become a central competitive advantage for firms, its rise in importance has also rendered economic action more uncertain. Spot exchange has increasingly given way to transactions of experience and credence goods, and information asymmetry and quality uncertainty accompany the exchange of goods and services. Management consultancy is a case in point. Consultants provide the cognitive abstractions and analyses that clients demand in the knowledge economy. At the same time, consulting services themselves exhibit experience and credence good features and carry quality uncertainty. In this way, management consultancy fully embodies the changes that have occurred over the past decades, and the informal institutions that connect supply and demand (chapter 3) reflect them.

As mentioned in the preface, the literature on the knowledge society and economy tends to concentrate on the rise of knowledge workers as a general phenomenon and often abstracts from differences between them. This book has sought to specify management consultancy as a particular phenomenon. I have sketched some exemplary differences between biotechnology and management consultancy and argued that this called for a different use of theories. While both biotech researchers and management consultants are typical cases of knowledge workers, biotechnology is research-intensive while consultancy is customer-driven. If biotechnology brings about a marketable result then it is a fairly tangible product, whereas the results of consulting services are mostly intangible (apart from IT and financial consulting). In addition, management consultancy is a more stratified market than biotechnology, and more beset with symbolic resources.

These features have impacts on the market mechanisms. In both industries, access to talented human resources constitutes a bottleneck to success. In consultancy, though, this has a stronger symbolic component than in biotechnology. Moreover, it is access to clients, rather than to research resources via cooperating firms or universities, that represents the challenge. This makes cooperation among consulting firms a contradiction to the ambitions of individual providers, in addition to the fact that intangible products render the information costs of monitoring cooperation partners high. Finally, the stratified nature of the consulting market makes any association with other firms more complicated in terms of status differences, while the less stratified nature of the biotechnology market means that cooperation can focus on complementary knowledge. As a result, in the biotech sector inter-firm cooperation is not only a transitional stage but a significant organizational practice of mature firms (Koput and Powell 2000), and biotechnology represents a perfect case for the application of embeddedness theory. Understanding the mechanisms of the management consultancy market, by contrast, calls for more theories.

I have suggested that transaction cost economics, embeddedness theory, signaling theory, and sociological neoinstitutionalism represent the available tools for this purpose. Transaction cost economics outlines the costs that calculative dealing with quality uncertainty involves. Embeddedness theory addresses the intangible benefits and drawbacks of social ties as well as the limits of calculative cost considerations. Signaling theory looks at the costs of signaling quality under conditions of information asymmetry and quality uncertainty. Sociological neoinstitutionalism looks at the increased needs to certify or legitimize management decisions, requiring cognitive abstractions and symbolic resources. Chapter 1 has compared these theories with regard to their basic views on the consulting market and pointed out their differences and areas where they agree. As a central element, regarding the debate on theory incommensurability, chapter 1 has looked at critical rationalism and argued that the point is not to integrate different theories artificially but to use them as tools to check and correct each other. This notion has underpinned the subsequent analysis of market mechanisms and individual consultancy topics.

Part I has looked at the mechanisms of the consulting market. Chapter 2 outlined the reasons consulting firms exist and why this service sector grows. It first presented a transaction cost account and then outlined other causes for the rise in demand over the past three decades. Chapter 2 suggested that, regarding the growth of consultancy, economic and sociological accounts complement each other and do not necessarily represent contradictions.

Chapter 3 introduced the sources of quality uncertainty for clients in terms of institutional and transactional uncertainty, and then outlined the various institutions that bridge clients' uncertainty: public reputation, experience-based personal trust, and networked reputation. The price of consulting services, especially the fees per day and per consultant, was discussed as another market mechanism. Chapter 4 looked at another issue that is important for understanding the consulting market: power relations between clients and consultants. While much of the critical literature on management consulting portrays consultants as powerful actors, chapter 4 argued that consultancy is a buyer's market, in which client authority prevails and social institutions bridge quality uncertainty and preclude short-term opportunistic behavior by consultants.

Chapter 5 looked at the relationship between internal and external consulting. Depending on the frequency and expected similarity of tasks, an internal consultancy may under certain circumstances be more economical than external consultants. However, signaling effects account for self-selection mechanisms among job applicants and for better human resources in external consulting firms. Moreover, internal consultancies do not have the same certification effect as external advisors, and in many cases the quality of social relations makes the difference of whether clients prefer internal or external providers.

Part II looked at the drivers of managing consulting firms. Chapter 6 focused on the relationships between strategy and organization consultancy, IT consultancy, and accounting firms. From an economic viewpoint, the expansion of accounting firms into IT and strategy consulting is a typical case of related diversification. Potential clients lower their transaction costs when buying different services from known providers. Furthermore, the more accountancy became IT-based in the 1980s the more related that diversification into IT consultancy became. Strategy and organization consultancy, by contrast, could not take advantage of related diversification because it was less connected to IT and because status dissimilarity involved reputation risks. Tapping into IT consulting would have represented a step down in an institutionalized market hierarchy.

Chapter 7 analyzed the marketing behavior of management consulting firms. Rooted in the market mechanisms outlined in Part I, four clusters of consulting firms have been identified in terms of marketing approaches: marketing refusers, direct marketers, publicists, and marketing "champions." Although marketing champions could have been expected to achieve the highest growth rates, no significant growth difference from the other clusters could be identified. It was concluded that consulting firms grow on the basis of factors that are difficult to influence by marketing tools: clients' trust, based on increasing quality certainty, and their recommendations to other firms.

Chapter 8 looked at the internal management of consulting firms, especially to governance mechanisms, organizational structure, and knowledge management. Consulting firms focus on those tasks and activities that require not only analytical capabilities but also information from different sources across firms, industries, and regions. They seek to adopt an organizational structure and knowledge management principles that enable and foster a fast exchange of information. The use of information technology and the encouragement of firm-internal personal contacts take center stage. Active document management allows not only for the speedy retrieval of insights from other cases and projects but also – as the authors' names are on the documents – for contacts to be established quickly with those colleagues who have worked on related topics beforehand. Moreover, consulting firms try to promote weak ties and information exchange between different projects and regions. Cross-staffing, the one-firm principle, and competence centers are the means in this context, but turf creation, status differences among consulting staff, and embedded ties within the firm limit the free exchange of information.

Chapter 9 turned to the human resource aspects of the leading consulting firms. It first looked at the way consulting firms select personnel, and then at their promotion mechanisms. The case-study-based procedures of personnel selection have a strong symbolic component, namely the signaling effect of consulting quality and the fostering of an analytical elite status in the knowledge society. As far as promotion mechanisms are concerned, chapter 9 reiterated that the quality of social relations between clients and consultants plays a major role in assignment decisions, and that consulting firms must represent rationality and dispassion. This explains why women have considerable career difficulties in management consulting. While at the lower ranks they can still excel with sharp analyses, at the higher levels they are unable to build on homosociality and have greater difficulty in building trust relations to clients. Regarding both personnel selection and career discrimination, it is concluded that economic and sociological insights are interwoven.

Economics and sociology: paradigms, methods, or jargon?

The stakes are high in the relationship between theories, especially those from such different camps as economics and sociology. Economists are often convinced that they work in a conceptually and methodologically superior way, and sometimes have a clichéd image of sociologists as imprecise do-gooders who write wordy texts rather than analyzing things in detail. Sociologists, by contrast, are convinced that they are at the forefront of great insights, and sometimes have the clichéd image of economists as being so divorced from reality that they engage in debates over methodological particulars that have little to do with what is "out there," or as applied statisticians who build mathematically sophisticated models that lack meaningful variables. The mutually held clichés indicate that the academic disciplines are often internalized, and shape the identities of scholars. W. O. Coleman (2002) has analyzed the assumptions, identities, and errors of anti-economists perfectly, and a similar book could be written about anti-sociologists (for this discussion, see also Hirsch *et al.* 1990 and Smelser and Swedberg 1994).

However, attending to only one discipline has more than psychological reasons. In fact, and paradoxically, it can be explained by means of sociology and economics. Sociologically, the academic disciplines have institutionalized to such an extent that working beyond their boundaries generates considerable legitimation problems. Institutions operate normatively and shape the convictions of what is considered good science. As a result, academics either remain within their particular discipline or apply their methods to topics that were formerly the province of other disciplines. The latter approach enhances mutual checks and thus scientific knowledge, but would benefit from greater familiarity with the other camp's language and arguments. Moreover, academics, especially younger ones, are typically embedded in scholarly networks, and address a particular community as an academic audience. Even if they are interested in other theories, their strong and weak ties in the academic community often limit their exposure and possibilities (Becher and Trowler 2001).

An economic reason for working on the basis of only one discipline is that it saves much in terms of information and transaction costs. These costs occur in making oneself familiar with other disciplines or theories, because it takes time to read books, to contemplate how the information can be used for one's analyses, to interact with other scholars, to get involved with additional scientific communities, etc. Apart from this economics of attention and information, for younger individuals the central signal for future scholarly productivity is to have a few early publications in academic journals. Journal articles need to be relatively short, and academic journals are typically specialized or have theoretical preferences. Producing a job market signal at low costs means producing a concise piece of data analysis on the basis of a single theory. Hence, the more one specializes at an early stage of one's career the lower the costs of producing the job market signal. This signaling mechanism operates "efficiently" if the sheer quantity of publications is taken as the variable of academic productivity – even if the result for the academic landscape is detrimental. As a consequence it is economically rational to work with one theory only and to abstain from cross-disciplinary work.

The tragedy is not some assumed superiority of one or other discipline – a certain amount of pride rightly belongs to each professional group – but the lack of institutions and incentives to render cross-fertilization more likely. Burt (2004) shows how good ideas are created by those who have access to other networks. Although investigated in a business rather than academic context, his results seem equally relevant for the latter.

We specialize by method, theory, and topic. It is impossible to keep up with developments in other specialties. It would be inefficient even if it were possible. So there is a market for information arbitrage of network entrepreneurs, and the evidence of their work is that valuable new ideas in any one specialty are often a familiar concept in some distant specialty. Across the clusters in an organization or market, creativity is a diffusion process of repeated discovery in which a good idea is carried across structural holes to be discovered in one cluster of people, rediscovered in another, then rediscovered in still others – and each discovery is no less an experience of creativity for people encountering the good idea. Thus, value accumulates as an idea moves through the social structure; each transmission from one group to another has the potential to add value. In this light, there is an incentive to define work situations such that people are forced to engage diverse ideas (Burt 2004: 389).

We can easily find examples where economics and sociology present complementary insights that add up to a more comprehensive view (see chapter 2 on the growth of consultancy), and examples where cross-fertilization between economics and sociology has taken place. The notions and relevance of networks, and organizational culture, were analyzed first in sociology before being taken up in economics, while rational choice is the most obvious example that traveled in the opposite direction. Cooperation has been analyzed by both, and it is hard to say which discipline was first.

From this viewpoint, economics and sociology represent networks or clusters of scholars rather than paradigms. But proponents of incommensurability refer to ontological or epistemological notions rather than to networks. They claim that if theories are based on different ontological, epistemological, or methodological assumptions then they form "paradigms" and are mutually exclusive (Burrell and Morgan 1979; Jackson and Carter 1991). With regard to management consultancy, they may refer to the degree of calculativeness. For example, signaling theory is based on the assumption of calculativeness, while sociological neoinstitutionalism tends to sneak agency in (see chapters 1 and 9). The argument of incommensurability proponents is that one first needs to agree about such issues and terms before one can find a common language for cross-fertilization. To this, however, there is a powerful answer from the viewpoint of critical rationalism, as outlined in chapter 1. If one expects others to agree about ontological assumptions, then one is already trying to render one's viewpoint immune to critique. For example, personnel selection in management consulting has at least two functions: acquiring the appropriate human resources capable of performing cognitive abstractions, and signaling quality to the business community through a particularly selective procedure focusing on quantitative skills. While the former is fully intentional, the latter's intentionality is questionable. It would require research to ascertain the extent to which consultants selecting applicants are aware of it, and it might turn out that consultants differ substantially in this regard.

The point of different approaches is that ontological and epistemological assumptions can be questioned from other viewpoints, and this is a far cry from demanding theories to merge or agree. Critical rationalism suggests at least two reasons for rejecting the doctrine of incommensurability.

(1) Mutual critique represents the basis for scientific progress, even the mutual critique between different ontological, epistemological, or methodological assumptions. Empirical phenomena do not change from one framework to another. Different frameworks conceptualize a phenomenon on different bases, but these bases can criticize each other and thus nurture the understanding of an

empirical phenomenon and foster scientific progress. The rational discussion of disagreements, without expecting theories to agree ultimately, leads to insights into empirical phenomena.

(2) The doctrine of paradigm incommensurability is wrong in its assumption that communication or mutual understanding between ontological or epistemological assumptions is impossible. Rather, communicating between them is like learning a different language: it is difficult but not impossible. Empirical phenomena often have more than one cause or trigger. Theories are limited in their scope, however, and can only encapsulate elements of a phenomenon, not the totality. Referring to more than one theory opens the eyes to aspects that an individual theory cannot see, and allows for a more encompassing or more precise view.

The central point is the mutual critique of theories. It is precisely because of the fact that they are based on different assumptions or methods, not in spite of it, that theories can foster scientific progress by operating as institutionalized checks and balances against each other. An argument of mutual exclusivity would be based on the assumption that empirical phenomena change from one framework to another. But this is a relativistic viewpoint. At least the mechanisms of the consulting market do not change according to the theory used for their explanation. Clients and consultants act, and institutions emerge, without their awareness of scientific theories.

Again, as outlined in chapter 1 with reference to Popper (1994), this does not mean that theories need to agree or must be integrated. On the contrary, to call for agreement, or even a merger of disciplines or theories, would mean calling for a utopia. In the preface I mentioned Akerlof's (interview with Akerlof in Swedberg 1990: 70) call for greater integration between economics and sociology. More precisely, he feels that many articles he reviews for scientific journals do not manage to merge A and B into C, but remain A + B or B + A. Akerlof thus expresses this dream that critical rationalism rejects. If A and B are able to criticize or complement each other, there is no need to make them agree or integrate artificially. Their mutual checks and critique are more important for scientific progress. Indeed, a reminder of the critical-rational call for the mutual critique of theories, rather than either considering them incommensurable or demanding that they integrate, may represent a way forward for economics and sociology.

Economists may insist that most sociological insights can be incorporated into economics language and methods. For example, the sociological reasons of increasing needs for network forms of organization and increasing needs for the certification of management decisions can be expressed as an economics of social networks (e.g. Montgomery 1991; Lazerson 1993; Bertrand *et al.* 2000) or as an economics of certification (e.g. Franck *et al.* 2004). This application of the language of economics to formerly sociological problems does not contradict the critical-rational notion of mutual critique and correction. Using new language or methods is not immune to critique from the sociological side and is, therefore, compatible with the critical-rational notions above. The flexibility of economics that Williamson (interview with Williamson in Swedberg 1990: 122) mentions, and probably also economists' better access to financial resources, place economics in an advantageous position and puts sociology on the defensive. But sociology will not be replaced by economics. The reality checks that sociology provides, the limits to efficiency and rationality that economists do not see on their own, and the methodological critique all represent checks on economics and drive the frontier on insights. Even if economists are convinced that they are methodologically stronger, ignorance of sociology and other disciplines would lead to stasis in their discipline.

We can again refer to the example of signaling theory and sociological neoinstitutionalism. Signaling theory is rooted in economics in that it assumes a deliberate production of signals by economic actors in order to indicate human capabilities or service quality. However, implicitly it is also rooted in sociology, because such signals only work and succeed in a given set of norms and customs, which may emerge without intentionality. Deliberate signaling acts may only operate efficiently in a broader institutionalized context in which these signals indicate quality and provide legitimacy. Through the sociological neoinstitutional lens, it is equally important, or even more insightful, to look at the emergence of these institutions rather than at the behavior of actors within them. More significantly, neoinstitutionalism looks at the inefficiencies that signaling mechanisms incur, such as a decoupling between signals and actual practice. Vice versa, the persistence of institutions may be a result of continuous, deliberate signaling acts, as Giddens's (1984) structuration approach would also suggest. This makes sociological neoinstitution-alists see that deliberate signaling acts enable or reinforce the persistence of non-intentional institutionalization.

The relationship between transaction cost theory and embeddedness theory is another example. Even if it is possible to model clients' reluctance to switch provider based on information and transaction costs, or costs incurred by irritating relationships to third parties, this already assumes that clients conduct such deliberations. But social tie quality and the web of mutual obligations may hamper or even preclude the activation of tie reconsiderations. The point is that, in reality, market transactions do not always obey one or other of the alternative theories and their assumptions. There is no predetermined, true client–consultant relationship in which either the assumptions of transaction cost economics or of embeddedness theory apply. A small change in the circumstances may result in a new situation and different behavior by the market participants. An embedded relationship may be reconsidered and turn into a vague utility function. Even though the quality of a social tie may still be perfectly acceptable the client may already be considering alternatives. The reverse process is equally conceivable. In the process of selecting among arm's-length providers, a client may find a personal match with one of the prospective providers and politely terminate the selection process – a process of satisficing, as March (1994) would call it. Alternatively, a client may advertise a project for bids and examine the applying consulting firms in a beauty contest, yet in the end select those to whom there was a preexisting social tie, or one emerged in the selection process. This choice may then *ex post* be modeled as anticipated savings on monitoring, enforcement, and contract adjustment costs, but one cannot assume by default that it was these cost considerations that made the difference. The central insight of embeddedness theory is that calculative decision-making processes may be constrained by the influence of personal match, strong ties, and word-of-mouth recommendations.

In summary, economics and sociology often represent different methods and jargons, and if some scholars choose to label different ontological or epistemological assumptions as "paradigms" there is no problem with this. But it does not render them immune to critique from other "paradigms." Scientific progress is achieved not just by working within the boundaries of one approach but also, or in particular, from the mutual critique between them. Multitheoretical approaches have contributions to make: to clarify and explain empirical phenomena — and to clarify the theories themselves. The contours of a theory, its strengths and weaknesses, emerge only in comparison to others, and with this awareness of the benefits and limits of theories we learn more about the subjects they seek to explain than by using only a single theory. Once the language of another theory has been learned, scholars recognize the limits of their own approach and gain further interpretive capacities for empirical results. Theories gain rather than lose clarity when other theories are taken into account. While lip service is constantly paid to the need for cross-fertilization, chances are that, in the current institutional structure, scholars will be punished for putting it into practice. As Burt's (2004) research suggests, academia pays a high price for this. The essence of both Burt's insights and of critical rationalism is that academia needs to improve the institutional structure and incentives such that cross-disciplinary work becomes easier and less costly to pursue.

Theoretical extensions and future research options

In places in the book I have referred, in passing, to game theory as a useful extension. This is related to the notion of trust, as outlined in chapters 1 and 3. According to game theory, a party offers cooperation as a specific investment when he or she reckons with rents if cooperation is reciprocated or with somewhat lower costs if not. The other party, the decision-maker, reciprocates cooperation if it involves advantages (von Neumann and Morgenstern 1944; Fudenberg and Tirole 1991; Axelrod 1984; Raub and Weesie 1990; Kreps 1991). The result is mutual abstaining from short-term opportunism and an increasing mutual belief in the other's cooperation, which could be labeled trust. Even reputation then emerges as a result of iterated games of calculative refraining from monitoring (Raub and Weesie 1990). Hence, economists are perfectly able to model cooperating and gaining a reputation as a fair player as a result of calculative behavior (Ripperger 1998; Axelrod 1984).

Glückler's (2005, 2006) results are interesting in this context. In his interviews with consultants and clients in London, Frankfurt, and Madrid, both clients and consultants enthusiastically referred to "trust" as the fundamental feature of their relationships with transaction partners. After further enquiry, however, it turns out that clients and consultants use the same term for at least two different types of trust, and at least one type is clearly based on calculation. Based on Barber's (1983) notions, Glückler (2005) distinguishes between competence trust and goodwill trust. Competence trust refers to the expectation that someone has the capabilities to fulfill a task; goodwill trust refers to the expectation that someone will not behave opportunistically. The first kind refers to clients' expectation that the consultant will do a good job, and, based on repeated fulfillment of this expectation, competence trust evolves. Glückler (2005, 2006) finds that this kind of competence trust is little more than performance expectation. If a consultant does not meet the client's expectations, then what has previously been referred to as trust will soon be withdrawn. Thus, competence trust is only as robust as a consultant's performance, or as a client's performance evaluation. It is calculative, because a client grants this kind of trust only step by step, from project to project. Here is a quote that illustrates this notion:

We never award a large project to strangers. In such cases [if the consultants are new to the firm], we always start with a small project... In large projects you like to resort to acquaintances, and in small projects you are more ready to meet a new partner (client of internal and external consultants).

Typically, clients give consultants more responsible projects and larger budgets in a gradual way, project by project, which represents tit-for-tat behavior as outlined by Axelrod (1984). The application of game theory, with its notion of escalating commitment to cooperation, and higher switching costs the more cooperation has evolved, suggests itself.

Glückler also refers to goodwill (or intrinsic) trust as different from competence trust. It also emerges from mutual experience and is reinforced in gradual progression, but involves intentions and attitudes rather than only performance expectations. Glückler (2005) finds that this kind of trust cannot be engineered but emerges as external to the cooperation. And yet he writes, "[T]his trust was less vulnerable and sensitive to irritations in collaboration. However, the collaboration was ultimately based on economic returns so that intrinsic trust could, of course, not compensate for significant project failures" (Glückler 2005: 1737). Thus, so long as the provider delivers a good service, the personal relations are described by both parties as trustful. If a source of disagreement arises the personal relationship may persist, but the client may keep his or her options open and compare alternatives for the next project.

Another important point is that client—consultant relationships are embedded in webs beyond bilateral relations. Switching provider may irritate other business relations. These circumstances are much more difficult to chart than bilateral cost considerations. However, such webs can be modeled by game theory as webs of reputation built on cooperative behavior (Raub and Weesie 1990; Bienenstock and Bonacich 1993, 1997). Reputation effects on third and fourth parties render models or experimental settings more complex and come up against methodological limits, but they do not preclude the application of game theory. When the sociological notion of relationship strength is taken into account, third-party gossip can again be modeled as a factor of cooperation (Burt and Knez 1996).

There are limits to how far experimental designs or game-theoretical tests to simulate business interactions can be applied to the real world, especially if the tests are conducted with students for reasons of research practicality. Apart from this methodological limitation to game theory, if intrinsic trust is only analytically separate from calculative trust but limits it in practice then we have, again, a sociological constraint to economic efficiency. Moreover, the game-theoretical finding that mutually increasing fairness and reciprocity can replace contract forms of cooperation confirms sociological suggestions and challenges the previous assumptions of the economic camp. A sociological corrective to the game-theoretical model emerges from research on the effect of formal contracts on a mutually escalating commitment to cooperation. For example, Poppo and Zenger (2002) and Klein Woolthuis *et al.* (2005) outline contingencies under which contracts, sometimes taken as signals of distrust, either disturb or encourage the emergence of cooperation. Hence, the possibilities of cross-fertilization do not stop when game theory is applied.

Another emerging field that could evolve into an extension of the four theories applied here is an economics of certification. So far, this has been a topic only in accounting, food quality certification, and other specialties. However, Franck *et al.* (2004) have made an initial attempt to apply it to management consultancy. They outline the costs of hiring a top consulting firm as an investment in the certification of management decisions. The less expensive alternatives are not hiring advice at all, hiring an internal consultancy, or hiring a less expensive, small consulting firm. In the last instance, ex-consultants of top-tier consulting firms may work in a smaller consulting firm and deliver similar consulting quality, but with lower certification effects. The costs of these alternative solutions can be compared to the gains of the certification by a large consulting firm.

This field between sociological neoinstitutionalism and the economics of certification gives rise to another extension. The signaling circle outlined in chapter 1 could be expanded to a full model of a signaling economy. In a signaling economy, the different levels of economic action could be modeled as a series of signaling circles: graduates as seekers and consulting firms as providers of jobs; consulting firms as providers and clients as seekers of certification; and the financial market as a provider of resources to firms where the management has been certified by hiring renowned consulting firms. Extending this scenario, financial institutions may be modeled as providers of loans to graduates for education with high signaling effects. Such a signaling economy would consist of at least two circles.

- A high number of applications to top-tier consulting firms, in conjunction with a rigorous selectivity, leads to a high rejection rate of candidates. This signals elite status and consulting quality (Franck and Pudack 2000; Pudack 2004). Consulting quality leads to clients' willingness to pay premium fees, which enables top-tier consulting firms to pay higher salaries than competitors. This, in turn, leads to a high number of applications and allows top-tier consultancies to be particularly selective.
- The second signaling circle is based on the first one. A client firm that hires a top-tier consulting firm, and puts its advice into practice, signals management quality (Franck *et al.* 2004). The signaling of high management quality leads to a positive capital market reaction – e.g. higher scores at rating agencies, benevolent financial institutions, or optimism by mutual funds. This allows the client firm to obtain capital at lower costs and, in turn, enables it to pay higher fees for advice, for which it can hire top-tier consulting firms.

Arguments of this kind are certainly not unknown to sociology. For example, Stehr (1994: 150–2) outlines the emergence of the symbolic economy as a feature of the knowledge society. It is tempting to extend these signaling mechanisms by another circle, at least in the form of a thought experiment. Credit rating agencies may prefer to give higher scores to those financial institutions that carefully select their borrowers on the basis of signaled management quality. As a result, those financial institutions that can signal management quality by hiring renowned consulting firms may benefit from a positive capital market reaction and gain less costly access to financial resources themselves. In this case they can continue to give better conditions to beneficiaries who signal management quality themselves. As a last step, and here the signaling mechanism would come full circle, financial institutions that benefit from the signaling mechanisms provide less costly loans to students with a prospectively excellent career, fostering their ability and willingness to pay for an expensive "Ivy League" education. A positive signaling effect to clients, in turn, promotes the willingness of top-tier consulting firms to hire the best candidates from top-of-the-range universities.

However, these last steps may overstretch the signaling argument. There is too much friction in the circle, and too many other variables of management quality and rating scores come into play. For example, in times of growth, top-tier consulting firms are in a recruitment frenzy. They do not find enough qualified candidates and need to make tradeoff decisions between compromising on applicant selectivity and turning down projects, and thus revenue, due to a lack of consultants. Overemphasizing the signaling mechanism would mean playing down actors' ability to assess management quality irrespective of human resource or consultancy inputs as proxies. Most importantly, it would overestimate the cost differentials that good versus average providers have to produce a quality signal. In fact, overstretching the signaling circle would merge with an exaggerated version of a sociological neoinstitutional argument – an economy in which agency is oriented totally at institutionalized norms rather than dispassionate calculation.

Nevertheless, the thought experiment points to an important intersection between signaling theory and sociological neoinstitutionalism. For the signaling circles to operate, top-rate business schools do not need to provide an education far superior to non-top-rate business schools; they just need to host better candidates thanks to self-selection. Renowned consulting firms do not always have to provide better consulting quality than less renowned providers, as reputation and self-selection account for better personnel. The signals to the market work in an institutionalized context of established norms — in this case the shared view of top-tier consultancies as elite organizations. This decoupling unites signaling theory and sociological neoinstitutionalism, even though sociological neoinstitutionalism adds a healthy dose of skepticism as to whether the signaling mechanisms lead to an efficient outcome and clear the market (see chapter 1). In any case, this connection of signaling theory and sociological neoinstitutionalism gives rise to considerable research opportunities, not only for the job preferences of university graduates regarding consultancy but also for the work of rating agencies and for the decision-making processes of clients about consulting firms and of financial institutions about borrowers.

Before becoming too enthusiastic about such research opportunities, embeddedness theory emerges, again, as an important corrective. The above signaling circles between consultants, clients, and the capital market tend to assume arm's-length relationships between these entities. In Spence's (1974) signaling models, job market participants (graduates and employers) may indeed be unknown to each other (critical on this assumption: Granovetter 1974). In business relationships, however, many individual actors from the three institutions may know each other pretty well. For example, in a country such as Germany, the relationships between banks and industry are institutionally interwoven through the supervisory board; banks and industry may hire the same consulting firms; and there are many long-term relationships between banks, borrowers, and consultants (Armbrüster 2005). In other countries, or even in international finance, the situation is not that different (Mintz and Schwartz 1985; Mizruchi 1992; Knorr Cetina and Brügger 2002). These social ties transfer much thicker information about performance and management quality than the signaling circle does. The economics of certification, then, hinges on the type and quality of social relations among the entities involved. From this perspective, a different research program evolves: an analysis of elite networks in which top-tier consultants are interwoven. While data are certainly difficult to obtain, such analyses would represent a fascinating extension of current research into management consultancy.

In summary, this book has given center stage to several phenomena of the consulting sector and has sought to show that the reconciliation of different theories about specific topics enables a more comprehensive account. It has sought to present a phenomenon-oriented rather than a paradigm-oriented approach. Not only do the different elements on which the theories focus broaden the view of management consulting, but their mutual critique generates an improved understanding of the phenomena and the theories alike. This may reduce the fear of many academics of falling between the various stools when drawing on more than one approach.

Learning another theory involves transaction costs, recombinations of social ties, and legitimacy issues. It is worth as much the effort as it is worth learning a language other than one's own. Academic institutions have increasingly embraced cross-disciplinarity, and new intersections such as neuro-economics have emerged, creating a mighty river to which not only economists and psychologists but also physicists and sociologists contribute. Cooperation of this kind may bring about not only new results through mutual corrections but also, hopefully, new institutions that help to reshape academia according to topics rather than discipline.

References

Abbott, A. 1988. *The System of Professions: An Essay on the Division of Expert Labor*. Chicago: University of Chicago Press

Abrahamson, E. 1996. "Management fashion," *Academy of Management Review* 21: 254–85

Aigner, D. J., and G. G. Cain 1977. "Statistical theories of discrimination in labor markets," *Industrial and Labor Relations Review* 30: 175–87

Akerlof, G. 1970. "The market for 'lemons': quality uncertainty and the market mechanism," *Quarterly Journal of Economics* 84: 488–500

1976. "The economics of caste and of the rat race and other woeful tales," *Quarterly Journal of Economics* 90: 599–617

Alchian, A. A., and H. Demsetz 1972. "Production, information costs, and economic organization," *American Economic Review* 62: 777–95

Allanson, S. P. 1985. "Interne Beratung: Strukturen, Formen, Arbeitsweisen," PhD dissertation no. 937. University of St Gallen

Allen, D. G., and K. McDermott 1993. *Accounting for Success: One Hundred Years of Price Waterhouse in America, 1890–1990*. Boston: Harvard Business School Press

Alpha Publications 1996. *The Market for Management Consultancy Services in Western Europe*. London: Alpha Publications

Alvesson, M. 1993. "Organizations as rhetoric: knowledge-intensive firms and the struggle with ambiguity," *Journal of Management Studies* 30: 997–1015

1995. *Management of Knowledge-Intensive Companies*. Berlin: de Gruyter

2000. "Social identity and the problem of loyalty in knowledge-intensive companies," *Journal of Management Studies* 37: 1101–23

2004. *Knowledge Work and Knowledge-Intensive Firms*. Oxford: Oxford University Press

Alvesson, M., and Y. Due Billing 1998. *Understanding Gender and Organizations*. London: Sage

Anand, N., T. Morris, and H. Gardner 2004. *The Process of New Practice Development in Mature Professional Service Firms*, working paper. Said Business School, University of Oxford

Andersen, N., and P. Herriot (eds.) 1997. *International Handbook of Selection and Assessment*. Chichester: Wiley

Angell, I. O. 1989. *The Mind-Set of Mathematical Logic in Management Consultancy*, Working Paper 19. Department of Information Systems, London School of Economics

Appleyard, M. M. 1996. "How does knowledge flow? Interfirm patterns in the semiconductor industry," *Strategic Management Journal* 17: 137–54

Argyris, C. 1970. *Intervention Theory and Method*. Reading, MA: Addison-Wesley
   2000. *Flawed Advice and the Management Trap*. New York: Oxford University Press

Argyris, C., and D. Schön 1978. *Organizational Learning: A Theory of Action Perspective*. Reading, MA: Addison-Wesley

Armbrüster, T. 2005. *Management and Organization in Germany*. Aldershot: Ashgate

Armbrüster, T., and A. Kieser 2001. "Unternehmensberatung: Analysen einer Wachstumsbranche," *Die Betriebswirtschaft* 61: 688–709

Armbrüster, T., and M. Kipping 2002. "Types of knowledge and the client–consultant interaction," in K. Sahlin-Andersson and L. Engwall (eds.). *The Expansion of Management Knowledge: Carriers, Flows, and Sources*. Stanford, CA: Stanford University Press, 96–110

Armbrüster, T., and R. Schmolze 1999. "Milkrounds, case studies, and the aftermath," paper presented at the Second International Conference on Management Consulting, 20 February 1999. King's College, London

Armour, J., and M. J. Whincop 2004. "An economic analysis of shared property in partnership and close corporations law," in J. A. McCahery, T. Raaijmakers and E. P. M. Vermeulen (eds.). *The Governance of Close Corporations and Partnerships: US and European Perspectives*. New York: Oxford University Press, 73–92

Arrow, K. J. 1973. "The theory of discrimination," in O. Ashenfelter and A. Rees (eds.). *Discrimination in Labor Markets*. Princeton: Princeton University Press, 3–33

Asher, M., and M. Lerner (eds.) 1999. *Vault.com Guide to the Case Interview*. New York: Vault.com

Ashford, M. 1998. *Con Tricks: The World of Management Consulting and How to Make It Work for You*. London: Simon and Schuster

Axelrod, R. 1984. *The Evolution of Cooperation*. New York: Basic Books

Bachmann, R. 2001. "Trust, power and control in trans-organizational relations," *Organization Studies* 22: 337–65

Backhaus, K., B. Erichson, W. Plinke, and R. Weiber 1994. *Multivariate Analysemethoden*, 7th edn. Berlin: Springer

Barber, B. 1983. *The Logic and Limits of Trust*. New Brunswick, NJ: Rutgers University Press

Barchewitz, C., and T. Armbrüster 2004. *Unternehmensberatung: Marktmechanismen, Marketing, Auftragsakquisition*. Wiesbaden: DUV Gabler

Barley, S. R., and P. S. Tolbert 1997. "Institutionalization and structuration: studying the links between action and institution," *Organization Studies* 18: 93–117

Bartlett, C. A. 1998. *McKinsey & Company: Managing Knowledge and Learning*, Case Study 9-396-357. Harvard Business School, Boston

Bartlett, C. A., and S. Ghoshal 1993. "Beyond the M-form: toward a managerial theory of the firm," *Strategic Management Journal* 14: 23–46

Becher, T., and P. R. Trowler 2001. *Academic Tribes and Territories: Intellectual Enquiry and the Culture of Disciplines*, 2nd edn. Buckingham: Open University Press

Becker, G. S. 1957. *The Economics of Discrimination*. Chicago: University of Chicago Press

Beckert, J. 1999. "Agency, entrepreneurs, and institutional change: the role of strategic choice and institutionalized practices in organizations," *Organization Studies* 20: 777–99

Beckman, C. M., and P. R. Haunschild 2002. "Network learning: the effects of partners' heterogeneity of experience on corporate acquisitions," *Administrative Science Quarterly* 47: 92–124

Bell, D. 1973. *The Coming of Post-Industrial Society*. New York: Basic Books

Benders, J., M. van Bijsterveld, and R.-J. van den Berg 1998. "Hitch-hiking on a hype: Dutch consultants engineering re-engineering," *Journal of Organizational Change Management* 11: 201–15

Berglund, J., and A. Werr 2000. "The invincible character of management consulting rhetoric: how one blends incommensurates while keeping them apart," *Organization* 7: 633–55

Bergström, O. 1998. "Cultural match: recruitment in a knowledge-intensive firm," paper presented at the European Group of Organisation Studies conference, 9–11 July. Maastricht

Bergström, O., H. Hasselbladh, and D. Kärreman 2004. "Discipline and reward: organizing disciplinary power in a knowledge organization," paper presented at the Twentieth European Group of Organisation Studies Colloquium, 1–3 July. Ljubljana, Slovenia

Berry, J. 1995. "Did I hear you say that consulting firms are equal opportunity employers?," *Journal of Management Consulting* Fall: 23–5

1996. "Women and consulting – the downside," *Journal of Management Consulting* **Spring**: 34–8

Bertrand, M., E. F. P. Luttmer, and S. Mullainathan 2000. "Network effects and welfare cultures," *Quarterly Journal of Economics* **115**: 1019–55

Besanko, D., D. Dranove, and M. Shanley 2000. *Economics of Strategy*, 2nd edn. New York: Wiley

Bessant, J., and H. Rush 1995. "Building bridges for innovation: the role of consultants in technology transfer," *Research Policy* **24**: 97–114

Bhide, A. 1994. *McKinsey and Company (A): 1956*, Case Study 9-393-066. Harvard Business School, Boston

  1995. *Building the Professional Firm: McKinsey and Co., 1939–1968*, Working Paper 95–010. Harvard Business School, Boston

Biech, E. 1999. *The Business of Consulting: The Basic and Beyond*. San Francisco: Jossey-Bass

Bienenstock, E. J., and P. Bonacich 1993. "Game-theory models for exchange networks: experimental results," *Sociological Perspectives* **36**: 117–35

  1997. "Network exchange as a cooperative game," *Rationality and Society* **9**: 37–65

Bloomfield, B. P., and A. Best 1992. "Management consultants: systems development, power and the translation of problems," *Sociological Review* **40**: 533–60

Bloomfield, B. P., and A. Danieli 1995. "The role of management consultants in the development of information technology: the indissoluble nature of socio-political and technical skills," *Journal of Management Studies* **32**: 23–46

Bogenrieder, I., and B. Nooteboom 2004. "Learning groups: what types are there? A theoretical analysis and empirical study in a consultancy firm," *Organization Studies* **25**: 287–313

Bower, M. 1940. *Supplementing Successful Management*. New York: McKinsey and Company

  1982. *The Will to Manage*. New York: McGraw-Hill

Brint, S. 1994. *In an Age of Experts: The Changing Role of Professionals in Politics and Public Life*. Princeton, NJ: Princeton University Press

Brockhaus, W. L. 1977. "Prospects for malpractice suits in the business consulting profession," *Journal of Business* **50**: 70–5

Brown, J. S., and P. Duguid 1996. "Organizational learning and communities of practice," in M. D. Cohen and L. S. Sproull (eds.). *Organizational Learning*. London: Sage, 58–82

  1998. "Organizing knowledge," *California Management Review* **40**: 90–111

Burrell, G., and G. Morgan 1979. *Sociological Paradigms and Organisational Analysis: Elements of the Sociology of Corporate Life*. London: Heinemann

Burt, R. S. 1992. *Structural Holes: The Social Structure of Competition*. Cambridge, MA: Harvard University Press

  1997. "The contingent value of social capital," *Administrative Science Quarterly* 42: 339–65

  2004. "Structural holes and good ideas," *American Journal of Sociology* 110: 349–99

Burt, R. S., and M. Knez 1996. "Trust and third-party gossip," in R. M. Kramer and T. R. Tyler (eds.). *Trust in Organizations: Frontiers of Theory and Research*. Thousand Oaks, CA: Sage, 68–89

Canbäck, S. 1998a. *Transaction Cost Theory and Management Consulting: Why do Management Consultants Exist?*, Working Paper 9810002. Henley Management College, Henley-on-Thames

  1998b. "The logic of management consulting (part one)," *Journal of Management Consulting* 1012: 3–11

  1999. "The logic of management consulting (part two)," *Journal of Management Consulting* 1013: 3–12

Chambers, E., M. Foulon, H. Handfield-Jones, S. Hankin, and E. Michaels 1998. "The war for talent," *McKinsey Quarterly* 1998/3: 44–57

Chandler, A. D. 1962. *Strategy and Structure: Chapters in the History of the Industrial Enterprise*. Cambridge, MA: MIT Press

Chung, S., H. Singh, and K. Lee 2000. "Complementarity, status similarity and social capital as drivers of alliance formation," *Strategic Management Journal* 21: 1–22

Clark, T. 1993. "The market provision of management services, information asymmetries and service quality – some market solutions: an empirical example," *British Journal of Management* 4: 235–51

  1995. *Managing Consultants: Consultancy as the Management of Impressions*. Buckingham: Open University Press

Clark, T., and R. Fincham (eds.) 2002. *Critical Consulting: New Perspectives on the Management Advice Industry*. Oxford: Blackwell

Clark, T., and G. Salaman 1998. "Creating the right impression: towards a dramaturgy of management consultancy," *Service Industries Journal* 18: 18–38

Clegg, S., M. Kornberger, and C. Rhodes 2004. "When the saints go marching in: a reply to Sturdy, Clark, Fincham and Handley," *Management Learning* 35: 341–4

Coase, R. H. 1937. "The nature of the firm," reprinted in R. H. Coase 1988. *The Firm, the Market, and the Law*. Chicago: University of Chicago Press, 33–55

Coleman, J. S. 1988. "Social capital in the creation of human capital," *American Journal of Sociology* **94,** Supplement: 95–120

1990. *Foundations of Social Theory.* Cambridge, MA: Harvard University Press

Coleman, W. O. 2002. *Economics and Its Enemies: Two Centuries of Anti-Economics.* Houndsmill: Palgrave Macmillan

Connor, D., and J. Davidson 1997. *Marketing Your Consulting and Professional Services.* New York: Wiley

Cortada, J. W. 1998. *Rise of the Knowledge Worker.* Boston: Butterworth-Heinemann

Coulter, K., and R. Coulter 2002. "Determinants of trust in a service provider: the moderating role of length of relationship," *Journal of Services Marketing* **16**: 35–50

Covaleski, M. A., M. W. Dirsmith, J. B. Heian, and S. Samuel 1998. "The calculated and the avowed: techniques of discipline and struggles over identity in Big Six public accounting firms," *Administrative Science Quarterly* **43**: 293–327

Crémer, J. 1993. "Corporate culture and shared knowledge," *Industrial and Corporate Change* **2**: 351–86

Czarniawska-Joerges, B. 1990. "Merchants of meaning: management consulting in the Swedish public sector," in B. Turner (ed.). *Organizational Symbolism.* New York: de Gruyter, 139–50

Czerniawska, F. (ed.) 1999. *Management Consultancy in the 21st Century.* Houndsmill: Macmillan

Dacin, M. T., M. J. Ventresca, and B. D. Beal 1999. "The embeddedness of organizations: dialogue and directions," *Journal of Management* **25**: 317–56

Danieli, A., S. Shaw, and P. Hornby 2003. *Gender and Management.* London: Sage

Das, T. K., and B.-S. Teng 2001. "Trust, control, and risk in strategic alliances: an integrated framework," *Organization Studies* **22**: 251–83

Dawes, P., G. R. Dowling, and P. G. Patterson 1992. "Criteria used to select management consultants," *Industrial Marketing Management* **21**: 187–93

Deetz, S. 1996. "Describing differences in approaches to organizational science: rethinking Burrell and Morgan and their legacy," *Organization Science* **7**: 191–207

de Wit, B., and R. Meyer 2004. *Strategy: Process, Content, Context: An International Perspective,* 3rd edn. Minneapolis: Thompson Learning

Dicken, P. 2003. *Global Shift: Reshaping the Global Economic Map in the 21st Century,* 4th edn. New York: Guilford Press

DiMaggio, P. J. 1988. "Interest and agency in institutional theory," in L. G. Zucker (ed.). *Institutional Patterns and Organizations: Culture and Environment*. Cambridge, MA: Ballinger, 3–21

1997. "Culture and cognition," *Annual Review of Sociology* 23: 263–87

DiMaggio, P. J., and H. Louch 1998. "Socially embedded consumer transactions: for what kinds of purchases do people most often use networks?," *American Sociological Review* 63: 619–37

DiMaggio, P. J., and W. W. Powell 1983. "The iron cage revisited: institutional isomorphism and collective rationality in organizational fields," *American Sociological Review* 48: 147–60

1991. "Introduction," in W. W. Powell and P. J. DiMaggio (eds.). *The New Institutionalism in Organizational Analysis*. Chicago: University of Chicago Press, 1–38

Drucker, P. 1969. *The Age of Discontinuity*. Boston: Butterworth-Heinemann

Dunford, R. 2000. "Key challenges in the search for the effective management of knowledge in management consulting firms," *Journal of Knowledge Management* 4: 295–302

Durvasula, S., S. Lysonski, and S. Mehta 1999. "Testing the SERVQUAL scale in the business-to-business sector: the case of ocean freight shipping service," *Journal of Services Marketing* 13: 132–50

Dyer, J. H., and K. Nobeoka 2000. "Creating and managing a high-performance knowledge-sharing network: the Toyota case," *Strategic Management Journal* 21: 345–67

Eriksson, K., A. Majkgard, and D. Sharma 1999. "Service quality by relationships in the international market," *Journal of Services Marketing* 13: 361–75

Ernst, B. 2002. *Die Evaluation von Beratungsleistungen: Prozesse der Wahrnehmung und Bewertung*. Wiesbaden: DUV Gabler

Ernst, B., and A. Kieser 2002. "In search of explanations for the consulting explosion," in K. Sahlin-Andersson and L. Engwall (eds.). *The Expansion of Management Knowledge: Carriers, Flows, and Sources*. Stanford, CA: Stanford University Press, 47–73

Farrell, J., and S. Scotchmer 1988. "Partnerships," *Quarterly Journal of Economics*, 103: 279–97

Faust, M. 2002. "Consultancies as actors in knowledge arenas: evidence from Germany," in M. Kipping and L. Engwall (eds.). *Management Consulting: Emergence and Dynamics of a Knowledge Industry*. Oxford: Oxford University Press, 146–63

FEACO 1998. *Survey of the European Management Consultancy Market 1997*. Brussels: European Federation of Management Consulting Associations

2002. *Survey of the European Management Consultancy Market 2001.* Brussels: European Federation of Management Consulting Associations

2005. *Survey of the European Management Consultancy Market 2004.* Brussels: European Federation of Management Consulting Associations

2006. *Survey of the European Management Consultancy Market 2005–2006.* Brussels: European Federation of Management Consulting Associations

File, K. M., D. S. P. Cermak, and R. A. Prince 1994. "Word-of-mouth effects in professional services buyer behavior," *Service Industries Journal* 14: 301–14

Fincham, R. 1995. "Business process reengineering and the commodification of managerial knowledge," *Journal of Marketing Management* 11: 707–19

1999. "The consultant–client relationship: critical perspectives on the management of organizational change," *Journal of Management Studies* 36: 335–51

Fligstein, N. 1983. "The intraorganizational power struggle: rise of finance personnel to top leadership in large corporations, 1919–1979," *American Sociological Review* 52: 44–8

1990. *The Transformation of Corporate Control.* Cambridge, MA: Harvard University Press

Franck, E., and T. Pudack 2000. "Unternehmensberatungen und die Selektion von Humankapital: eine ökonomische Analyse," *Die Unternehmung* 54: 145–55

Franck, E., T. Pudack, and M.-A. Benz 2004. "Unternehmensberatung als Legitimation: eine ökonomische Analyse," in M. Nippa and D. Schneiderbauer (eds.). *Erfolgsmechanismen der Top-Management-Beratung: Einblicke und kritische Reflexionen von Branchenkennern.* Heidelberg: Physica, 27–38

Franck, E., T. Pudack, and C. Opitz 2001. *Zur Funktion von Topmanagement-Beratungen als "Karrieresprungbrett" für High Potentials,* Working Paper 3. Lehrstuhl für Unternehmensführung und -politik, University of Zurich

Friedland, R., and A. F. Robertson (eds.) 1990. *Beyond the Marketplace: Rethinking Economy and Society.* New York: de Gruyter

Fudenberg, D., and J. Tirole 1991. *Game Theory.* Cambridge, MA: MIT Press

Ghoshal, S. 1993. "Andersen Consulting (Europe): entering the business of business integration (1992 INSEAD case)," in J. Hendry and T. Eccles (eds.). *European Cases in Strategic Management.* London: Chapman and Hall, 30–58

Giddens, A. 1984. *The Constitution of Society: Outline of the Theory of Structuration.* Cambridge: Polity Press

1990. *The Consequences of Modernity.* Stanford, CA: Stanford University Press

Gioia, D. A., and E. Pitre 1990. "Multiparadigm perspectives on theory building," *Academy of Management Review* 15: 584–602

Glückler, J. 2004. *Reputationsnetze: Zur Internationalisierung von Unternehmensberatern: eine relationale Theorie.* Bielefeld: Transcript Verlag

2005. "Making embeddedness work: social practice institutions in foreign consulting markets," *Environment and Planning* A 37: 1727–50

2006. "A relational assessment of international market entry in management consulting," *Journal of Economic Geography* 6: 369–93

Gouldner, A. W. 1979. *The Future of Intellectuals and the Rise of the New Class.* New York: Continuum

Gounaris, S., and K. Venetis 2002. "Trust in industrial service relationships: behavioral consequences, antecedents and the moderating effect of the duration of the relationship," *Journal of Services Marketing* 16: 636–55

Granovetter, M. 1974. *Getting a Job: A Study of Contacts and Careers.* Chicago: University of Chicago Press

1985. "Economic action and economic structure: the problem of embeddedness," *American Journal of Sociology* 91: 481–510

Granovetter, M., and R. Swedberg (eds.) 1992. *The Sociology of Economic Life.* Boulder, CO: Westview

Grant, R. M. 1996a. "Prospering in dynamically-competitive environments: organizational capability as knowledge integration," *Organization Science* 7: 375–87

1996b. "Towards a knowledge-based view of the firm," *Strategic Management Journal* 17 (Winter special issue): 109–22

Greiner, L. E., and R. O. Metzger 1983. *Consulting to Management.* Englewood Cliffs, NJ: Prentice Hall

Grey, C. 1994. "Career as a project of the self and labor process discipline," *Sociology* 28: 479–97

Grönroos, C. 2000. *Service Management and Marketing: A Customer Relationship Management Approach,* 2nd edn. New York: Wiley

Hagedoorn, J., and J. Schakenraad 1994. "The effect of strategic technology alliances on company performance," *Strategic Management Journal* 15: 291–309

Hagedorn, H. 1955. "The management consultant as transmitter of business techniques," *Explorations in Entrepreneurial History*: 164–73

Hall, J. 1999. "Statement on 'segmenting the consulting industry of the future,'" in F. Czerniawska (ed.). *Management Consulting in the 21st Century*. Houndsmill: Macmillan, 153–5

Hamel, G. 1991. "Competition for competence and inter-partner learning within international strategic alliances," *Strategic Management Journal* 12: 83–103

Hammer, M., and J. Champy 1993. *Reengineering the Corporation: A Manifesto for Business Revolution*. London: Brealey

Hansen, M. T. 1999. "The search-transfer problem: the role of weak ties in sharing knowledge across organization subunits," *Administrative Science Quarterly* 44: 82–111

    2002. "Knowledge networks: explaining effective knowledge sharing in multiunit companies," *Organization Science* 13: 232–48

Hansen, M. T., and M. R. Haas 2001. "Competing for attention in knowledge markets: electronic document dissemination in a management consulting company," *Administrative Science Quarterly* 46: 1–28

Hansen, M. T., N. Nohria, and T. Tierney 1999. "What's your strategy for managing knowledge?," *Harvard Business Review* 77/2: 106–16

Harrison, B. 1999. "Statement on 'recruiting and retaining people,'" in F. Czerniawska (ed.). *Management Consulting in the 21st Century*. Houndsmill: Macmillan, 210–11

Hassard, J., and D. Pym (eds.) 1990. *The Theory and Philosophy of Organizations: Critical Issues and New Perspectives*. London: Routledge

Hausman, A. V. 2003. "Professional service relationships: a multi-context study of factors impacting satisfaction, re-patronization, and recommendations," *Journal of Services Marketing* 17: 226–42

Havelock, R. G., and A. Guskin 1971. *Planning for Innovation through Dissemination and Utilization of Knowledge*. Center for Research on Utilization of Scientific Knowledge, University of Michigan, Ann Arbor

Held, D., A. McGrew, D. Goldblatt, and J. Perraton 1999. *Global Transformations: Politics, Economics and Culture*. Cambridge: Polity Press

Hermalin, B. E. 2000. "Economics and corporate culture," http://papers.ssrn.com/sol3/papers.cfm?abstract_id=162549

Higdon, H. 1969. *The Business Healers*. New York: Random House

Hirsch, P., S. Michaels, and R. Friedman 1990. "Clean models vs. dirty hands: why economics is different from sociology," in S. Zukin and P. DiMaggio (eds.). *Structures of Capital: The Social Organization of the Economy*. Cambridge: Cambridge University Press, 39–56

Högl, M., and H. G. Gemünden 2001. "Teamwork quality and the success of innovative projects: a theoretical concept and empirical evidence," *Organization Science* 12: 435–49

Högl, M., K. Weinkauf, and H. G. Gemünden 2004. "Interteam coordination, project commitment, and teamwork in multiteam R&D projects: a longitudinal study," *Organization Science* 15: 38–55

Holmstrom, B., and S. N. Kaplan 2001. "Corporate governance and merger activity in the United States: making sense of the 1980s and 1990s," *Journal of Economic Perspectives* 15: 121–44

Holzer, H. J., and K. R. Ihlanfeldt 1998. "Customer discrimination and employment outcomes for minority workers," *Quarterly Journal of Economics*, 113: 835–67

Hördt, O. 2002. *Frauen in der Unternehmensberatung: Empirische Analyse zur geschlechtsspezifischen Segregation.* Wiesbaden: DUV Gabler

Hoskisson, R. E., C. W. L. Hill, and H. Kim 1993. "The multidivisional structure: organizational fossil or source of value?," *Journal of Management* 19: 269–98

Hoyer, H. 2000. "Internes Consulting in Deutschland: Ergebnisse einer Marktuntersuchung," in C. Niedereichholz (ed.). 2000. *Internes Consulting: Grundlagen, Praxisbeispiele, Spezialthemen.* Munich: Oldenbourg, 55–81

Iles, P., and G. Salaman 1995. "Recruitment, selection and assessment," in J. Storey (ed.). *Human Resource Management: A Critical Text.* London: Routledge, 203–33

Ivaldi, M., B. Jullien, P. Rey, P. Seabright, and J. Tirole 2003. *The Economics of Tacit Collusion,* Working Paper 186. Institut d'Economie Industrielle Toulouse. Available at http://europa.eu.int/comm/competition/mergers/review/the_economics_of_tacit_collusion_en.pdf [accessed November 2005]

Jackall, R. 1988. *Moral Mazes: The World of Corporate Managers.* New York: Oxford University Press

Jackson, N., and P. Carter 1991. "In defense of paradigm incommensurability," *Organization Studies* 12: 109–27

James, M. 2001. "Multinational management consultancies: world market leaders," in B. Curnow and J. Reuvid (eds.). *The International Guide to Management Consultancy: The Evolution, Practice and Structure of Management Consultancy Worldwide.* London: Kogan-Page, 33–41

Johnson, M., and G. M. Zinkhan 1998. "The impact of outcome, competency and affect on service referral," *Journal of Services Marketing* 12: 397–416

Jones, E. 1995. *True and Fair: A History of Price Waterhouse.* London: Hamish Hamilton

Jones, G. R. 1983. "Transaction costs, property rights, and organizational culture: an exchange perspective," *Administrative Science Quarterly* 28: 454–67

Kahn, C., and G. Huberman 1988. "Two-sided uncertainty and 'up-or-out' contracts," *Journal of Labor Economics* 6: 423–44

Kandel, E., and E. P. Lazear 1992. "Peer pressure and partnerships," *Journal of Political Economy* 100: 801–17

Karlson, D., and M. D. Crisp (eds.) 1988. *Marketing Your Consulting or Professional Services*. Menlo Park, CA: Crisp Publications

Karsten, M. F. 1993. *Management and Gender*. New York: Praeger

Katz, E., M. L. Levin and H. Hamilton 1963. "Traditions of research on the diffusion of innovation," *American Sociological Review* 28: 237–52

Keeble, D., and J. Schwalbach 1995. *Management Consultancy in Europe*, Working Paper 01. Economic and Social Research Council Centre for Business Research, University of Cambridge

Kehrer, R., and C. Schade 1995. "Interne Problemlösung oder Konsultation von Unternehmensberatern?," *Die Betriebswirtschaft* 55: 465–79

Kelley, R. E. 1979. "Should you have an internal consultant? Companies find that staff specialists often can be quicker, cheaper and more effective than external ones," *Harvard Business Review* 57/6: 110–20

Kennedy Information 2002. *The Global Consulting Market Place: Key Data, Forecasts and Trends*. Fitzwilliam, NH: Kennedy Publications

Kieser, A. 2002. "Managers as marionettes? Using fashion theories to explain the success of consultancies," in M. Kipping and L. Engwall (eds.). *Management Consulting: Emergence and Dynamics of a Knowledge Industry*. Oxford: Oxford University Press, 167–83

Kipping, M. 1996. "The U. S. influence on the evolution of management consultancies in Britain, France, and Germany since 1945," *Business and Economic History* 25: 112–23

1997. "Consultancies, institutions and the diffusion of Taylorism in Britain, Germany and France, 1920s to 1950s," *Business History* 39/4: 67–83

1999. "American management consulting companies in western Europe, 1920 to 1990: products, reputation and relationships," *Business History Review* 73: 193–222

2002. "Trapped in their wave: the evolution of management consultancies," in T. Clark and R. Fincham (eds.). *Critical Consulting: New Perspectives on the Management Advice Industry*. Oxford: Blackwell, 28–49

Kipping, M., and L. Engwall (eds.) 2002. *Management Consulting: Emergence and Dynamics of a Knowledge Industry*. Oxford: Oxford University Press

Kishel, G., and P. Kishel 1996. *How to Start and Run a Successful Consulting Business*. New York: Wiley

Klein Woolthuis, R., B. Hillebrand, and B. Nooteboom 2005. "Trust, contract and relationship development," *Organization Studies* 26: 813–40

Knorr Cetina, K., and U. Brügger 2002. "Global microstructures: the virtual societies of financial markets," *American Journal of Sociology* 107: 905–50

Kollock, P. 1994. "The emergence of exchange structures: an experimental study of uncertainty, commitment, and trust," *American Journal of Sociology* 100: 313–45

Koput, K. W., and W. W. Powell 2000. "Science and strategy: organizational evolution in a knowledge-intensive field," paper presented at the annual meeting of the Scandinavian Consortium of Organizational Research, 30 September–1 October. Stanford University, Stanford, CA

Kotler, P., T. Hayes, and P. N. Bloom 2002. *Marketing Professional Services*, 2nd edn. San Francisco: Prentice-Hall

Kreps, D. M. 1990. "Corporate culture and economic theory," in J. E. Alt and K. A. Shepsle (eds.). *Perspectives on Positive Political Economy*. Cambridge: Cambridge University Press, 90–143

1991. *Game Theory and Economic Modelling*. New York: Oxford University Press

Kreps, D. M., and R. Wilson 1982. "Reputation and imperfect information," *Journal of Economic Theory* 27: 253–79

Kubr, M. (ed.) 1986. *Management Consulting: A Guide to the Profession*, 2nd edn. Geneva: International Labour Organization

1996. *Management Consulting: A Guide to the Profession*, 3rd edn. Geneva: International Labour Organization

Lane, C., and R. Bachmann 1996. "The social constitution of trust: supplier relations in Britain and Germany," *Organization Studies* 17: 365–95

Larsen, J. N. 2001. "Knowledge, human resources and social practice: the knowledge-intensive business service firm as a distributed knowledge system," *Service Industries Journal* 21: 81–102

Larwood, L., and U. E. Gattiker 1985. "Rational bias and interorganizational power in the employment of management consultants," *Group and Organization Studies* 10/1: 3–17

Lazear, E., and S. Rosen 1981. "Rank order tournaments as optimal labor contracts," *Journal of Political Economy* 89: 841–64

Lazerson, M. 1993. "Factory or putting-out? Knitting networks in Modena," in G. Grabher (ed.). *The Embedded Firm: On the Socioeconomics of Industrial Networks*. New York: Routledge, 203–26

Lechler, T., and H. G. Gemünden 1998. "Kausalanalyse der Wirkungsstruktur der Erfolgsfaktoren des Projektmanagements," *Die Betriebswirtschaft* 58: 435–50

Lee, M., and L. F. Cunningham 2001. "A cost/benefit approach to understanding service loyalty," *Journal of Services Marketing* 15: 113–30

Levine, S. S. 2004. *The Strength of Performative Ties: Dynamics of Network Exchange in a Knowledge Intensive Firm*, working paper. Wharton School of Business, University of Pennsylvania, Philadelphia

Levitt, T. 1981. "Marketing intangible products and product intangibles," *Harvard Business Review* 59/3: 94–102

Levy-Leboyer, C. 1992. "Selection and assessment in Europe," in H. C. Triandis, M. D. Dunnette and L. Hough (eds.). *Handbook of Industrial and Organizational Psychology*, vol. 4, 2nd edn. Palo Alto, CA: Consulting Psychologists Press, 173–91

Lie, J. 1997. "Sociology of markets," *Annual Review of Sociology* 23: 341–60

Lindahl, D. P., and W. B. Beyers 1999. "The creation of competitive advantage by producer service establishments," *Economic Geography* 75: 1–20

Lorenz, E. 1999. "Trust, contract and economic cooperation," *Cambridge Journal of Economics* 23: 301–15

Lovelock, C. 2000. *Services Marketing: People, Technology, Strategy*, 4th edn. San Francisco: Prentice-Hall

Mackay, M. M. 2001. "Application of brand equity measures in service markets," *Journal of Services Marketing* 15: 210–21

Maister, D. H. 1982. "Balancing the professional service firm," *Sloan Management Review* 24: 15–29

1993. *Managing the Professional Service Firm*. New York: Free Press

Mangold, W. G., Miller, F., and G. R. Brockway 1999. "Word-of-mouth communication in the service marketplace," *Journal of Services Marketing* 13: 73–89

March, J. G. 1991. "Organizational consultants and organizational research," *Journal of Applied Communication Research* 19: 20–31

1994. *A Primer on Decision Making: How Decisions Happen*. New York: Free Press

McCahery, J. A., T. Raaijmakers, and E. P. M. Vermeulen (eds.) 2004. *The Governance of Close Corporations and Partnerships: US and European Perspectives*. New York: Oxford University Press

McGivern, C. 1983. "Some facets of the relationship between consultants and clients in organizations," *Journal of Management Studies* 20: 367–86

MCI 2002a. "The contrasting fortunes of Accenture and PwC Consulting," *Management Consultant International* January: 1–3

2002b. "Creating client value in the shadow of Enron," *Management Consultant International* March: 8

2002c. "2001 a terrible year for strategy firms, finds KI report," *Management Consultant International* May: 7

2002d. "Profession's top 50 firms stagnated in 2001," *Management Consultant International* June: 9–15

2002e. "Cap Gemini's LEAP too late to stop its year-long fall," *Management Consultant International* July: 2–7

2002f. "IBM snaps up PwC's consulting unit in $3.5 billion deal," *Management Consultant International* August: 1–2

2002g. "The future is not so bright for Europe after all," *Management Consultant International* August: 10–11

McKenna, C. D. 1995. "The origins of modern management consulting," *Business and Economic History* 24: 51–8

2001. "The world's newest profession: management consulting in the twentieth century," *Enterprise and Society* 2: 673–9

2006. *The World's Newest Profession: Management Consulting in the Twentieth Century.* Cambridge: Cambridge University Press

Measelle, R. 1999. "Statement on 'key threats and challenges,'" in F. Czerniawska (ed.). *Management Consultancy in the 21st Century.* Houndsmill: Macmillan, 194–5

Meyer, J. W. 1996. "Otherhood: the promulgation and transmission of ideas in the modern organizational environment," in B. Czarniawska and G. Sevon (eds.). *Translating Organizational Change.* Berlin: de Gruyter, 241–52

2002. "Globalization and the expansion and standardization of management," in K. Sahlin-Andersson and L. Engwall (eds.). *The Expansion of Management Knowledge: Carriers, Flows, and Sources.* Stanford, CA: Stanford University Press, 33–44

Meyer, J. W., and B. Rowan 1977. "Institutionalized organizations: formal structure as myth and ceremony," *American Journal of Sociology* 83: 340–63

Michaels, E., H. Handfield-Jones, and B. Axelrod 2001. *The War for Talents.* Boston: Harvard Business School Publishing

Milgrom, P., and J. Roberts 1992. *Economics, Organization and Management.* Englewood Cliffs, NJ: Prentice Hall

Mills, A. J., and P. Tancred (eds.) 1992. *Gendering Organizational Analysis.* Newbury Park, CA: Sage

Mintz, B., and M. Schwartz 1985. *The Power Structure of American Business.* Chicago: University of Chicago Press

Mitchell, V.-W. 1994. "Problems and risks in the purchasing of consultancy services," *Service Industries Journal* **14**: 315–39

Mitra, K., M. C. Reiss, and L. M. Capella 1999. "An examination of perceived risk, information search and behavioral intentions in search, experience and credence services," *Journal of Services Marketing* **13**: 208–28

Mizruchi, M. S. 1992. *The Structure of Corporate Political Action.* Cambridge, MA: Harvard University Press

Mohe, M. 2002. "Inhouse Consulting: Gestern, heute – und morgen?," in M. Mohe, H. J. Heinecke and R. Pfriem (eds.). *Consulting: Problemlösung als Geschäftsmodell: Theorie, Praxis, Markt.* Stuttgart: Klett-Cotta, 320–43

    2004. *Klientenprofessionalisierung: Strategien und Perspektiven eines professionellen Umgangs mit Unternehmensberatung.* Marburg: Metropolis-Verlag

Montgomery, J. 1991. "Social networks and labor market outcomes: towards an economic analysis," *American Economic Review* **81**: 1408–18

Moore, G. L. 1984. *The Politics of Management Consulting.* Westport, CT: Greenwood

Moore, K., and J. Birkinshaw 1998. "Managing knowledge in global service firms: centers of excellence," *Academy of Management Executive* **12**: 81–92

Morris, T., and L. Empson 1998. "Organization and expertise: an exploration of knowledge bases and the management of accounting and consulting firms," *Accounting, Organizations and Society* **23**: 609–24

Mowery, D. C., J. E. Oxley, and B. S. Silverman 1996. "Strategic alliances and interfirm knowledge transfer," *Strategic Management Journal* **17**: 77–91

Muchinsky, P. M. 1986. "Personnel selection methods," in C. L. Cooper and I. T. Robertson (eds.). *International Review of Industrial and Organizational Psychology.* New York: Wiley, 37–71

Nayyar, P. R. 1990. "Information asymmetries: a source of competitive advantage for diversified service firms," *Strategic Management Journal* **11**: 513–19

Nayyar, P. R., and R. K. Kazanjian 1993. "Organizing to attain potential benefits from information asymmetries and economics of scope in related diversified firms," *Academy of Management Review* **18**: 735–59

Neef, D. (ed.) 1998. *The Knowledge Economy.* Boston: Butterworth-Heinemann

Neef, D., G. A. Siesfeld, and J. Cefola (eds.) 1998. *The Economic Impact of Knowledge*. Boston: Butterworth-Heinemann

Niedereichholz, C. (ed.) 2000. *Internes Consulting: Grundlagen, Praxisbeispiele, Spezialthemen*. Munich: Oldenbourg

Nonaka, I. 1994. "A dynamic theory of organizational knowledge creation," *Organization Science* **5**: 14–37

Nonaka, I., and H. Takeuchi 1995. *The Knowledge Creating Company*. New York: Oxford University Press

Nooteboom, B. 1996. "Trust, opportunism and governance: a process and control model," *Organization Studies* **17**: 985–1010

2000. "Institutions and forms of coordination in innovation systems," *Organization Studies* **21**: 915–39

North, D. C. 1990. *Institutions, Institutional Change and Economic Performance*. Cambridge: Cambridge University Press

Noyelle, T. J., and A. B. Dutka 1988. *International Trade in Business Services: Accounting, Advertising, Law, and Management Consulting*. Cambridge, MA: Ballinger

Oefinger, T. 1986. "Erfüllung von Berateraufgaben in Unternehmen durch interne und externe Berater: eine theoretisch-empirische Analyse," PhD dissertation. University of Augsburg

Oliver, E. 1999. "Statement on 'key threats and challenges,'" in F. Czerniawska (ed.). *Management Consultancy in the 21st Century*. Houndsmill: Macmillan, 195

O'Rorke, B. 1999. "Statement on client-consultant relations," in F. Czerniawska (ed.). *Management Consultancy in the 21st Century*. Houndsmill: Macmillan, 168–9

O'Shea, J., and C. Madigan 1997. *Dangerous Company: The Consulting Powerhouses and the Businesses They Save and Ruin*. London: Brealey

Page, C. 1998. "How clients pick management consultants in Australia and New Zealand," *Journal of Management Consulting* **10**: 56–8

Palmer, A., and M. O'Neill 2003. "The effects of perceptual processes on the measurement of service quality," *Journal of Services Marketing* **17**: 254–74

Pejovich, S. 1997. *Economic Analysis of Institutions and Systems*. Berlin: Springer

Petmecky, A. 2004. "Management von Management Consultants: Eine Rolle für den Einkauf?," paper presented at the conference "Grenzen der Strategieberatung," 14–16 October. Ludwig Maximilian University, Munich

Pfeffer, J., and R. Salancik 1978. *The External Control of Organizations: A Resource Dependence Perspective*. New York: Harper and Row

Phelps, E. S. 1972. "The statistical theory of racism and sexism," *American Economic Review* **62**: 659–61

Pinault, L. 2000. *Consulting Demons: Inside the Unscrupulous World of Global Corporate Consulting*. New York: Harper Business

Podolny, J. M. 1994. "Market uncertainty and social character of economic exchange," *Administrative Science Quarterly* **39**: 458–83

Popper, K. R. 1994. *The Myth of the Framework*, by M. Notturno (ed.). London: Routledge

Poppo, L., and T. Zenger 2002. "Do formal contracts and relational governance function as substitutes or complements?," *Strategic Management Journal* **23**: 707–25

Porter, M. E. 1980. *Competitive Strategy*. New York: Free Press
    1985. *Competitive Advantage: Creating and Sustaining Superior Performance*. New York: Free Press

Porter, T. M. 1995. *Trust in Numbers: The Pursuit of Objectivity in Science and Public Life*. Princeton, NJ: Princeton University Press

Portes, A. 1998. "Social capital: its origins and applications in modern sociology," *Annual Review of Sociology* **24**: 1–24

Powell, W. W. 1990. "Neither market nor hierarchy: network forms of organization," *Research in Organizational Behavior* **12**: 295–336
    1996. "Inter-organizational collaboration in the biotechnology industry," *Journal of Institutional and Theoretical Economics* **152**: 197–215
    1998. "Learning from collaboration: knowledge and networks in the biotechnology and pharmaceutical industries," *California Management Review* **40**: 228–40

Powell, W. W., and P. J. DiMaggio (eds.). 1991. *The New Institutionalism in Organizational Analysis*. Chicago: University of Chicago Press

Powell, W. W., K. W. Koput, and L. Smith-Doerr 1996. "Interorganizational collaboration and the locus of innovation: networks of learning in biotechnology," *Administrative Science Quarterly* **41**: 116–45

Pudack, T. 2004. *Signale für Humankapital: Die Rolle von Unternehmensberatungen beim Berufseinstieg von Hochschulabsolventen*. Wiesbaden: DUV Gabler

Ramsay, H., and D. Scholarios 1999. "Selective decisions: challenging orthodox analyses of the hiring process," *International Journal of Management Reviews* **March**: 63–89

Rassam, C., and D. Oates 1992. *Management Consultancy: The Inside Story*. London: Mercury Books

Raub, W., and J. Weesie 1990. "Reputation and efficiency in social interactions: an example of network effects," *American Journal of Sociology* **96**: 626–54

Reagans, R., and B. McEvily 2003. "Network structure and knowledge transfer: the effects of cohesion and range," *Administrative Science Quarterly* **48**: 240–67

Rees, B. A. 2004. *The Construction of Management: Competence and Gender Issues at Work*. Cheltenham: Edward Elgar

Reich, R. 1992. *The Work of Nations*. New York: Vintage Books

Reimus, B. 1997. "Knowledge sharing within management consulting firms Report on how U.S.-based management consultancies deploy technology, use groupware and facilitate collaboration," http://www.kennedyinfo.com/mc/gware.html [accessed 15 June 1999]

Richter, A. 2004. "The changing balance of power in the consulting market and its effects on consulting firms," in Jean-Paul Thommen and Ansgar Richter (eds.). *Management Consulting Today: Strategies for a Challenging Environment*. Wiesbaden: DUV Gabler, 111–29

Richter, A., and K. Lingelbach 2004. *Allokation von Eigentumsrechten in Unternehmensberatungen: Inside versus Outside Ownership*, working paper. European School of Business, Oestrich-Winkel, Germany

2005. *The Allocation of Ownership Rights in Management Consulting Firms: An Institutional Economics Approach*, working paper. European School of Business, Oestrich-Winkel, Germany

Ripperger, T. 1998. *Ökonomik des Vertrauens: Analyse eines Organisationsprinzips*. Tübingen: Mohr Siebeck

Ritter, T., and H. G. Gemünden 2003. "Network competence: its impact on innovation success and its antecedents," *Journal of Business Research* **56**: 745–55

Robertson, I. T. 1996. "Personnel selection and assessment," in P. Warr (ed.). *Psychology at Work*, 4th edn. London: Penguin, 121–61

Robertson, M., J. Swan, and S. Newell 1996. "The role of networks in the diffusion of technological innovation," *Journal of Management Studies* **33**: 333–59

Rogers, E. M. 1995. *Diffusion of Innovations*. New York: Free Press

Ruef, M. 2002. "At the interstices of organizations: the expansion of the management consulting profession, 1933–1997," in K. Sahlin-Andersson and L. Engwall (eds.). *The Expansion of Management Knowledge: Carriers, Flows, and Sources*. Stanford, CA: Stanford University Press, 74–95

Sahlin-Andersson, K., and L. Engwall (eds.) 2002. *The Expansion of Management Knowledge: Carriers, Flows, and Sources*. Stanford: Stanford University Press

Salaman, G. 2002. "Understanding advice: towards a sociology of management consulting," in T. Clark and R. Fincham (eds.). *Critical*

Consulting: New Perspectives on the Management Advice Industry.
Oxford: Blackwell, 247–59

Sarvary, M. 1999. "Knowledge management and competition in the
consulting industry," *California Management Review* 41: 95–107

Saver, M. 1991. *Outplacement-Beratung.* Wiesbaden: DUV Gabler

Schade, C. 1997. *Marketing für Unternehmensberatung: Ein institutionen
ökonomischer Ansatz.* Wiesbaden: DUV Gabler

Schein, E. 1969. "The mechanisms of change," in W. G. Bennis, K. D. Benne
and R. Chin (eds.). *The Planning of Change.* New York: Holt,
Rinehart and Winston, 98–108

Scherer, A. G. 1998. "Pluralism and incommensurability in strategic
management and organization theory: a problem in search of a
solution," *Organization* 5: 147–68

Schmidt, L., N. Brandt, and F. Ahlers 2000. "Inhouse-Consulting in der
betrieblichen Praxis – Ergebnisse einer Befragungen," *Zeitschrift für
Führung und Organisation* 69: 260–7

Shenson, H. L. 1990. *Shenson on Consulting: Success Strategies from the
Consultant's Consultant.* New York: Wiley

Simonin, B. L. 1997. "The importance of collaborative know-how: an
empirical test of the learning organization," *Academy of Management
Journal* 40: 1150–74

Sloan, A. 1964. *My Years with General Motors.* Garden City, NY:
Doubleday

Smelser, N. J., and R. Swedberg 1994. "The sociological perspective on
the economy," in N. J. Smelser and R. Swedberg (eds.). *Handbook of
Economic Sociology.* Princeton: Princeton University Press, 3–26

Smith, M., and D. George 1994. "Selection methods," in C. L. Cooper
and I. T. Robertson (eds.). *Key Reviews in Managerial Psychology.*
New York: Wiley, 54–97

Sorge, A., and A. van Witteloostuijn 2004. "The (non)sense of organizational change: an essai about universal management hypes, sick consultancy metaphors, and healthy organization theories," *Organization
Studies* 25: 1205–31

Spence, M. 1973. "Job market signaling," *Quarterly Journal of Economics*
87: 355–74

    1974. *Market Signaling: Informational Transfer in Hiring and Related
Screening Processes.* Cambridge, MA: Harvard University Press

    1976. "Competition in salaries, credentials, and signaling prerequisites
for jobs," *Quarterly Journal of Economics* 90: 51–74

Spender, J. C. 1996. "Making knowledge the basis of a dynamic theory
of the firm," *Strategic Management Journal* 17 (Winter special issue):
45–62

Stanback, T. M. 1979. *Understanding the Service Economy: Employment, Productivity and Location.* Baltimore: Johns Hopkins University Press

Stanback, T. M., P. J. Bearse, T. J. Noyelle, and R. A. Karasek 1981. *Services: The New Economy.* Totowa, NJ: Allanheld and Osmun

Starbuck, W. H. 1992. "Learning by knowledge-intensive firms," *Journal of Management Studies* 29: 713–40

Stegemeyer, W. 2002. *Der Vergleich von Abschlussprüfung und Unternehmensberatung aus der Perspektive der Agency- und der Signaling-Theorie.* Marburg: Tectum

Stehr, N. 1994. *Knowledge Societies.* New York: Sage

Stehr, N., and V. Meja (eds.) 2005. *Society and Knowledge: Contemporary Perspectives in the Sociology of Knowledge and Science.* New Brunswick, NJ: Transaction

Stewart, A. H. 1991. "The role of narrative structures in the transfer of ideas," in C. Bazerman and J. Paradis (eds.). *Textual Dynamics of the Professions.* Madison, WI: University of Wisconsin Press, 120–44

Stigler, G. J. 1961. "The economics of information," *Journal of Political Economy* 69: 213–25

Strang, D., and J. W. Meyer 1993. "Institutional conditions for diffusion," *Theory and Society* 22: 487–511

Sturdy, A. 1997. "The consultancy process: an insecure business," *Journal of Management Studies* 34: 389–413

Sturdy, A., T. Clark, R. Fincham, and K. Handley 2004. "Silence, Procrustes and colonization: a response to Clegg et al.'s 'Noise, Parasites and Translation: Theory and Practice in Management Consulting,'" *Management Learning* 35: 337–40

Suchman, M. C. 1995. "Managing legitimacy: strategic and institutional approaches," *Academy of Management Review* 20: 571–610

Suddaby, R., and R. Greenwood 2001. "Colonizing knowledge: commodification as a dynamic of jurisdictional expansion in professional service firms," *Human Relations* 54: 933–53

Svensson, G. 2002. "A triadic network approach to service quality," *Journal of Services Marketing* 16: 158–79

Swedberg, R. (ed.) 1990. *Economics and Sociology: Redefining Their Boundaries: Conversations with Economists and Sociologists.* Princeton, NJ: Princeton University Press

Theuvsen, L. 1994. *Interne Beratung: Konzept, Organisation, Effizienz.* Wiesbaden: DUV Gabler

Tolbert, P. S., and L. G. Zucker 1996. "The institutionalization of institutional theory," in S. R. Clegg, C. Hardy, and W. R. Nord (eds.). *Handbook of Organization Studies.* London: Sage Publications, 175–90

Tordoir, P. 1995. *The Professional Knowledge Economy: The Management and Integration of Professional Services in Business Organizations.* Dordrecht: Kluwer

Townley, B. 1989. "Selection and appraisal: reconstituting 'social relations'?," in J. Storey (ed.). *New Perspectives on Human Resource Management.* London: Routledge, 92–108

  1993. "Foucault, power/knowledge and its relevance for human resource management," *Academy of Management Review* 18: 518–45

  1994. *Reframing Human Resource Management: Power, Ethics and the Subject at Work.* London: Sage

Tsai, W. 2001. "Knowledge transfer in intraorganizational networks: effects of network position and absorptive capacity on business unit innovation and performance," *Academy of Management Journal* 44: 996–1004

Turner, A. N. 1982. "Consulting is more than giving advice," *Harvard Business Review* 60/5: 120–9

UNCTAD 1993. *Management Consulting: A Survey of the Industry and Its Largest Firms.* New York: United Nations Conference on Trade and Development, Program on Transnational Corporations

  1995. *World Investment Report 1995: Transnational Corporations and Competitiveness.* New York: United Nations Conference on Trade and Development

Uzzi, B. 1996. "The sources and consequences of embeddedness for the economic performance of organizations: the network effect," *American Sociological Review* 61: 674–98

  1997. "Social structure and competition in interfirm networks: the paradox of embeddedness," *Administrative Science Quarterly* 42: 35–67

von Neumann, J., and O. Morgenstern 1944. *Theory of Games and Economic Behavior.* Princeton, NJ: Princeton University Press

Wajcman, J. 1998. *Managing Like a Man: Women and Men in Corporate Management.* Pittsburgh: Pennsylvania State University Press

Waldman, M. 1990. "Up-or-out contracts: a signaling perspective," *Journal of Labor Economics* 8/2: 230–50

Werr, A. 1999. *The Language of Change: The Roles of Methods in the Work of Management Consultants.* Stockholm: Stockholm School of Economics

  2002. "The internal creation of consulting knowledge: a question of structuring experience," in M. Kipping and L. Engwall (eds.). *Management Consulting: Emergence and Dynamics of a Knowledge Industry.* Oxford: Oxford University Press, 91–108

Werr, A., T. Stjernberg, and P. Docherty 1997. "The functions of methods of change in management consulting," *Journal of Organizational Change Management* 10: 288–307

Wet Feet Press 1996. *Ace Your Case! The Essential Management Consulting Case Workbook*, vol. 2.1. San Francisco: Wet Feet Press

Wharton MBA Consulting Club 1997. *The Wharton MBA Case Interview Study Guide*, vol. 1. Wharton MBA Consulting Club, University of Pennsylvania, Philadelphia

Wickham, P. A. 1999. *Management Consulting*. London: Financial Times/ Pitman

Wiemann, E.-M. 2004. "Die Etablierung und der Nutzen einer Berater-Governance," paper presented at the conference "Grenzen der Strategieberatung," 14–16 October. Ludwig Maximilian University, Munich

Williams, C. L. 1991. *Gender Differences at Work: Women and Men in Nontraditional Occupations*. Berkeley, CA: University of California Press

Williamson, O. E. 1975. *Markets and Hierarchies: Analysis and Antitrust Implications*. New York: Free Press

1985. *The Economic Institutions of Capitalism*. New York: Free Press

1986. *Economic Organization*. Brighton: Wheatsheaf

1988. "The logic of economic organization," *Journal of Law, Economics and Organization* 4: 65–93

1991. "Comparative economic organization: the analysis of discrete structural alternatives," *Administrative Science Quarterly* 36: 269–96

1993. "Calculativeness, trust, and economic organization," *Journal of Law and Economics* 36: 453–86

Willmott, H. 1990. "Beyond paradigmatic closedness in organizational enquiry," in J. Hassard and D. Pym (eds.). *The Theory and Philosophy of Organizations: Critical Issues and New Perspectives*. London: Routledge, 44–62

1993. "Breaking the paradigm mentality," *Organization Studies* 14: 681–720

Wirtz, K.-E. 1985. *Wettbewerbsdruck und Problemlösungsinitiative: Determinanten der Nachfrage nach externer Unternehmensberatung*. Berlin: Duncker und Humblot

Wood, P. 1996. "Business services, the management of change and regional development in the UK: a corporate client perspective," *Transactions of the Institute of British Geographers* 21: 644–65

(ed.) 2002. *Consultancy and Innovation: The Business Service Revolution in Europe*. London: Routledge

Zimmermann, T. 2004. "Was gute Strategieberatung ausmacht," paper presented at the conference "Grenzen der Strategieberatung," 14–16 October. Ludwig Maximilian University, Munich

Zucker, L. G. 1986. "Production of trust: institutional sources of economic structure, 1840–1920," *Research in Organizational Behavior* 8: 53–111

Zukin, S., and P. J. DiMaggio (eds.) 1990. *Structures of Capital: The Social Organization of the Economy*. Cambridge: Cambridge University Press

Index

Accenture 121, 122, 130, 138, 169
accounting firms 42, 71, 119–39, 151,
  170, 186, 189, 208
administrative fiat 107, 109
alliances 131, 134–6, 150
Andersen Consulting 123, 169
Arthur Andersen 42, 137
asset specificity 12, 13, 24, 45–7, 49,
  58, 60, 63, 64, 87–9, 103, 105–6,
  110, 152, 153
associations of consulting 69, 71, 73,
  122, 130, 141
A.T. Kearney 138

Bain 169
BDU 141
biotechnology 135–6, 206
Booz Allen and Hamilton 123, 132,
  133, 136
Boston Consulting Group 132, 136,
  138, 169

Cap Gemini Ernst and Young
  Consulting 138, 169
career 99–100, 107, 162, 180,
  189–201, 209, 211
case-study job interviews 180–8, 190,
  209
certification
  economics of 107, 115, 214, 218–21
  of management 7, 63, 64, 91, 107,
    115, 208, 214, 218–21
CMC 69
communities of practice 16–17, 158–9
compensation 156
competence center 130, 132, 136, 153,
  156, 160–5, 168, 173, 174, 209
confidentiality 72–3, 108, 172
Congress 64
consultants' stress 97–100, 165

consulting approaches 1, 4, 6, 52–5, 73,
  76, 81, 99, 102, 107, 112, 133, 134,
  157, 159, 162, 163, 165, 168, 172,
  174, 176, 183
consulting instruments, see consulting
  tools
consulting methods 2, 3, 14, 45, 50–5,
  73, 88, 94, 153, 158, 166–7, 179
consulting tools 50–5, 88, 105, 106,
  153, 158–9, 166, 168, 179
corporate governance 64
crisis of the consulting market from
  2001 to 2003, see stagnation
critical rationalism 18, 34–7, 207,
  212–14, 216
critical view on consulting 3–6, 8, 54–5,
  74–5, 86–7, 183, 207
cross-fertilization 211, 212, 216, 218

decoupling 10, 27, 113, 221
Deloitte Touche Tohmatsu 42, 122
demand frequency 12–13, 24, 45, 46,
  51, 61, 103–4, 106, 208,
  see also demand intensity
demand intensity 50–1, 53, 106,
  see also demand frequency
deregulation 60
discrimination 193–201
  customer 195, 199
  signaling-based 194
  statistical 90, 193–5, 199
  taste-based 90, 193–5, 199
diversification 133, 134, 139
  related diversification 125–6, 137,
    208
divisionalization 25, 126, 131–4

economies of scale 47, 49, 109, 120–2,
  125–8, 152, 157, 205

economies of scope 47, 49, 109, 120,
 125–8, 137, 138, 157, 205
EDS 138
Enron 42, 124, 137, 138
enterprise resource planning 121–3
Ernst and Young 42, 169
ERP, see enterprise resource planning

fads of management, see critical view
 on consulting
fashions of management, see critical
 view on consulting
FDI 55–6, 58, 152, 205
FEACO 71, 130
fees, see price
functionalist view on consulting 2–3,
 5–6, 8

game theory 19–21, 137–8, 164,
 216–18
gender 193–201
Glass–Steagall Banking Act 64
globalization 55–8, 66, 85, 152, 205–6
governance of consulting firms 123–4,
 132–9, 152–77, 208
growth of consulting firms 69, 78–81,
 141, 147–9, 151, 156
growth of the consulting market 2, 3,
 41–2, 55–67, 75, 92–5, 101, 128,
 132, 137, 207, 211

Harvard Business School (HBS) 180,
 181, 183, 186
Hewlett-Packard 121
hiring, see recruitment
hold-up 46, 47, 87–9, 98
homosociality 195–6, 209
human resource management in
 consultancy 157–8, 178–201, 206,
 208, 209, 212

IBM 121, 124, 138
ICMCI 69
implementation 3, 4, 25, 43, 47, 96,
 103, 113, 122, 123, 127–30, 169
incommensurability 18, 32–7, 207,
 212–13
information asymmetry 9, 26, 27, 29,
 69, 95–9, 125, 126, 137, 138, 191,
 206, 207

Initial Public Offering (IPO) 123–4,
 190
intangibility 4, 20, 61–2, 72–4, 135–6,
 140, 153, 206–7
internal consulting 26, 50–1, 101–15,
 208
internationalization 25, 26, 65, 85,
 see also globalization
isomorphism 7–8, 26, 113, 172, 190
IT outsourcing 120–1, 123–5
Ivy League 220–1

knowledge
 explicit 161, 164, 166–72
 management of 3, 16, 17, 72,
  153–77, 209
 tacit 61, 158, 161, 166–72
knowledge economy 46, 61, 62, 205–7,
 220
knowledge society, 209,
 see also knowledge economy
KPMG 42, 123

legitimacy 4, 7–8, 10, 11, 25, 31, 54,
 63–4, 66, 82, 83, 91, 107, 109, 113,
 115, 125, 126, 187, 188, 207, 210,
 214, 222

malpractice suits 70, 72, 74
Management Consultancies
 Association (UK), see MCA
management development 103, 130,
 134
market entry 70, 76, 85, 129, 138
marketing consulting services 84, 126,
 140–51, 186–7, 208
market power 27, 87–95, 188, 207
MBA 2, 133, 157, 193
MCA 122
McKinsey 7, 44, 123, 130, 132–4, 136,
 138, 169, 176–7, 181, 190
mergers and acquisitions 59–60, 121,
 124, 126–7, 152, 155
M-form 25–6, 134
mobility of consultants 73, 162, 172
Monitor Consulting 138

networked reputation 75–85, 95, 186,
 207, see also referrals
niche strategy 119, 131–2, 137

offshoring 57
one-firm concept 3, 133, 154, 160–5, 209
one-stop business model 133, 137
organizational culture 134, 160–5, 211
organizational development 1

partnership 123, 134, 154–7, 199, 200
personnel selection in management consultancy 165, 178–90, 192, 209, 212
  homogenization by 165, 178, 187–9
  validity of 179, 180, 182–6, 190
price 68, 69, 74, 81, 82, 99, 130–1, 207
PricewaterhouseCoopers 42
privatization 55, 58, 59, 63, 205
project organization 153, 157–60
promotion mechanisms 9, 20, 100, 107, 133–4, 156, 163, 178, 190–201, 209
PwC Consulting 124, 138

rat race 178, 192–3
recommendations 29, 75, 80, 82, 85, 150, 215, see also referrals
recovery 92
recruitment 3, 11, 129, 133, 134, 151, 179, 184–9, 199, 220
referrals 75–85, 95, 98, 139–51, 171, 172, 189, 191, 193, 207, 215
regulation of the consulting market 69, 71–2
reputation 11, 16, 31, 71, 75–85, 125–6, 129, 130, 136–8, 140–51, 175, 186–7, 207, 216

Second World War 25, 59
shareholders 65, 66, 114, 154–6
shareholder value 63
Siemens 121

Silicon Valley 63
slowdown of the consulting market from 2001 to 2003, see stagnation
spinoff 134, 138
stagnation of the consulting market from 2001 to 2003 41, 65, 92, 99, 119, 124, 130, 132, 137, 138, 179
stakeholders 65, 66, 114
status similarity 81, 128–9, 136, 137, 172, 177, 206, 208
strategy
  in knowledge management 169, 170
  of consulting firms 119–39
strategy-as-practice 119, 124
stratification 76, 81, 91, 135–6, 141, 146, 206
symbolism 4, 28, 63, 66, 83, 114, 115, 181, 186–8, 197, 206, 207, 209, 219

task complexity 46, 49–51, 53, 59, 63, 105–6, 110, 178
task similarity 50–3, 55, 58, 60, 61, 64, 103, 106, 110, 152, 153, 156, 208
trade 41, 55–8, 64, 152, 205
  intra-firm 57–8
  intra-industry 57, 152, 205
tournaments 178, 191–3, 200
trust 16, 19, 21–4, 69, 75–85, 95, 112, 126, 137, 139–51, 189, 191, 193, 195, 207, 209, 216–18

uncertainty 5, 7, 9, 12–13, 16, 19, 24, 46, 69–81, 83, 84, 98, 140, 164, 191, 193, 206, 207
up-or-out system 100, 154, 178, 191–3, 199

word-of-mouth 16, 20, 75, 78, 80, 95, 98, 99, 139–51, 189, 191, 215, see also referrals